WILD CARD OD

No Wild Cards | Joker Wild

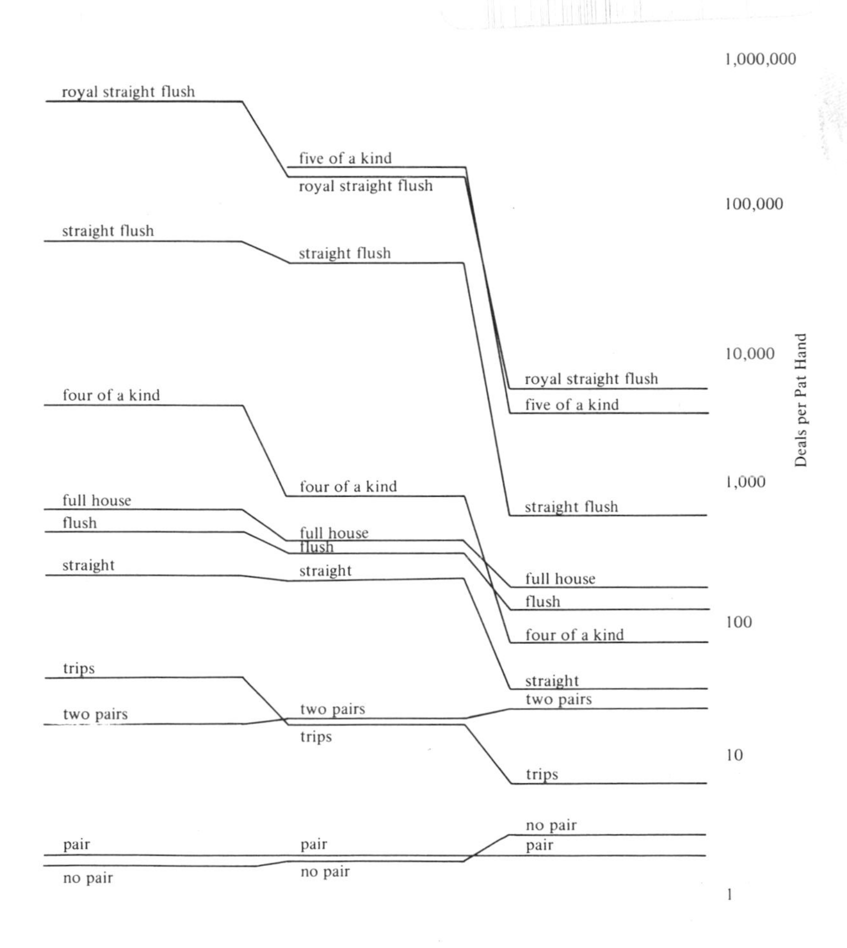

Various Hands

Rational selfishness—man's greatest virtue.
Through it, greed grows beautiful; life becomes joyful.
Serve only the highest cause—man the individual—you.

ERIC FLAME

POKER

A GUARANTEED INCOME FOR LIFE

by using the

ADVANCED CONCEPTS OF POKER

by

Frank R. Wallace, Ph. D

I & O Publishing Company
Wilmington, Delaware

Standard Book Number 911752-05-6
Library of Congress Catalog No. 68-58702
1st printing, November 1968
2nd printing, September 1969
3rd printing, June 1970
4th printing, November 1970
5th printing, March 1971
6th printing, October 1971
7th printing, March 1972 (revised)

Published by
I & O Publishing Company
Post Office Box 644
Wilmington, Delaware 19899

Manufactured in the United States of America

FOREWORD

You can earn $50,000 a year by playing poker . . . yes, even more if you want to. Any man or woman can get rich by applying the "Advanced Concepts of Poker".

This book is for the penny-ante novice as well as the professional poker player; it is for anyone who will ever pick up a poker hand. Once familiar with the "Advanced Concepts of Poker", your only limitation in winning money is the extent you choose to apply these concepts.

What is your goal in poker? Do you want to get rich, be the biggest winner in the game, gain confidence, punish another player, or just have more fun? Define what you want, then increasingly apply the "Advanced Concepts of Poker" until you reach your goal. How far should you go? . . . That depends on you and your goals.

INTRODUCTION

Every week millions of poker players lose more money* than many nations spend in a year. Around the world, considerable money awaits those knowing more than the basic concepts and techniques of poker. ... The opportunities for the good player are great.

Over one hundred and thirty books have been published about poker ... none focus on the concept of extracting maximum money from a poker game. ... This book details the methods to win maximum money from any game, and also describes methods to generate more money by quickening the betting pace, raising the stakes, expanding the game, creating new games, and finding bigger games.

The player who knows and applies the "Advanced Concepts of Poker" is a rare person . . . few have ever played against him. He can win money so fast that he could bankrupt most games at will. But he controls his winnings and preserves the game in order to extract maximum money from his opponents. He camouflages his poker skill, and his opponents seldom realize that he is taking all their money.

Once familiar with the "Advanced Concepts of Poker", one can -

- recognize the good player
- guard against the good player
- develop into a good player.

** A LIFE magazine article (August 16, 1968) about poker reported that 47,000,000 poker players in the United States alone wager 45 billion dollars annually.*

The "Advanced Concepts of Poker" are objective and realistic. Many involve deception. Some are ruthless. A few are immoral*. Know them and be wiser. Apply them and get rich**.

* *None of the "Advanced Concepts of Poker" employ cheating, but a few are immoral because they involve deception outside of the poker game. The good player, however, does not need to use a single immoral concept to achieve his goals. So why include immoral concepts? This book is a definitive treatment of poker and, therefore, all concepts are included. Also by identifying the immoral concepts, the reader can recognize them and take defensive measures when such concepts are used against him.*

** *This book identifies the true nature of winning poker as a highly profitable but a time-consuming nonproductive activity that requires bringing out the worst in one's opponents. In certain cases, therefore, poker can work against the good player's self-esteem and happiness no matter how much he wins.*

THE ADVANCED CONCEPTS OF POKER

CONTENTS

PAGE

FOREWORD III

INTRODUCTION V

PART ONE

DEFINITIONS

I. Game of Poker (1) 1

II. Odds (2) 3

1. Card odds (3) 3
2. Investment odds (4) 6
3. Edge odds (5) 8

III. Betting (6) 10

1. Betting stakes (7) 11
2. Betting pace (8) 11

IV. Poker Players (9) 13

1. Good player (10) 13
2. Other players (11) 15

V. Emotions (12) 18

VI. Poker Concepts (13) 21

1. Common concepts (14) 21
2. Advanced concepts (15) 29

PART TWO

TECHNIQUE
(DTC Method)

VII. Discipline (16) 31

VIII. Thought (17) 41

X. Control (18) 44

PAGE

PART THREE

STRATEGY

X. Ingredients of Strategy (19) 49

1. Understanding game (20) 49
2. Knowing opponents (21) 51
3. Situation and position (22) 53

XI. Tailor-Made Game (23) 56

1. Increasing the betting pace (24) . . . 56
   a. Twist (25) 57
   b. Split pot, high-low (26) 58
   c. Check raise and pick-up checks (27) 59
   d. Right to bet (28) 59
   e. Early bet (29) 59
   f. Bet or get (30) 60
   g. Additional cards (31) 60
   h. Novel games (32) 60
   i. Wild cards and freak hands(33). 60
   j. Table stakes and pot limit(34). 61
2. Increasing the betting stakes (35). . 62
3. Increasing the edge odds (36). 65

XII. Behavior (37) 67

1. Systemization and blandness (38). . 68
2. Personality (39) 69
   a. Unfriendly (40) 69
   b. Congenial (41) 71
   c. Introvert and extrovert (42). . 71
3. Practicing deceit (43) 72
   a. Concealing desires (44). 72
   b. Concealing facts (45) 73
   c. Lying (46) 74
4. Creating an atmosphere (47) 75
   a. Carefree (48) 75
   b. Relaxed (49) 76
   c. Pleasant (50) 76

PAGE

5. Observation (51) 77
a. Reading opponents (52) 77
b. Remembering exposed cards and ghost hands (53) 81
c. Seeing flashed cards (54) 82
d. Intentional flashing (55) 85
e. Peekers (56) 85
6. Non-game behavior (57) 88

XIII. Policies (58) 90

1. Money (59) 90
a. Maintaining proper attitude (60) 90
b. Stimulating poor attitude in opponents (61) 90
c. Increasing money in game(62) . 91
2. Credit (63) 92
a. Extending credit (64) 94
b. Refusing credit (65) 94
c. Cashing checks (66) 95
d. Bad debts (67) 95
3. Rules (68) 98
a. Modified rules (69) 99
b. Disputed plays (70) 99
c. Inequitable rules (71) 100
d. House rules (72) 100
4. Arguments and emotional situations (73) 102

XIV. Cheaters (74) 103

1. Cheating (75) 103
2. Accepting cheaters (76) 105
3. Rejecting cheaters (77) 106
4. Robin Hood cheater (78) 108
5. Detection (79) 109

XV. Taxes and Laws (80) 111

PAGE

PART FOUR

OPPONENT

XVI. Involvement (81) 124

1. Emotional (82) 124
2. Financial (83) 127

XVII. Exploitation (84) 128

1. Personal weaknesses, favors, and bribes (85) 128
2. Play of cards and betting (86) 132
3. Hypnosis (87) 134
4. Distractions (88) 135
5. Agreements (89) 138

XVIII. Money Extraction (90) 139

1. Winning too fast (91) 139
2. Uncontrolled money flow (92) . . . 139
3. Controlled money flow (93) 140

PART FIVE

GAME

XIX. Other Games (94) 145

1. Finding game (95) 145
2. Becoming a permanent player (96) 147
3. Quitting game (97) 148
4. Breaking-up game (98) 149

XX. Organization (99) 149

1. Regular game (100) 150
2. Starting time (101) 150
3. Quitting time (102) 151
4. Contacting players (103) 153
5. A place to play (104) 157

PAGE

XXI. Expansion (105) 159
1. New players (106) 159
a. Keeping players (107) 160
b. Rejecting players (108)...... 161
c. Women players (109) 165
2. Improving attendance (110)...... 167

XXII. Maintenance (111).................. 168
1. Making game attractive (112) 168
2. Helping losers (113)............ 169
3. Raising morale of losers (114) 170
4. Off-days (115)................. 172
5. Leaving game early (116)........ 173

XXIII. Major and Minor League Games (117) 174
1. Major league (118) 175
2. Minor league (119) 175
3. Farm system (120)............. 176

CONCLUSION 178

APPENDIX

A. History.......................... 179

B. Bibliography 183

C. Glossary 203

D. Odds 248

E. Review.......................... 264

INDEX 269

ADDENDUM NOTES 277

Here is knowledge.
Come, light your torch.
JOHN FLAGG

THE ADVANCED CONCEPTS OF POKER

How much money can you win at poker? It makes no difference if you are a professional poker player, a novice, or have never played poker before* . . . the following one hundred and twenty "Advanced Concepts of Poker" can guide any man or woman to unlimited winnings. How much you win depends on how *fully* and how *many* of these concepts you choose to apply.

PART ONE - DEFINITIONS

Definitions of the broadest aspects of poker (the game, odds, betting, players, emotions, and concepts) are given below in the form of contextual descriptions**:

I. GAME OF POKER (1)

The object of poker is to win maximum money. Poker is not a card game; it is a game of money management. Cards are merely the tools for manipulating money. From the smallest penny-ante game to the largest table-stake game, all money eventually goes to the good player. His key weapons are his mind and a license to use unlimited deception.

Poker is unique among money making situations. In business, for example, opportunities to apply the proper business concepts are limited in number. The financial outcome, therefore, cannot be certain. But in poker, while chance may influence each separate hand, the opportunities

---

* *For the complete beginner, the basic rules and concepts of poker are quite simple and can be learned after a few hours exposure to any poker game. The best all-around book for the basic rules and concepts of poker is Jacoby, OSWALD JACOBY ON POKER. This book is recommended reading, not only for beginners, but for all players who are not already consistent winners. Jacoby's poker book may be purchased from the I & O Publishing Company for $4.95 plus 50c for postage and handling. (No postage and handling charge if ordered with MAN'S CHOICE.)*

For an in-depth psychological understanding of each type of poker player from the sad-sack loser to the confident winner, F. R. Wallace's novel MAN'S CHOICE is recommended reading for all poker players. This $6.95 hardbound book is available from I & O Publishing Company for $5.95 (postpaid).

** *Definitions of specific words or phrases used in poker are given in the glossary in Appendix C.*

(hands) are so numerous that "luck"* becomes insignificant. Application of the proper poker concepts assures financial success.

Poker concepts are best illustrated by players in actual game situations. The following five players are the nucleus of a weekly, Monday night game:

Sid Bennett
Ted Fehr
John Finn
Quintin Merck
Scotty Nichols

Although other men play in this game from time to time, most of the poker situations in this book are illustrated with these five players.

*** * ***

"Four in the morning," Quintin Merck grunts at the dark whiskered men still sitting around the rectangular poker table. It is not a real poker table, not the kind with trays for money and a green felt top ... it is the dining room table at Scotty Nichols' house. They have played here every Monday night for the past six years.

Rising layers of gray smoke mushroom around the overhead cluster of electric bulbs that push light down to a leather table mat covered with ten and twenty dollar bills. The largest pile of money is in front of John Finn, a twenty-eight year old social worker.

In the sticky summer heat, the men slouch in squeaking, wooden chairs. Only John Finn appears alert. The tall, black haired man slips on his glasses and hooks the gold rims around his ears. His dark eyes move from player to player.

On his left sits Sid Bennett, a thirty-five year old paving contractor. His large smiling head flops in a semicircle as straight yellow hair falls over his forehead and nearly touches his faded blue eyes. He's in a daze, John says to himself. Look at him grin.

On John's right sits Ted Fehr, a thirty year old gambler and restaurant owner. He coils a fifty dollar bill around his skinny

** Luck is a mystical illusion that does not exist in reality (see pages 18 and 226).*

fingers while waiting for the next hand. Under bristly red hair, his freckled face wrinkles. His sagging, bloodshot eyes watch John Finn's arm hook around the huge pot. "The biggest pot of the night," he moans, "and look who wins it. You . . . "

John interrupts, "Wake up, Professor, it's your deal."

With a growling noise, Professor Merck deals. John watches the deck and sees the bottom card plus two other cards flash. He then studies Quintin Merck's green eyes . . . they are watering from the cigarette smoke curling over his moustache and into his leathery face. Wearing a sweaty beret and an opened polo shirt, the wiry fifty-five year old college professor hunches over the table. Suddenly he looks up and frowns at John Finn.

Without flinching, John refocuses and looks into the kitchen. Then his eyes return to the game . . . he studies Scotty Nichols. The plump, forty-two year old stockbroker slumps half dozing in his chair. His mouth droops open to expose a cluster of gold capped teeth. His thick glasses magnify his eyes into brown globes that float in circles between each squeezing blink. A tie droops from the frayed collar of his scorched white shirt.

They're all valuable to me, John Finn tells himself as his eyes draw into narrow slits.

II. ODDS (2)

Three types of odds are important in poker. Most players are familiar with the *card* odds, and most players base their playing and betting decisions on them. The card odds, however, can be meaningless unless the *investment* odds are also considered. Another type of odds is the *edge* odds, which evaluate the relative performance of each player. These three types of odds are described below:

1. Card Odds (3)

The card odds are the probabilities of being dealt or drawing to various hands. These odds are reviewed in most books about poker. The following table is based on the card odds and shows the statistical frequency that different poker hands occur.

High Hands	*Approximate Deals per Pat Hand*	*Hands Possible*
Total hands	1	2,598,960
No pair	2	1,302,540
One pair	2.5	1,098,240
Two pairs	20	123,552
Three of a kind	50	54,912
Straight	250	10,200
Flush	500	5,108
Full house	700	3,744
Four of a kind	4,000	624
Straight flush	70,000	36
Royal straight flush	650,000	4
Five Aces (with Joker)	3,000,000	1

Low Hands (pairless hands)		
Ace high (+)	5	502,860
King high (+)	8	335,580
Queen high (+)	12	213,180
Jack high (+)	20	127,500
Ten high (+)	37	70,360
Nine high (++)	36	71,860
Eight high (++)	70	35,840
Seven high (++)	170	15,360
Six high (++)	500	5,120
Five high (++)	2,500	1,024

(+) - No straights or flushes. Ace is high.
(++) - Including straights and flushes. Ace is low.

There are 2,598,960 different poker hands in a fifty-two card deck. If a player is dealt 100,000 hands in his lifetime, he will never hold (on his first five cards) more than four percent of all the possible hands.

Other poker probabilities based on the card odds are tabulated in Appendix D.

The card odds can reveal interesting information. For example, how many pat straight flushes will Sid Bennett get during his life? To figure this, the expected number of hands that will be dealt to him during his life is estimated by the following calculation:

10 hands/hr. X 5 hrs./game X 50 games/yr. X 40 yrs./ poker life = 100,000 hands/poker life

Now the number of pat (on the first five cards) poker hands that Sid should get during his lifetime is calculated from the card odds and tabulated below:

	Approximate Number of Pat Hands in a Lifetime
No pair	**50,000**
One pair	**40,000**
Two pairs	**5,000**
Three of a kind	**2,000**
Straight	**400**
Flush	**200**
Full house	**170**
Four of a kind	**25**
Straight flush	**1.4**
Royal straight flush	**0.15**

So statistically, Sid should get a pat straight flush (on his first five cards) once or twice during his life. Of course, he will catch straight flushes on the draw or in seven card stud more often.

. . . Sid wins a big pot with a full house. He throws back his massive head and shouts, "I'm on a spinner! I'm going to break this game!" His head drops; he shakes his finger at the players and continues, "Just watch my luck. I'm getting a whole round of pat straight flushes . . . starting next deal."

"That won't happen till the sun burns out," Quintin Merck snorts.

Statistically, Quintin is right. Sid will be dealt five consecutive straight-flushes once in every 1.7 x 10^{24} deals, or once in every 700,000,000,000,000,000,000 years. Yet his five consecutive straight-flushes could start coming with the next deal.

Let him hope, John Finn says to himself.

2. *Investment Odds (4)*

Investment odds are the estimated returns on money that is bet. These odds are approximated by the following formula:*

$$\frac{\text{(potential size of pot, \$) (probability of winning pot)}}{\text{potential loss, \$}} = \text{Investment odds}$$

For example, if a player estimates that a $40 potential pot would require an average $10 betting investment (his potential loss), and if he estimates that his probability of winning that pot is .4 (40%)**. then his investment odds would be

$$\frac{(40)\ (.4)}{10} = 1.6.$$

When the investment odds are greater than 1.0, the play is favorable and should be made.

Investment odds are important for making correct betting and playing decisions. Most players rely only on card odds, which often lead to wrong decisions. For example, investment odds sometimes favor drawing to an inside straight. At other times, investment odds may favor folding three Aces before the draw. In both cases, the wrong play may have resulted if the decisions were based on the card odds alone.

* *The beginner should not be dismayed or get bogged down by this formula. Read on. With experience, one will realize that accurate estimations of investment odds are achieved by the proper thinking methods and not by mathematical problem solving. This formula is merely a shorthand expression of the proper thought process for evaluating a bet.*

** *How does one estimate the probability of winning a pot? This is done by assessing one's own hand and position against the behavior and betting of one's opponent. Initially, these estimates may be little more than guesses. Accuracy will improve with practice, experience and application of the various concepts described in this book.*

Determination of investment odds is not a mathematical problem. Numbers plugged in the above formula are quick estimations or guesses derived by objectively evaluating together the facts of the game, players, and situation. These estimations become more valid with increased thinking effort and experience. While the good player may never actually use or even think about this formula, it does express his thought process for evaluating bets.

Quintin, Ted and Scotty each draw one card. John Finn holds two low pair, tens and fours. What does he do? He considers the card odds, the past betting, probable future betting, his observations (e.g., of flashed cards), and his reading of each opponent . . . he then estimates the following investment odds:

Draw one card to his two pair . . .

$$\frac{(\$200)(.2)}{\$60} = .66 = \text{fold.}$$

Draw three cards to his pair of fours . . .

$$\frac{(\$300)(.1)}{\$20} = 1.5 = \text{play.}$$

So instead of folding his two pair (and often the investment odds favor folding two small pair), he breaks up his hand and draws to the pair of fours at favorable investment odds. The low $20 estimate of his potential loss is the key to making this play favorable. John figures his chances for catching and having to call the last bet are small.* When the high probability of a no-bet or drop hand (zero dollars) is averaged into the numerator, the potential loss becomes relatively small–even though the last round bet may be large if he improves his hand. In other words, he will fold with no additional cost unless he catches three of a kind or better, which would let him bet heavily with a good possibility of winning.

---

* *The weakness of hands such as small pairs, four flushes and four card straights after the draw increases the investment odds because failure to improve these hands causes an immediate fold, thereby minimizing the potential loss.*

In another hand, Sid and Ted draw three cards. Again John has two little pair. After objectively weighing all factors within the framework of the investment odds formula, he estimates his most favorable play is to stay pat then bet the last round as if he had a straight or a flush:

Play pat . . .

$$\frac{(\$100)\ (.8)}{\$60} = 1.33 = \text{play.}$$

The advantages of this play are: if either Sid or Ted catch two pair or even trips, they may fold and let John win on a pat bluff. If either catches a strong hand and shows any betting strength, John folds with no additional cost. Also, neither will try to bluff into John's pat hand And finally if Sid or Ted do not improve, John Finn wins additional money if either one calls.

3. Edge Odds or Edge Percentage (5)

Edge odds indicate the relative performance of a player in a poker game. These odds are calculated by the following formula:

$$\frac{\text{average winnings (or losses) of player, \$}}{\text{average winnings of the biggest winner,\$}} \times 100\% = \text{Edge Odds \%} \quad *$$

For example, if the biggest winner of *each* game averages plus $150, and if a player averages plus $75 per game, then the edge odds for this player are +75/150 X 100% = +50%. The more games used to calculate edge odds, the more significant they become. Edge odds based on ten or more games should reflect the relative performance of a player fairly accurately. The good poker player usually maintains edge odds ranging from 25% to 65%, depending on the game and abilities of the other players. An approximate performance grading of poker players based on the edge odds is tabulated below:

* *If you are not mathematically inclined and do not understand this or other formulae and ratios presented in this chapter, do not worry, and read on for these formulae are not necessary to understand and utilize the concepts identified in this book.*

EDGE ODDS*, %

Grading	*Game Without A Good Player*	*Game With One Good Player*
Good Player	-	25 - 65
Sound Player	10 - 25	5 - 20
Average Player	0 - 15	(-5) - 10
Weak Player	(-10) - 5	(-15) - 0
Poor Player	(-20) - (-5)	(-65) - (-10)

*These odds are estimated for an average, seven-man game.

The good player is a very expensive person as indicated by the sharp decreases in everyone's edge odds when he plays.

In a black leather notebook, John Finn keeps records of every player. After each game, he estimates their winnings and losses. After every ten games, he calculates their edge odds as shown below:

Ten Game Average (December, 1961 - February, 1962)

Player	*Estimated Average Win or Loss per game, $*	*Edge Odds,* %*	*Grading*
John Finn	**+262**	**+59**	**Good**
Quintin Merck	**+ 45**	**+10**	**Sound**
Scotty Nichols	**- 10**	**- 2**	**Average**
Sid Bennett	**- 95**	**- 21**	**Poor**
Ted Fehr	**-100**	**- 22**	**Poor**
Other Players	**-135**	**- 30**	**Poor**

***The biggest winner for each game averaged +$445.**

By reviewing his long term edge odds data (shown below), John notices slow changes in the players . . . Quintin is gradually improving, Scotty and Ted are deteriorating, while Sid remains stable.

Ten Game Average Edge Odds, %
(1961-1962)

Ten game period #	1	2	3	4	5	6	7
John Finn	+61	+53	+62	+59	+55	+60	+56
Quintin Merck	- 2	+ 2	- 5	+10	+ 8	+12	+15
Scotty Nichols	+ 4	+ 7	+ 6	- 2	+ 1	- 10	- 18
Sid Bennett	- 22	- 20	- 23	- 21	- 20	- 18	- 12
Ted Fehr	- 18	- 20	- 19	- 22	- 28	- 30	- 31
Other Players	- 23	- 24	- 26	- 30	- 25	- 22	- 20
Average biggest winner, +$	295	315	430	445	570	650	630

The steady increase in profit for the biggest winner also indicates John Finn's progress in driving up the betting stakes and pace.

III. BETTING (6)

Few players differentiate between the betting stakes and the betting pace. The betting *stakes* are the size of bets and raises permitted. The stakes are established by the house rules. The betting *pace* is the tempo or frequency of bets and raises. The pace depends on the games played and the willingness of players to bet. Both the stakes and pace determine how expensive the game is . . . or how much money can be won or lost.

The good player is seldom characterized as a tight player. His betting pattern is generally (but not always) aggressive, and often lopsidedly aggressive. Pushing hard whenever he has an advantage (favorable investment odds) and quickly dropping against genuine strength lets him maximize his wins and minimize his losses. A lopsided aggressiveness quickens the betting pace and offers the good player psychological advantages (builds fear in opponents).

As the bets increase, the losses of the other players tend to increase faster than the potential losses of the good player. Therefore, the investment odds formula on page 6 suggests that a steeper progression in betting for each round (causing the numerator to increase more rapidly than the denominator) permits greater aggressiveness and lets the good player bet with poorer hands.

1. Betting Stakes (7)

Most players think only of the betting stakes when they consider the size of the game.

The betting stakes in John Finn's Monday night game are as follows: In draw, $25 is the maximum bet and raise on the first rounds.This maximum increases to $50 in subsequent rounds of betting. In stud, the maximum bet is $5 on the first up card. The bet then increases in $5 increments on each subsequent round of betting to $10, $15, $20, and so on. Only three raises are allowed, except when only two players remain and then raises are unlimited. Check raising is permitted.

2. Betting Pace (8)

The betting pace is often more significant than the betting stakes in determining the size of the game. The good player knows the betting pace of both the game and of each individual hand. The betting pace of the *game* (game pace) is determined by comparing the betting done on various hands to the betting normally done on these hands. The pace may differ markedly among different poker games. In a fast pace game, for example, two pair after the draw may be worth two raises. In a slow pace game, these same two pair may be worth not even a small bet.

The good player controls his offensive and defensive game by altering his betting pace.

The betting pace of *each hand* (hand pace) is determined by comparing the extent of betting, calling, raising, and bluffing to the size of the pot. Often this pace is too slow during certain phases of a hand and too fast during other phases. The following ratios reflect betting paces during the various phases of a poker hand.

Phase	*Ratio**	*Slow Pace* → *Fast Pace*
Open	$\frac{\text{(opening bet, \$) (\#callers)}}{\text{pot, \$}}$	Increasing Ratio →
Raise	$\frac{\text{(raise bet, \$) (\# callers)}}{\text{pot, \$}}$	Increasing Ratio →
Final Bet	$\frac{\text{(last bet, \$) (\#callers)}}{\text{pot, \$}}$	Increasing Ratio →
Bluff	$\frac{\text{(\# bluffs) (average \# final callers)}}{\text{\# hands played}}$	Increasing Ratio →

The optimum betting pace is usually opposite to the actual pace. For example, if the betting pace is relatively slow the optimum pace will be somewhat faster. The closer one plays to the optimum pace, the more he increases his edge odds.

In the Monday night game, John realizes that the betting in seven card stud moves at a fast pace during the early rounds, but slows considerably in the late rounds of big bets. He takes advantage of this imbalance by laying back during the early rounds as players get drawn in and disclose their betting tendencies. Then in the later rounds, he quickens the pace by betting aggressively.

The following ratios illustrate how John Finn estimates the pace of this seven card stud game.

---

* *If you are not mathematically inclined and do not understand this or other formulae and ratios presented in this chapter, do not worry, and read on for these formulae are not necessary to understand and utilize the concepts identified in this book.*

Phase	Without John Finn			With John Finn		
	Estimate	*Ratio*	*Pace*	*Estimate*		*Ratio*
Open	$\frac{\$5 \times 4}{\$25}$	= .8	**Too fast**	$\frac{\$5 \times 5}{\$30}$	=	.8
Raise (first round)	$\frac{\$5 \times 3}{\$40}$	= .4	↓	$\frac{\$5 \times 4}{\$45}$	=	.4
Final Bet	$\frac{\$20 \times 2}{\$200}$	= .2	**Too slow**	$\frac{\$25 \times 3}{\$300}$	=	.4
Final Raise	**Best hand should raise, usually does not**			**John Finn often takes the final raise**		

IV. POKER PLAYERS (9)

There are good poker players and poor poker players. Most players fall in between these two extremes. The good player works hard to maintain maximum edge odds . . . he never compromises his advantage for the sake of others. He shares his abilities or earnings with no one. The poor player displays laziness and a lack of discipline. He has no resources to the advantages or earnings of others.

1. Good Player (10)

The good player plays solely for his own benefit. He is not a gambler* because he bets only when the odds are favorable. (Gamblers bet money at unfavorable odds and eventually lose all the money they risk.) The good poker player cannot lose; he eventually wins all the money that gambling players will risk.

---

* *See page 124 for a definition of gambling.*

Ability to play good poker does not correlate with intelligence or ability to play games such as bridge or chess. What makes a good poker player? . . . The good player can subjugate his impluses and motivate all his actions toward meeting the objective of poker, which is to win maximum money. He never gives anything away or helps others without the motive of eventual profit. The good player thinks ahead and plans his moves in advance. He disciplines himself and maintains an emotional consistency. He objectively analyzes the game as well as each individual player, hand and bet; he then adapts to any situation. The good player continually expands his skill by soaking up the experience of every play made by each player.

Good poker players are rare, and their paths seldom cross . . . in fact, most players have never encountered a good player. In the rare event that two good players are in the same game, their effective control is diluted and their edge odds are reduced by each other's presence. A good player searches for weaknesses in his opponents, but two good players will not waste time in trying to analyze each other. They direct their mental effort more profitably toward studying the game and the other players.

When involved in a hand against the good player, meaningful investment odds can be difficult to estimate, and the card odds may be the best basis for a decision. The strategy of the good player often depends on creating impulse reactions in his opponents. The proper move, therefore, can sometimes be made against a good player by acting oppositely to one's initial impulse. For example, when undecided about calling a good player and the impulse is to fold, the best move may be to call or even raise.

John Finn is the only good player in the Monday night game. He works hard, thinks objectively, and adapts to any situation. By applying the "Advanced Concepts of Poker", he wins maximum money from the game.

To overcome mental laziness and restrictive thinking, he forces himself to think constantly and imaginatively about the game. This lets him make more profitable plays. For example, he breaks up a pat full house* to triple the size of the pot while decreasing his chances of winning only slightly (from 98% down to 85%). This play increases his estimated investment odds from

$$\frac{(100)\,(.98)}{\$20} = 4.9 \text{ up to } \frac{(300)\,(.85)}{\$40} = 6.4.$$

Everyone knows John wins, but his opponents refuse to realize that they are paying him thousands of dollars every year to play in their game.

2. *Other Players (11)*

The other players supply income to the good player. They are working for him and are his assets. He treats them with care and respect. He plans his actions to extract maximum money from them.

The differences in attitude between the good player and the other players are listed on pages 16 and 17:

* *The opportunity to profitably break a full house by drawing to three of a kind rarely occurs. The above case results when several players with weak hands would fold if the full house were played pat, but would call if a draw were made. Also the full house would be broken to draw to four of a kind if sufficient evidence existed that the full house was not the best hand.*

Situation	*Mystical Feelings of Many Players*	*Objective Attitude of Good Player*
Poker game	A relaxing mental diversion to escape reality.	A mental discipline requiring full focus on reality.
Evaluation of a play	Winning the pot is most important.	Playing the hand properly is most important.
Winner or loser	Play according to winnings or losses.	Never be influenced by winnings or losses.
Streaks of luck	Changes or odds are influenced by previous events. Luck runs in cycles.	Past means nothing, except for psychological effects it has on other players.
Wild games	Such games are not real poker and require less skill. "Good" poker players will not play these games.	Complex or wild games require more skill and offer greater advantages to the good player.
Ante increase	Attitudes are mixed.	A bigger ante encourages looser play and decreases the advantage of a tight player.
Table stakes	Winner has an advantage when he takes money off the table.	The good player has more advantage with maximum money on the table.

Situation	*Mystical Feelings of Many Players*	*Objective Attitude of Good Player*
Play past time limit	Chances of winning decrease.	Advantages for the good player increase as opponents get tired and think less.
Violation of rules	Enforce rules equally.	*Apply* rules rigidly to better players and more liberally to weaker players. *Interpret* rules consistently and equitably.
Change in sequence of cards	The run of cards is broken ...misdeal.	Makes no difference ... keep playing.
Playing errors such as betting out of turn	Scold or penalize the culprit.	Usually benefits the good player. Encourage sloppy play.
Cheater	Throw him out of game.	If he is a loser, say nothing and let him play.

The major enemy of poker players is their rationalization for their failure to think. They continually find excuses for their weaknesses and lack of self-control. Their losses are directly proportional to their mental laziness. The poor player evades thinking by letting his mind sink into irrational fogs. His belief in luck short-circuits his mind by excusing him from the responsibility to think. Belief in luck is a great mystical rationalization for the refusal to think. . . . In method of thought, the good player is right and the poor player is wrong.

John Finn uses the mystical attitudes of his opponents to extract more money from them. In his black notebook, he has a table that summarizes everyone's attitude:

Situation	*Mystical Attitude*	*Objective Attitude*
Evaluation of a play	**Quintin, Scotty, Sid, Ted**	**John**
Winner or loser	**Scotty, Sid, Ted**	**John, Quintin**
Streaks of luck	**Scotty, Sid, Ted**	**John, Quintin**
Wild games	**Quintin, Scotty, Ted**	**John, Sid**
Play past time limit	**Scotty, Sid**	**John, Quintin, Ted**
Violation of rules	**Quintin, Ted**	**John, Sid, Scotty**
Cheaters	**Scotty, Ted**	**John, Quintin, Sid**

V. EMOTIONS (12)

Money affects emotions, and emotions control most players. Poker involves the winning and losing of money.

Common emotions of anger, excitement, greed, masochism, sadism, and self-pity often take control of players during the action. Most players fail to recognize or are unable to suppress these emotional influences that decrease their objectivity and poker ability. The good player recognizes his own emotions and prevents them from influencing his actions . . . he avoids acting on his whims and feelings.

Players respond emotionally to various experiences during the game. The good player uses their emotional reactions to his financial advantage. Some typical reactions and their causes are listed below:

Emotional Reactions	*Cause*
Playing loose to recover losses Playing tight to minimize losses	A losing streak
Pushing good luck by playing loose Playing tight to protect winnings	A winning streak
Extending good luck by playing recklessly	Winning a big hand or several hands
Playing poorly to avenge a loss or to retaliate for injured feelings	Losing a big hand or hurt feelings
Acting comical or silly	Lack of confidence, nervousness, fear, or desire for mental diversion
Becoming prone to impulsive actions and mistakes	Fear or nervousness
Losing concentration and decreasing awareness of situation	Laziness, other thoughts, fatigue

Recognition and control of one's own emotions are difficult and require thinking effort. This is one reason why good poker players are rare. . . . The good player directs his actions to produce desirable emotions (of pleasure and self-esteem); the poor player lets his emotional whims produce undesirable actions.

Poker is a unique medium for studying men. Where else can one stare at and intensely observe another person for hours every week?

The opportunity to study players, often in highly emotional situations, is probably better than most psychoanalysts get to analyze their patients. The observant, good player will soon understand his opponents better than their own families do.

Poker players are often fatigued and under emotional stresses that expose their characters. On another page in John's notebook, he summarizes the emotional characteristics of his opponents:

Player	*Emotional Characteristics*
Quintin Merck	**Fairly stable and objective. Can be roused by insulting or humiliating, then his playing disintegrates. Becomes less objective during late hours as he fatigues.**
Scotty Nichols	**Has inferiority complex and lack of confidence. Plays extremely tight if winning. He loosens up and plays recklessly after suffering a heavy loss or after losing several consecutive hands.**
Sid Bennet	**Hides his lack of confidence with silly behavior. Humor him and keep atmosphere relaxed to bring out his worst. Be careful not to hurt his feelings, or he will sulk and play tight. Goes wild when winning.**
Ted Fehr	**A compulsive gambler. Wants to punish himself. Wants to lose. Deteriorates easily into a desperate condition. Insensitive to insults. Low level of pride.**

VI. POKER CONCEPTS (13)

Ideas on how to play poker can be assembled into concepts. The normal concepts described in most poker books are popular ideas based on a combination of common sense and generalizations. These concepts can help some poor players improve their game. But good poker requires a much sharper definition of the problems followed by actions based on advanced concepts. The "Advanced Concepts of Poker" are the objective approaches to each aspect of the game and are specifically designed to win maximum money.

1. Common Concepts (14)

The commonest concept for winning at poker has always been to play conservatively (tight) and to play according to the card odds. Most books on poker stress this concept. They usually include some basic techniques as well as some rules for betting, raising, and bluffing. They also present some common ideas about strategy and psychology. . . . But none of these books offer a maximum-win approach to poker.

Appendix B (pages 183-202) lists all the known books about poker published since 1872. The following table summarizes and analyzes the typical concepts presented in these books:

EXAMPLES OF COMMON CONCEPTS IN POKER LITERATURE

Book	*Concept*	*Failure of Concept*
1. Abbott, J. - 1881 Jack Pot Poker	Never lend or borrow money.	Credit is necessary to keep most high stake games going week after week.
2. Allen, G. W. - 1895 Poker Rules in Rhyme	"It's the game the boys like best Two or three times a week One man often beats the rest With nothing else but cheek."	Action on objectively thought out plans (not cheek) is needed to win consistently.
3. Blackbridge, J. - 1880 The Complete Poker-Player	To play for a minimum loss or gain is what a gentleman should hope for.	To play for maximum gain is what the good player strives for.
4. Cady, Alice H. - 1895 Poker	Bluffing should be shunned for only an old player can experiment in this.	Only the weakest players will shun bluffing.
5. Coffin, G.S. - 1949 Fortune Poker	Shrewd players in bad luck should call for a new deck of cards to break the cycle.	A sign of a poor player is one who calls for a new deck of cards to break his bad luck... he fails to understand poker.

Book	*Concept*	*Failure of Concept*
6. Crawford, J. R. - 1953 How to be a Consistent Winner	Treat every bet as though it were your first one. Forget the money already in the pot.	Must consider the money in the pot to estimate the potential return on the present bet (investment odds).
7. Culbertson, E. - 1950 Culbertson's Hoyle	Never raise early unless the purpose is to drive out players.	Raise early to start bluffs, build pots, control betting, keep players in, drop players out - depending on the situation.
8. Curtis, D. A. - 1901 The Science of Draw Poker	New fangled high-low poker is mental weakness and should soon die out, even among the feeble minded.	High–low poker requires more skill and offers greater advantages to the good player.
9. Dowling, A.H. - 1940 Confessions of a Poker Player	Players acting out-of-turn should be penalized.	Players acting out-of-turn benefit the good player.
10. Encyclopedia Britannica - 1965 Poker	In high-low seven-card stud, never play for high unless first three cards are trips.	When to play depends on the investment odds, not on fixed dogma.

Book	*Concept*	*Failure of Concept*
11. Florence, W.J. - 1891 Handbook on Poker	A good player will at times purposely play poorly to vary his game.	The good player never purposely plays poorly. With thinking, he finds infinite ways to vary his game at favorable investment odds.
12. Foster, R.F. - 1904 Practical Poker	The compulsory ante is not based on judgement and has been the ruin of the scientific poker player.	The ante helps the loose player and usually benefits the good player.
13. Frey, R.L. - 1947 The Complete Hoyle	Never open unless the probability is that you hold the highest hand.	Open without best hand to establish betting position, to defend against a larger bet, or to set up a play at favorable investment odds.
14. Henry, J.R. - 1890 Poker Boiled Down	Elements of poker success are good luck, good cards, cheek, good temper and patience.	Good "luck" and good cards have no bearing on ultimate success in poker ... every player eventually gets the same "luck" and cards.

Book	*Concept*	*Failure of Concept*
15. Jacoby, O. - 1947 Oswald Jacoby on Poker	The most successful bluffs are likely to be the innocent ones.	The most successful bluffs are likely to be the well thought out and properly executed ones.
16. Keller, J.W. - 1887 Draw Poker	Playing poker without money is really an intellectual and scientific game. Playing poker with money becomes mere gambling.	Poker is a game of money management, not a card game.
17. Morehead, A.H. - 1956 New Complete Hoyle	The most widespread mistake is to play long hours in a futile losers' game.	The greatest advantages occur in a game consisting of tired losers ... they are usually the poor players at their poorest. Also, the losers' game will usually move at a faster pace.
18. Morehead, A.H. - 1967 The Complete Guide to Winning Poker	Many of the finest poker exploits are inspirational and intuitional.	The only fine poker exploits are the ones consciously thought out.

Book	Concept	Failure of Concept
19. Moss, J. - 1955 How To Win At Poker	Beware of poor players. Stay out of games in which there are fish.	Poor players are the most profitable opponents. Seek poor players and games in which there are fish.
20. Ostrow, A.A. - 1945 The Complete Card Player	Seven-stud, wild card, and high-low poker increase the element of luck so greatly that rules for improving one's play cannot be set down.	The more complex the poker variations, the less the element of "luck" affects the outcome.
21. Philips, H. - 1960 Profitable Poker	No sillier resolution is uttered than, "Well, I must see it through."	If the pot is large and the final bet is small, the investment odds may heavily favor "seeing it through".
22. Radner, S.H. - 1957 The Key to Playing Poker	To assure a night's winnings, sit to the left of loose bettors and to the right of tight players.	The good player usually sits to the right of loose bettors and to the left of tight players.
23. Reese, T. and Watkins, A.T. - 1964 Secret of Modern Poker	To win consistently you must play tight.	To win consistently, you must adapt to the game pace.

Book	*Concept*	*Failure of Concept*
24. Rottenberg, I. - 1965 Friday Night Poker	High stake games are played by grim, salty players.	High stake games are played by all types of players.
25. Scarne, J. - 1965 Scarne on Cards	Do not lend money. It often comes back to break you.	The good player lends money in order to win more money.
26. Schenick, R.C. - 1872 Rules for Playing Poker	The dealer has no special advantage.	The dealer has an advantage in draw games and a large advantage in low ball and twist stud games.
27. Smith, R.A. - 1925 Poker to Win	The yellowest, most contemptible form of cheating is welching.	The welcher has lost his money in the game before borrowing, therefore, he has been an asset.
28. Steig, I. - 1959 Poker for Fun and Profit	When someone says, "There isn't much to poker," walk away from him; he is a lout.	When someone says, "There isn't much to poker," get him in the game; he will be a valuable loser.
29. Wickstead, J.M. - 1938 How To Win At Stud Poker	In poker, fortune favors the brave.	In poker, the objective thinker makes fortune favor him.

Book	Concept	Failure of Concept
30. Winterblossom, H.T. - 1875 Draw Poker	The bluffing element in draw poker is fictitious.	The importance of bluffing depends on the stakes, not on the type of game.
31. Yardley, H.O. - 1957 Education of a Poker Player	In all my life, I've never lost at over three consecutive sittings.	A good player at theoretical maximum edge odds (an impossible situation) will lose about once every four sessions ... or lose in four consecutive sittings about once every 250 sessions. Also, the good player never brags about his success.
32. General Advice in most poker books from 1872 to 1966	Keep stakes down, hold to a rigid quitting time, play tight and according to the card odds.	The good player drives the stakes up, usually avoids a rigid quitting time, and plays according to the investment odds.

By applying the *common* concepts of poker, one can win moderately in small stake games that consist mainly of poor players. But in regular high stake games, continual losses force most poor players to quit or to improve. High stake games, therefore, often consist of experienced poker players advanced beyond these common concepts.

When a player using the common concepts enters a high stake game, he usually feels confident that by playing tight he must eventually win over his looser playing opponents. Bewilderment then replaces his confidence as he continually loses against players whom he considers inferior competition.

Scotty Nichols usually plays sensibly . . . he bets only good hands and is the tightest player in the game. He has studied many books about poker and faithfully follows their techniques and strategy. According to these books, he should be a consistent winner, particularly in this game with its loose and wild players. Why is he a loser? John Finn knows the answer . . . Scotty plays too tight. The pots he wins are usually small, and the pots he loses are often large. Why? Whenever Scotty shows betting strength or even stays in a hand, the other players either fold or stop betting. When he wins, therefore, the pots are smaller than normal. When players do bet against him to make a large pot, they usually hold a powerful enough hand to beat him. In other words, Scotty is a tight player who, as the wild player, has not adjusted to the game pace.

2. Advanced Concepts (15)

To extract maximum money from a poker game, the "Advanced Concepts of Poker" must be applied. Application of these concepts involves -

- opponents who do not fully understand poker
- a pot that separates players from their money*
- an interaction among the good player, the other players, and a pot.

By using the "Advanced Concepts of Poker", the good player eventually wins all the money that his opponents are willing to lose.

Objective, planned deception is the strategic basis for the "Advanced Concepts of Poker". Unlimited deception is accepted and ethical in poker. John Finn makes full use of this unique license and will do anything (except cheat) that brings him an advantage.

The other players in the Monday night game believe they are deceptive. Their deception, however, is generally unimaginative and repetitive . . . it seldom fools John Finn.

The application of the "Advanced Concepts of Poker" is detailed in Part Two of this book.

** Unattached money in a pot belongs to no one and can be won by any deceptive means, except cheating. Use of normal poker deception would be unethical and often fraudulent if the money were taken directly from an individual rather than from an ownerless pot.*

PART TWO

TECHNIQUE
(DTC Method)

Discipline, Thought, and Control are the techniques of good poker. The DTC method is the application of these three techniques.

VII. DISCIPLINE (16)

Discipline is the mechanism of good poker. Self-control develops through discipline. Self-control is necessary to -

- prevent emotions from affecting actions
- allow total concentration to focus on the game
- permit continuous objective thinking in order to analyze past action, to carry out present action, and to plan future action.

Self-control develops by practicing the following disciplines during the game:

Discipline Practiced	*Self-Control Developed*
Consume no food or beverage	Awareness
Do not swear or display feelings	Emotional control
Maintain good posture . . . sit straight and keep both feet flat on the floor	Alertness
Memorize important hands played and the performance of each opponent	Concentration
Mentally review and criticize each play	Objectivity

The good player increases his advantage as the game grinds into late hours. His disciplines become more nagging and thus more effective for maintaining self-control. At the same time, the concentration and playing ability of his tired opponents decrease. Also, as his opponents develop into big winners or losers for the evening, they become less objective and respond more to their feelings.

A decrease in self-control has a cumulative effect that can cause even a sound player to deteriorate into a poor player. For example, if a loss of self-control generates a breakdown in discipline, then a process of deterioration starts. Deterioration may be only temporary . . . but can be permanent especially with compulsive gamblers. Deterioration can be induced or can start spontaneously by -

- a long losing or winning streak
- entering a higher or a lower stake game
- a close loss of a big hand
- a bad play or bet
- an upsetting remark
- a personal problem.

The good player recognizes any loss of his own self-control during the game. He adopts the following attitudes to prevent deterioration of his play:

- Actual winning or losing of a pot is not important.
- Each well-played hand, won or lost, is a victory.
- Each poorly played hand is a defeat (even if the pot is won).
- Each move lacking self-control will eventually cost more money than is in any pot.

A continuous string of flawless* plays can produce a reciprocating momentum that perfects discipline. If a bad play spoils this momentum, the resulting loss of confidence can lead to poorer quality poker. A bad play to the good poker player is like a cigarette to an ex-smoker . . . one slip (betrayal of one's self) breaks his momentum of discipline and can bring disaster.

A few minutes of post-game discipline are necessary to record valuable information and data about the game. In addition to his notes written after each game, the good player periodically re-evaluates the game and players. These evaluations point out slow changes occurring in the game and often suggest changes in strategy necessary to maintain optimum edge odds.

John Finn uses convenient, mimeographed outlines as shown on pages 34, 36, 38 and periodically fills them out as shown on pages 35, 37 and 39. These outlines provide him with a consistent form of information on the game and players.

---

* *The good player does not consider an honest error in judgement as a flaw. To him, the flaw is the failure to think and act rationally. The flawless play, therefore, is one based on full, rational thought.*

WEEKLY GAME NOTES*

GAME –

DATE –

Highlights –

Evaluation of game –

Evaluation of own performance –

(a) errors

(b) unusual plays –

(c) number of wins –

(d) calculated edge odds –

Information on opponents

(a) observations

(b) performance

(c) winnings, losses, and debts,$

(d) bluffs, tried/called –

Statistics

(a) number of hands played –

(b) starting and quitting time –

(c) maximum win –

(d) maximum loss –

Miscellaneous –

** Collecting and remembering the data for these Weekly Game Notes require discipline and concentration. Indeed, the chief value in acquiring these notes is not the data themselves, but is the forced mental attention on the game that is required to collect these data.*

WEEKLY GAME NOTES

GAME – *Monday, weekly*

DATE – *9/10/62*

Highlights –

Sid cheats Quintin out of $700 pot. Have talk with Quintin. Everything okay. ...New player Jeff Klien is a good addition. Will be permanent loser. ...Ted absent. Broke from playing horses. ...Sid plays wildly and poorly, but won big.

Evaluation of game –

Continues at fast pace. Near optimum stakes for now. Only Charlie appears in financial trouble. Scotty is starting to hurt.

Evaluation of own performance – *$550 win*

(a) errors – *2*
(details in black book, pg.52)

(b) unusual plays – *3*
(details in black book, pg. 78)

(c) number of wins – *12*
(7 full, 5 split)

(d) calculated edge odds –
550/650x100 = 85%

Information on opponents

(a) observations

Jeff blinks eyes when a bet is made against his weak hand. Keeps eyes open wide when he has a strong hand.

(b) performance

Aaron - fair
Quintin - good to fair
Scotty - fair to poor
Charlie - very poor
Jeff - fair
Mike - fair
Sid - poor
John - good

(c) winnings, losses, and debts,$

Sid - +650
John - +550
Mike - +400
Jeff - +200
Aaron - -250
Scotty - -300
Quintin - -350
Charlie - -900 (borrows $300)

(d) bluffs, tried/called – *30/19*

Aaron - 3/2
Quintin - 1/0
Scotty - 0
Charlie - 6/5
Jeff - 1/1
Mike - 0
Sid - 15/10
John - 4/1

Statistics

(a) number of hands played – *108*
(%won = 12/108 = 11%)

(b) starting and quitting time –
8:15 PM - 5:00 AM

(c) maximum win –
+$650 (Sid)

(d) maximum loss –
-$900 (Charlie)

Miscellaneous –

- *Need another regular player.*
- *Everyone absorbing losses okay, except Charlie who is getting desperate.*
- *Problem about Ted's debts and bounced checks.*

**SEMI-ANNUAL
GAME PROFILE**

GAME –
PERIOD –

Pace and Stakes –

Average maximum win –

Average maximum loss –

Performance of opponents –

Regular players –

New or occasional players –

Games played –

Ante per player –

Betting –

Raising –

Attitudes –

Personal performance –

Miscellaneous –

SEMI-ANNUAL GAME PROFILE

GAME – *Monday, weekly*
PERIOD – *1/8/62 - 6/4/62*

Pace and Stakes – *Fast pace is near maximum. Pressure for higher stakes.*

Average maximum win – *+$550*

Average maximum loss – *-$450*

Performance of opponents – *Average and fairly stable. Quintin is improving. Scotty, Aaron, and Ted are deteriorating.*

Regular players – *John Finn, Quintin Merck, Sid Bennett, Ted Fehr, Scotty Nichols.*

New or occasional players – *Aaron Smith, Mike Bell, Charlie Holland, Mac Zimmerman, Jim Todd, Jake Fehr, Lee Pennock, Jeff Klien.*

Games played – *Draw and stud with twists, high-low and qualifiers. Occasionally use wild cards and the Bug.*

Ante per player – *$1.00 for stud. $5.00 for draw.*

Betting – *In draw, $25 open then $50 in subsequent rounds. In stud, $5 first card then increase by $5 for each additional card. Twists are free. . . . 80% of bets are at the maximum.*

Raising – *Right to bet rule. Normally three raises. With only two players, raises are unlimited. Check raises okay.*

Attitudes – *Generally good. Sid continues to cheat without problems. No one resentful or in danger of quitting.*

Personal performance – *Good, but leveling off in effort. Areas to improve - Increase focus on broader aspects of the game. Increase flexibility in style during early rounds.*

Miscellaneous – *Stakes are ready to move up to next level. Try doubling stakes for the last round in the next few games.*

SEMMI-ANNUAL
PLAYER PROFILE

NAME –

PERIOD –

Classification –

Motive –

Attitude –

Performance –

Average won or lost/game –

Edge odds –

Behavior

Open –

Bet –

Call –

Raise –

Last bet –

Bluff –

Fold –

Weaknesses –

Strengths –

Changes –

Miscellaneous –

**SEMMI-ANNUAL
PLAYER PROFILE**

NAME – *Quintin Merck*

PERIOD – *1/8/62 - 6/4/62*

Classification – *Sound player and improving.*

Motive – *Pass time. Satisfy ego. ...Shifting to motive of making money.*

Attitude – *Grouchy but improving.*

Performance – *Above average.*

Average won or lost/game – *+$50 and increasing.*

Edge odds – *+10% and increasing.*

Behavior

Open – *When under the gun, he holds back good hands.When dealing, he will almost always open.*

Bet – *Bets too light in early rounds. Same give-away habits (listed in black book, pg. 17).*

Call – *Calls with much weaker hands than he is willing to bet.*

Raise – *Too conservative. Seldom raises a good winning hand if it is of low value.*

Last bet – *Bets only when sure, but calls with weak hands.*

Bluff – *Seldom. Averages once every two sessions. Same give-away habits (listed in black book, pg. 17).*

Fold – *Folds too easily early in hand and too hard late in hand.*

Weaknesses – *Play deteriorates when he gets angry from personal insults or from humiliating losses. Betting is out of proportion. Too conservative, but tires in late hours then plays too loose.*

Strengths – *Fairly objective. Conservative. Tries to concentrate.*

Changes – *Improving and becoming more objective. Making conscious effort to improve. Better control over emotions.*

Miscellaneous – *He becomes less valuable as he improves. If improvement and winnings continue, he will be a liability. May have to eliminate him from the game.*

A few minutes of pre-game discipline is needed to review past notes. Also, a nap before the game improves discipline and thought. A bath and a shave before the game help retain the freshness necessary to sustain peak performance through an all-night session.

How valuable is discipline? Obviously it is important in poker. But, how valuable is discipline to the extent of not eating refreshments? Did you ever eat a seven hundred and fifty dollar sandwich? Well, such costly sandwiches are sometimes eaten in John Finn's game.

Consider Scotty Nichols who tries hard to play a good game. . . .Sid deals draw poker. Scotty seems nervous, as if desperate to win a pot. He opens for $25 with a pair of Aces, and Sid raises to $50. Now Scotty is sucked in and calls. Nervous hunger seizes him. He rushes to the food table and rapidly piles many slabs of ham and cheese into a giant sandwich. In the meantime, Ted Fehr draws a card and carelessly flashes it . . . it is the Ace of Diamonds. Then the dealer, waving the deck around, exposes the bottom card for all to see - except Scotty who is laying pickles in his sandwich. The bottom card? It is the Ace of Clubs.

Now it is Scotty's turn to draw. Hurrying back to the table, he smiles at his sandwich. Then with a yawning mouth, his teeth chomp into the pile of food. Beads of mustard ooze over the crust and drip onto his slacks. Then with mustard-covered fingers, Scotty picks up his cards. . . . John Finn watches him play. Yes, the pair of Aces are still there. But wait . . . he also has four Spades. Scotty wonders what to do.

"Come on," Quintin grunts. "Speed up the game."

"Got to go with my best hand," Scotty finally blurts. He draws three cards to his pair of Aces and then jams the rest of the sandwich into his mouth. The first card off the deck is the King of Spades . . . his flush card. So what? he still catches another King to give him two pair, Aces and Kings . . . a pretty good hand.

This pretty good hand is enough to keep him in for a $50 bet then a $50 raise. Quintin Merck wins with a Queen high flush.

"What rotten luck", Scotty whines as he grabs an overflowing handful of potato chips. His words are followed by a slobbering crunch.

Rotten luck? Had Scotty stayed at the table, he would have seen the two flashed Aces and drawn to his four flush to win the $600 pot. Instead he loses $150. That ham and cheese sandwich cost him $750! . . . Also, John Finn uses the mustard stains on Scotty's cards to identify them in future hands.

VIII. THOUGHT (17)

Thought is the labor of good poker. Objectivity and steady concentration are needed to think properly; this requires discipline. *Analytical* thinking is necessary to understand and predict the actions of opponents. *Objective* thinking is necessary to plan the proper action.

The good player continually thinks about poker during the game. He looks at his cards quickly to allow maximum time for observation and thought. He never wastes precious time by slowly looking at or squeezing his cards. When involved in a hand, his thoughts concentrate on strategy. The good player gains a major advantage over other players by thinking ahead and forming several strategical plans based on anticipated hands. When an anticipated hand develops, he can make quicker and more accurate playing decisions. . . . When not involved in a hand, the good player studies the game, gathers data, and plans future strategy. Between hands, he analyzes the action of each concluded hand.

Intensive thought and concentration also help to overcome nervousness, which even a good player may experience when playing in an unfriendly or a high-stake game.

Since thinking is the labor of poker, maximum effort should yield maximum returns. How much is this effort worth in dollars? When a player wins an average of $40 per game, his winning rate is equivalent to a job paying $15,200 per year*. Average winnings of $150 per game are equivalent to a $57,000 per year job*.

Compare the effort in poker to the effort required in a job yielding similar earnings. For example, a winning rate of $5 per game is equivalent to a job paying only $1,900 per year*; such pay would not be worth the effort needed to play good poker.

Let us see how thinking pays off. John Finn is under the gun in draw poker. He has a four flush in Hearts and checks. Next is Sid Bennett, who opens for $25. John check-raises to $50. Sid and Scotty call the raise. Now John draws and immediately looks at his card . . . he misses his flush. Does he give up? No . . . by paying attention and thinking, there is still a chance to win that $250 pot. John stays alert, and this is what he sees and hears:

Sid Bennett draws one card, sticks it in the center of his hand then quickly looks at it. Is he drawing to a flush, a straight, or two pair? Probably two pair, because when he draws one card to the flush or straight he places the draw card at the back end of his hand then looks at it very slowly. This along with his betting pattern (opens then reluctantly calls a raise), suggests that Sid has two pair.

Ted Fehr flashes a black picture card when dealing Scotty's draw card. While ruffling the cards through his chubby fingers, Scotty exposes the deuce of Hearts. Therefore, if he were going for the flush or straight, he missed it. Scotty slowly squeezes his cards open to look at his new card then gives a blowing exhale. He usually inhales when he sees a good draw.

Now John has a good view of the situation. The opener (Sid

---

* *Calculated for a five hour weekly game . . . and 1900 hours of actual work per year (estimated from data in the U.S. Government Bulletin, "Employment, Earnings and Monthly Report on the Labor Force", volume 12, number 10, April, 1966).*

with two pair) looks weak with respect to the two, one-card draw hands behind him . . . especially after John raised the first round bet. Knowing that Scotty has a busted hand, John sits in a position of strength, despite his worthless hand. He has the last bet, and the other players respect his hand because of his first round raise followed by his single card draw. John has an excellent chance of buying the $250 pot with a bluff.

If Sid and Scotty check and John bets $50, Sid would probably drop his winning hand because he would also have to contend with Scotty's one card draw as well as John's one card draw. If Sid folds, Scotty would then fold his busted hand leaving John the pot. John figures his chances of a successful bluff under these circumstances are better than 1 to 2. The return for winning the pot would be about 5 to 1. He estimates his investment odds at $250 X 0.3/$50 = 1.5 . . . these are good odds.

What if Sid bets his two pair? Does John fold his hand or does he still bluff by raising back? He would probably fold for the following reasons:

- After already betting $50, Sid would probably call John's raise – out of pride if for no other reason.

- Sid's bet would drive out Scotty, thus eliminating a big factor needed to bluff Sid out. John's chances of a successful bluff would decrease sharply.

- John would have to risk $100 for a $300 pot - a 3 to 1 return on his bluff play rather than the 5 to 1 return if Sid does not bet. His investment odds would fall to $450 X 0.1/100 = 0.45 . . . a very unfavorable level.

What actually happens? Well, things turn out better than John hoped for. Sid checks, and Scotty hesitates then suddenly bets $50. This is his normal pattern when bluffing - hesitate then bet fast. Scotty's obvious bluff attempt makes John's bluff even easier. He casually raises to $100. Sid and Scotty fold immediately.

John wins a $300 pot with a worthless hand plus a little thinking.

Incidentally, in 1965 John Finn earns $42,000 while playing 400 hours in the Monday night game. This equals $105 per hour, which is equivalent to a job yielding $200,000 per year. . . . A job paying that much is worth a concentrated thinking effort.

IX. CONTROL (18)

Control is the result of good poker. When the good player achieves self-control through discipline and understands his opponents through thinking, he then can seize control of the game. When in control, he becomes the center of attention. His opponents spend a major portion of their effort trying to figure out his moves and then adjusting to them . . . they play according to his actions. From this controlling position he can -

- influence the betting, raising, and bluffing of his opponents
- force opponents into traps and wrong moves
- dilute opponents' attention toward one another so he can play them off against each other.

The player who continually strives for maximum *investment* odds cannot control the game. Always making the play that yields the maximum return reduces the flexibility needed to control the players and to achieve maximum *edge* odds. The good player, therefore, chooses from a wide variety of plays available at slightly less favorable odds. For example, by backing off from the maximum investment odds, the good player increases his flexibility in play-making so greatly that he can produce almost any desired effect. Also, by under-betting a hand then over-betting a subsequent similar hand with only an occasional bet made at the maximum investment odds, he makes his betting unpredictable. This flexibility and unpredictability allow the good player to control the betting.

Money flows toward the player who controls the betting. The best time to get this control is early in the hand while the bets are still cheap. The good player often gains control by unexpected or unusual plays (such as a raise into obvious strength of an opponent), by larger than usual first round bets, or by weird bets (such as a four dollar bet instead of the usual five dollar bet). He then makes subsequent offensive or defensive betting manipulations designed to influence the big, last round bets and raises.

Offensive manipulations designed to maximize a potential win are done by altering (increasing or decreasing) the betting pace in order to -

- build pots
- encourage players to stay for the large, last round bets
- set up bluffs
- induce opponents to bluff.

Defensive manipulations designed to minimize a potential loss are done by altering (increasing or decreasing) the betting pace in order to -

- suppress bets or raises
- prevent bluffs

- drive out or keep in players to change the investment odds for drawing to potential hands (such as two pair, or a four-flush) from unfavorable to favorable.

Confusion and fear decrease the ability of players to think objectively and to play their hands properly. Most players fear the confusing play and unpredictable betting of the good player. He further increases their fear of him by making shock or spectacular plays. Many opportunities occur where investment odds actually favor spectacular maneuvers such as -

- holding a high pair pat in draw poker
- breaking up a full house to draw to three of a kind
- raising then dropping out on the next bet
- making a colorful bluff such as holding pat and betting four Kings in a low-ball game
- raising a weak looking stud hand in the face of very strong appearing opposition
- dropping a strong looking stud hand in the face of weak appearing opposition.

John Finn has a big psychological advantage over his opponents. He confuses, shocks, bullies, frightens and worries them into concentrating their attention on him. They react strongly to his actions. Their moves and bets are often distorted because they base them on trivial moves by John while ignoring significant moves by other players. Knowing how they will react to his moves, John can often make them do what he wants, while he alone retains a balanced view of the game. The results? . . . he controls the game.

Watch how this control works. Immediately after bluffing Sid Bennett (on page 43), John spreads his cards face up across the table. Seeing John's four Hearts with a big black Club right in the middle, Sid moans and groans as the other players laugh at him. With his face blushing red, he mutters, "I'll sleep in the street before you bluff me out again."

The players are still talking about John's bluff as Scotty Nichols starts the next deal. Ted opens for $25. Sid fumbles with his money . . . an indication that he wants to raise. John has a pair of Aces that could be played with advantageous investment odds if he can gain an offensive betting position and prevent Sid's raise. This is an easy problem for John. He just throws some confusion at the players by making a weird $3 raise.

Sid drops the money he was fingering. "What's Finn up to?" he says wrinkling his nose. "He's either got nothing or a powerhouse. Uh . . . probably hoping for a raise."

Perfect. That is exactly the reaction John wanted . . . the silent players stare at him with opened mouths as they try to figure out his bet. The result? Everyone just calls and then anxiously waits for John's next move. With that three dollar bet, John prevents any raising, gets everyone's attention, and assumes the offensive betting position.

Now the draw. John Finn takes three cards, and Sid frowns at him. Immediately, John looks at his draw. He catches a pair of Jacks to give him Aces-up, two pair. His expression remains unchanged. Sid draws one card, glances at it and then grunts, "I had John beat all the time. Should've raised him out of his seat."

A convenient statement for John . . . it verifies that Sid still has two pair. Scotty also draws one. By knowing his betting and playing habits, John reads him for two pair also. Ted draws one card; his freckled face stiffens as he slowly squeezes his cards apart. Then with a burst of swear words, he flings the cards across the table.

"Miss your flush?" Quintin Merck smiles with a fluttering moustache. Ted just pouts his lips and looks at the ceiling.

John makes a nominal $1 bet. Sid, still mumbling about being bluffed out of the previous hand and then being tricked out of the first round raise, reacts emotionally, "You ain't getting off cheap this time," he snorts. "I raise fifty bucks."

Scotty Nichols hesitates a long time before calling. This confirms he has two pair. If Scotty had three of a kind or better, he would have called without hesitation. Now John is in a strong fundamental position with his Aces-up; he raises to $100. Both Sid and Scotty, having already bet their hands heavily, feel compelled to call and do. . . . John's Aces-up wins the four hundred dollar pot.

So with a normally unfavorable hand and position, John controls the betting and wins the pot. Also by controlling the players, he builds a potential one hundred dollar pot into a big, four hundred dollar pot by tickling Sid's emotions.

* * *

John Finn is a good player because he disciplines himself, thinks objectively, then takes control of the game. Discipline, thought, then control - the DTC method - is his technique for good poker.

Parts Three, Four and Five of this book show how the good player with the DTC Method achieves -

- improved edge odds (increased advantage)
- faster money flow (increased income)
- more players and games (increased future earnings).

PART THREE

STRATEGY

With discipline and objective thinking, the good player takes control of poker games. With the proper strategy, he molds these games to his maximum advantage. His prime strategical tool is deception.

INGREDIENTS OF STRATEGY (19)

Proper strategy depends on the game, opponents, and the situation. Certain phases of poker remain constant; other phases change from bet to bet, hand to hand, or game to game. The good player bases his long-term strategy on the constant phases of poker and his short-term strategy on the variable phases. Good strategy contains the following ingredients:

Strategy	*Principle Ingredient*
Long range	Understanding of game
Short range	Knowledge of opponents
Immediate action	Awareness of situation

1. Understanding Game (20)

The mechanics of poker are simple and can be learned in a few minutes. The strategy of poker, however, has infinite possibilities. Strategy depends more on proper technique than on experience. Even a novice can acquire an immediate strategic advantage over seasoned opponents by applying the DTC technique.

Long-range (general) strategy develops from an understanding of the game. The good player understands the game by appraising the -

- quality of players

- betting pace
- availability of cash
- credit situation
- general attitude and friendliness
- areas of resistance and resentment
- bluffing attitudes
- reasons for player turn-over.

When a player fails to appraise a game accurately, he experiences -

- decreased edge odds
- errors and missed opportunities
- less effective strategy.

The good player continually re-evaluates the game in order to detect changes and inaccurate appraisals.

All sorts of game and player information are in John Finn's black leather notebook. Every month he summarizes his observations in a section labeled "General Appraisal of Game and Players". Here is a typical summary:

"Monday - 7/9/62. The players have stabilized over the past month, except for the continued disintegration of Scotty's game . . . he gets desperate when losing heavily and then makes poor bets and bluffs. The betting pace is gradually increasing as wild modifications are added. The betting stakes remain stable. The cash situation is good despite heavy losses by Sid, Ted and Scotty. But Ted is in financial trouble; he runs up large debts then pays them off with borrowed money. He may soon go broke.

"Resentment is building up between Quintin and Sid. Quintin sarcastically questions Sid's honesty. Sid shouts back angry remarks about Quintin's stinginess. This quarrel must end before it hurts the game.

"The game is in good shape and yields a substantial income. No one seems about to quit, except Ted if he goes bankrupt. But the game needs one or two new players . . . Aaron Smith would be a profitable addition."

2. *Knowing Opponents* (21)

Short range strategy develops from knowledge of opponents. The good player knows his opponents by appraising their –

- personalities
- weaknesses and strengths
- behavior patterns
- motives for playing
- economic status
- betting and raising tendencies
- dropping and bluffing tendencies
- areas of confusion and errors.

Classification of opponents is a major step toward understanding them. Poker players usually can be put into one of the following classes:

Class of Player	*Ability to Control*	*Ability to Read*	*Performance*
Good	Hardest	Very difficult	Biggest winner
Sound	↓ Increase ease to control	Difficult	↓ Decrease winnings
Daring, unconventional		Medium	
Loose winner		Medium	
Tight winner		Medium	
Tight loser		Easy	Loser
Loose loser		Easy	↓ Increase losings
Very tight		Easy	
Wild		Medium	
Desperate		Medium	
Suicidal	Easiest	Medium	Biggest loser

Some players are a mixture of two classes. Also, the class of a player can change from moment to moment or over the long term as shown below:

Class Change	*Reasons for Change*
Over long term	Increased experience, personality changes
From game to game	Feelings, emotions, stakes, financial condition
From one type of game to another	Differences in understanding various games
From hand to hand	Winning, losing, tired, upset
During play of a hand	Improper perspective on different phases of betting

John classifies the players in the Monday night game as follows:

Player	*Class*	*Ability to control and read*	*Performance*	*Changes*
John Finn	**Good**	**Very difficult**	**Big winner**	**Stable. General long-term improvement.**
Quintin Merck	**Sound**	**Hard**	**Winner**	**Some deterioration when tired or insulted. General long-term improvement.**
Scotty Nichols	**Very tight**	**Easy**	**Loser**	**Deteriorates when losing heavily or on a long losing streak, then plays loose and poorly.**
Sid Bennett	**Wild**	**Medium**	**Big loser**	**Tightens up if feelings are hurt. Plays wild when winning.**
Ted Fehr	**Suicidal**	**Easy**	**Big loser**	**Plays tight early in game then disintegrates, especially if losing. His playing becomes even worse when on a horse betting spree.**

3. Situation and Position (22)

Action (immediate) strategy depends on the immediate situation. This strategy involves decisions about calling, opening, betting, raising, dropping and bluffing. In making these decisions, the good player correlates the following four factors to the immediate situation:

1. Estimated Strength* of Own Hand

2. Game

   pace
   temperament
   atmosphere
   time (such as first hand, a late hour, last hand)
   size of pot
   potential size of pot

3. Opponents

   indicated strength
   attitude
   attentiveness
   win or loss status
   effect of previous bet

4. Position

   fundamental
   technical

The good player appraises his situation from two positions- the fundamental and the technical. The *fundamental position* is the *statistical value*** of a hand relative to the other play-

---

** Estimated strength of a hand relative to estimated strengths of opponents' hands is a function of one's evaluations.*

*** Statistical value of a hand relative to other hands is a function of the number of players. The statistical value of a hand decreases with increasing number of players.*

ers' hands. The *technical position* is his strategical and psychological advantage over his opponents at a given moment. An important factor in his technical position is his *seat position.*

Seat position is important in nearly every decision. The good player adjusts his strategy according to his position relative to the dealer, opener, bettor, raiser, and the strong and weak hands. He considers his seat position in decisions about -

Increasing importance of seat position ↑

- bluffing
- betting or raising
- declaring hand (in split pot games)
- calling or dropping
- playing of cards
- influencing opponents to call or drop
- inducing opponents to bet or raise
- planning long range strategy.

The best seat position depends on where the other players sit. The good player generally positions himself as shown below:

Good player prefers to bet before these types of players -	*Good player prefers to bet after these types of players -*
Weak	Strong
Wild but readable	Impulsive, erratic, not readable or predictable
Loose but predictable	Tight
Plays dealer-advantage games (such as twist and draw games)	Plays conventional stud games
Fast	Slow

The good player usually gets a desirable seat at the start of a game because his opponents seldom care where they sit.If an opponent is conscious of position, he generally tries to sit behind (bet after) the wildest player . . . a position the good player seldom wants. A player can pick a good position by arriving after the players are seated and then squeezing into the best seat position. But continuous late arrival for this purpose can hurt a game. The good player will use the excuse of "changing his luck" to swap seats with a player in a better position. This move also gives his opponents the erroneous but advantageous impression that he is superstitious.

The dealer has an advantage in draw or closed hands because he bets last. This advantage can be eliminated by using a marker or a buck to determine the first bettor. The good player, however, usually avoids or discourages the use of any controls such as a marker.

Most regular players get into a habit of sitting in the same position. In the Monday night game, John arranges the seating to his advantage, then game after game the players sit approximately in the same order. He maintains this seating arrangement by preventing the players from realizing that they are sitting in habitual patterns advantageous to him.

Ted Fehr's betting is erratic and impulsive. While John can usually read Ted's hands, he can seldom predict his betting actions. By positioning himself so Ted bets first, John can adjust his strategy according to Ted's play. Sid Bennett's betting is wild but predictable. By betting before him, John can often check his strong hands and let Sid do the betting for him. It makes less difference to John where Quintin (a sound player) or Scotty (a tight player) sit. The ideal seating arrangement for John is illustrated below:

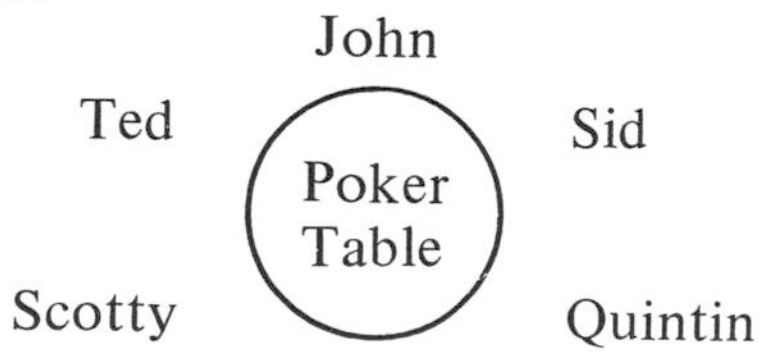

XI. TAILOR-MADE GAME (23)

The good player designs poker games to his maximum advantage by increasing the betting pace, the betting stakes, and his edge odds. A major step in this direction is to complicate the game by orienting the action around stud poker rather than draw poker. Stud poker offers the following advantages to the good player:

- More skill and effort are needed to assimilate the additional information and variables offered by the exposed cards.*
- Added rounds of progressively higher bets effectively increase the betting *stakes.*
- Faster and more bets effectively increase the betting *pace.*

1. Increasing the Betting Pace (24)

The good player increases the money flow in a poker game to maximize his profits. Opposition to higher stakes, however, exists in most games. An effective and subtle way to increase the money flow is to increase the betting pace rather than the betting stakes. A faster pace usually increases excitement in a way that is attractive to most players, especially the weaker players.

The betting pace is increased by adding modifications to the game such as listed below:

Modification	*Effects*
Twist	Provides additional large, last-round bets Induces players to stay for twist cards Increases confusion Amplifies players' weaknesses

***** *The good player will add further variables by inconspicuously altering the order of his exposed cards.*

Modification	*Effects*
Split pots (high-low)	Allows more bets and raises Provides more playing opportunities Increases confusion Amplifies players' weaknesses
Check Raise	Allows more, large raises
Pick-up checks	Permits larger bets
Right to bet	Allows more raises
Early bet	Early build-up of pot keeps players in for large last-round bets
Bet or get	Allows more bets
Additional cards	Produces more calls
Novel games	Increases confusion Amplifies players' weaknesses
Wild cards and freak hands	May or may not increase betting pace Increases confusion
Table stakes or pot limit	Allows direct control over the betting stakes.

The good player can gradually work many of these modifications into most games - even into games that are not dealer's choice. These modifications increase the circulation of money, which lets the good player win more because the faster pace lets his opponents lose more. The following paragraphs describe these modifications:

a. Twist (25)

The twist increases the betting pace. At the normal conclusion of a poker hand, a card or cards may be exchanged (twisted) for a new card or cards. An additional round of betting follows each twist. As players grow accustomed to this modification, they usually become addicted to it and make the twist a permanent part of the game.

A single twist played with five-card stud is the gentlest way to introduce this modification; most players will accept a twist as a good way to convert normally dull five-card stud into a more interesting six-card stud game. As players get accustomed to this twist, other twist modifications can be added such as -

Faster betting pace ↓

- twist in seven-card stud
- twist in draw poker
- pay for each twist (for example, an amount equal to the ante)
- double twists
- giant twist in stud (as many cards as the player desires are exchanged on each twist)
- progressive paying for unlimited twists (second twist costs twice the first twist, third twist costs twice the second, and so on)
- unlimited, giant twists.

b. Split pot, high-low (26)

The betting pace increases markedly by splitting pots between highest and lowest hands (high-low poker) because of the dynamic betting between the strongest high and the strongest low hands. Many players are hostile to high-low poker until they understand it. Seven-card stud high-low is perhaps the gentlest way to introduce split pot games. With patience and persistence, the good player can usually generate great interest in high-low poker. Other high-low modifications that can be added are -

Faster betting pace ↓

- high-low five-card stud
- high-low draw
- high-low with qualifiers (minimum hands required to win, such as two pair for high and nine for low)
- high-low with twist
- high-low with qualifiers and twists.

c. Check raise and pick-up checks (27)

Player A checks; player B bets; now player A raises . . . this is called *check raising.* Player A checks; player B checks; player C makes a bet three times larger than the maximum bet by making A's bet, B's raise, and then his own raise . . . this is called *picking-up checks.* Check raising and picking-up checks increase the betting flexibility as well as the number of large bets and raises. If these modifications cause a defensive attitude among players, however, a decrease in the betting pace occurs. Also, house rules of many games prohibit check raising and picking-up checks.

d. Right to bet (28)

Every player has a chance to bet or raise during each round of betting. With this rule, a player holding a strong hand cannot be shut out of his bet or raise by three minimal raises made in front of him. Right to bet increases the betting pace, particularly in split pot games. Players seldom object to this seemingly equitable modification.

e. Early bet (29)

An indirect method to increase the ante is to permit a small bet after dealing the first hole-card in stud or the second card in draw. This early bet holds more players in for the later rounds of large betting. If most players stay or drop on the basis of their cards rather than on the size of the pot, however, this modification can drive out potential players and thus decrease the betting pace.

f. Bet or get (30)

No checking is permitted with this rule . . . each player must either bet or drop. This modification gets players involved early and keeps them in for the big, last-round bets. Most players are unaccustomed to this modification and may object vigorously to it.

g. Additional cards (31)

An additional sixth card is dealt to each draw hand. The hands are then reduced to five cards during the draw. This additional card keeps more players in the hand, particularly in low-ball draw. Players seldom object when this simple modification is introduced.

h. Novel games (32)

Poorer playing normally results when a new or novel game is introduced because the players do not understand the changes in odds that occur. Novel games may range from a simple one such as Lowball Draw or Hold Me to a complex one such as Place-and-Show-Tickets-Split-Pot-with-Twist-Your-Neighbor. (This game is played as follows . . . at the conclusion of a stud or draw game, each player draws a card from the hand of an adjacent player for use in his own hand. The pot is then split between the second and third best hands.)

A decreased betting pace may result, however, if players become frightened by wild games or modifications that are introduced too rapidly or are too extreme.

i. Wild cards and freak hands (33)

Wild cards increase the betting pace and loosen up certain games. But if hands such as five of a kind or straight flushes become so common that any betting strength suggests a maximum value hand, suppressed betting results. Fear of very strong hands usually decreases as players become accustomed to playing with wild cards.

The bug card (the Joker used as a wild card for completing straights and flushes and as an Ace in all other hands) can increase the betting pace without causing fear of maximum value hands.

The good player rarely encourages the use of freak hands such as blazes, tigers, dogs, kilters and skeets. While such hands could temporarily increase his edge odds by adding confusion, the use of freak hands may discourage players from accepting more profitable modifications such as twists and split pots with qualifiers.

j. Table stakes and pot limit (34)

Table stakes or pot limit betting gives the good player direct control over the betting stakes. But this type of betting can slow down the betting pace and normally cannot be used with split pot games. In many games, therefore, table stakes or pot limit betting would decrease the financial opportunities for the good player.

Six years ago, Sid Bennett insisted that good poker players liked only straight draw and stud games. He claimed five-card stud was the greatest gambling game of all. As John Finn gradually increased the betting pace by adding one modification after another, Sid went to the other extreme as shown below:

Sid is winning; his pale lips are smiling. He grabs the deck, shoves his face over the table and announces, "New game!" He then deals two separate hole cards to everyone.

"What's this?" Quintin says with his face twisting into a knotted shape.

"Seven stud high-low. Everyone plays two hands. You can even raise yourself," Sid says through a snorting laugh. "And the hand to the left of the highest hand wins high and the hand to the right of the lowest hand wins low."

"I'm going home," Quintin says as he grabs his ante from the pot and stands up to leave.

"Sit down; we aren't going to play that," John Finn says. He then turns to Sid and explains, "I know it's dealer's choice, but that's no poker game. You can't have hands next to the winners as winners."

"Bunch of ribbon clerks," Sid whines. "Okay, straight high-low . . . play your left hand for high and right hand for low. And you can still raise yourself."

"That's more like it," John says.

"Uh, that's just as bad," Quintin grunts while slumping back into his chair.

Sid's toothy grin stretches wider as he continues to deal.

2. Increasing the Betting Stakes (35)

After an increase in the betting pace, the good player can often increase the betting *stakes.* Most games can withstand as much as a ten to a hundred fold increase in the betting stakes! Even when the financial limits of the big losers seem reached, the stakes can usually be increased appreciably.

The good player increases the stakes in carefully planned steps. Several temporary increases may be necessary before higher stakes become permanent. In some games, however, stakes can be increased rapidly. Opportunities to increase the stakes occur when players want -

- a chance to get even by increasing the ante or stakes in the late hours or during the last round
- a more equitable relationship to the ante by increasing the first round or opening bets
- a chance to protect a hand by increasing the middle round bets
- an opportunity to bet a good hand by increasing the last round bets.

The stakes are normally easier to increase after the betting pace increases. Opposition to higher stakes and game modifications usually lessens when the resisting player is -

- tired
- losing heavily or winning big for the evening
- on a long losing or winning streak
- upset by some occurrence during the game
- affected by personal problems
- drinking.

John Finn starts playing in the Monday night game on June 6, 1960. The game is already seven years old, and the stakes have stabilized over the past five years. A dollar is the maximum bet, and only straight draw and stud games are allowed. . . . The following table shows how both the betting pace and stakes steadily increase after John takes control of the game:

			Money Flow		
Date	*Pace*	*Stakes,$*	*Average Big Winner,$*	*John Finn's Average Winnings,$*	*John Finn's Edge Odds,%*
6/60	**Straight stud and draw**	**0.50- 1**	**25**	**8**	**30**
7/60		**1- 2**	**40**	**14**	**35**
8/60	**Add twist**		**70**	**32**	**45**
9/60		**2- 4**	**100**	**40**	**40**
1/61	**Add high-low**		**170**	**94**	**55**
2/61		**5- 10**	**210**	**105**	**50**
6/61		**10- 20**	**260**	**130**	**50**
12/61	**Add qualifiers**		**360**	**234**	**65**
1/62		**25- 50**	**450**	**270**	**60**
7/62		**50-100**	**600**	**210**	**35**
8/62		**25- 50**	**550**	**358**	**65**
3/64		**50-100**	**700**	**350**	**50**
1/65	**Add complex and wild modifications**	**50-100**	**1400**	**840**	**60**

The above data show three interesting phenomena:

1. When the *stakes* increase, there is not a proportional increase in the average winnings (money flow). This is because players tighten up their play at higher stakes. An increase in the *pace,* however, causes a relatively large increase in the money flow.
2. John's edge odds go up when the *pace* increases and down when the *stakes* increase. This is because his opponents play poorer as the pace increases, but more cautiously at higher stakes.
3. An increase in the pace stimulates an increase in the stakes.

These data also show how the increases in stakes and pace affect John's profits. The doubling of stakes during July, 1962 results in his edge odds dropping sharply from 60% down to 35%. At these higher stakes, he must spend a much greater portion of his income to hold the valuable losers in the game. On realizing this, he drops the stakes back to the previous level and brings his edge odds up to a healthy 65%. Why the big increase in John's edge odds when he lowers the stakes? After getting a taste of larger bets, the players bet looser and play more carelessly when the stakes are lowered to the old level. A year and a half later, John increases the stakes again . . . and this time the increase is more profitable and permanent.

John usually tries raising the stakes soon after increasing the betting pace. Under the pretense of giving the losers a break, he increases the stakes during the last round. The following dialog shows how he manipulates the last round to his advantage:

"You're getting blasted again," Sid Bennett says to Ted Fehr. "Must be losing a grand."

"That's only four thousand hamburgers at my drive-in," Ted smiles. "Wait till I get the deal. I'm doubling the stakes like we did last week. Got to make a big comeback."

"No sir, none of that," Quintin Merck interrupts as his cigarette falls from his mouth. "Next thing you know, we'll be playing the whole game at doubled stakes."

"You're right," John says trying hard to sound sincere. "If anything, we should ban that last round of double stakes . . . it's too expensive."

"Yeah," Scotty Nichols says while counting his winnings.

. . .Two hours later, John announces the last round.

"Hey, double the stakes for the last round," Ted cries.

"Well . . . we made a rule against it," John shrugs. He then turns to the other players and continues, "We gave the losers a break last week. Ted is stuck bad. Let's double the ante and play a round of high-low poker."

"Yeah," Scotty says as he checks his freshly emptied wallet.

"I'm in," Ted says throwing his double ante into the pot.

"High-low draw? That's a stiff game," Quintin grumbles while slowly anteing. "Guess it's better than doubling the stakes."

What does John accomplish by this? He introduces the fast pace, high-low draw game. He doubles the ante, which will make it easier to increase the stakes at a later date. He creates the images that he is both helping a loser and opposing higher stakes . . . while actually setting up conditions for both higher stakes and a faster pace.

3. Increasing the Edge Odds (36)

The good player designs a game to yield maximum edge odds. The theoretical, maximum edge odds occur only when the perfect player is in the most complex game, under the most confusing circumstances against the poorest players. While the theoretical maximum edge odds can never be achieved, the good player strives to approach them. The perfect situation is represented by completion of The Diamond shown on page 66. The Diamond measures the idealness of a poker game for the good player.

THE DIAMOND

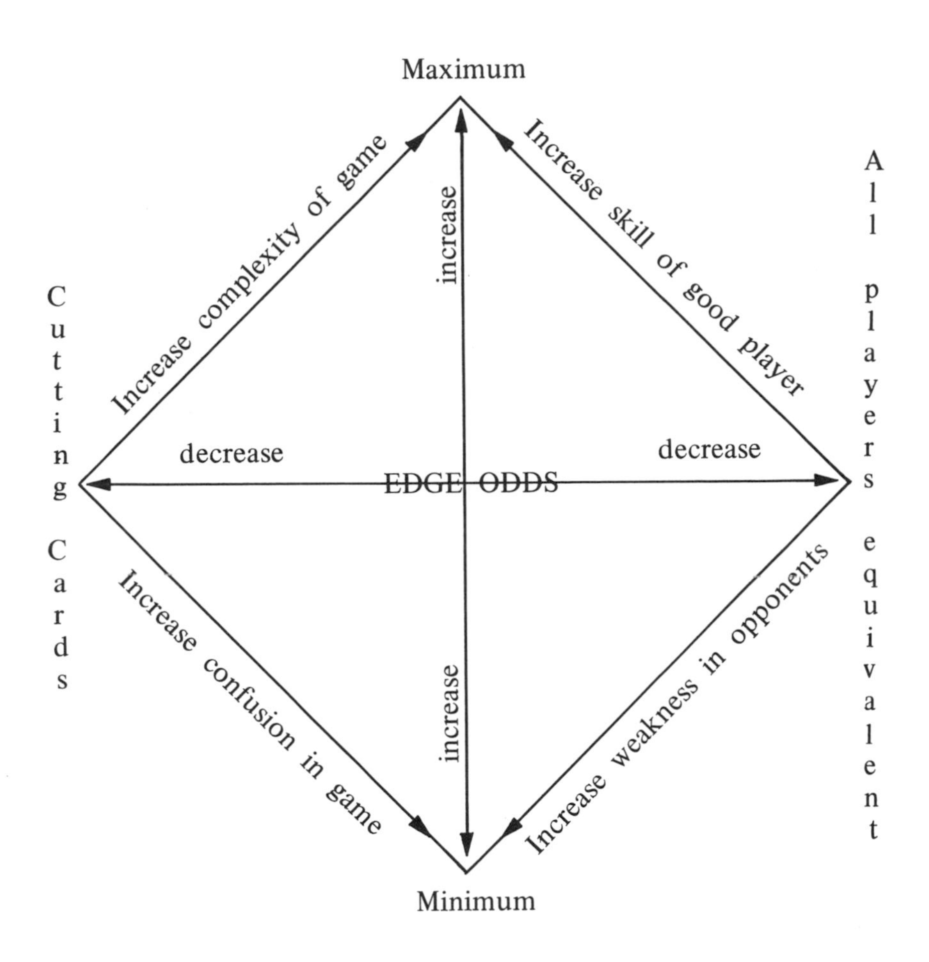
Maximum
Increase complexity of game
increase
Increase skill of good player
All players equivalent
Cutting Cards
decrease
decrease
EDGE ODDS
Increase confusion in game
increase
Increase weakness in opponents
Minimum

How far does John Finn go toward completing the hypothetical Diamond on page 66? How much further could he increase his edge odds in the Monday night game? He makes the following estimations:

	Estimations		
Side of Diamond	*% Completed*	*Maximum Possible %*	*Limitation*
Increase skill of good player	**95**	**100**	**None**
Increase weakness in opponents	**45**	**65**	**Availability of weak players capable of large losses**
Increase confusion in game	**70**	**80**	**Human tolerance**
Increase complexity of game	**90**	**95**	**Opponent's capacity to comprehend**
Total (average), %	**75**	**85**	

Playing with the Diamond 75% complete, John's edge odds are about 65%. He estimates, therefore, that under optimum conditions the Diamond would be 85% complete and his edge odds could improve to a maximum of 74%. This estimation of maximum edge odds establishes a goal that John Finn strives for by continually increasing his thinking effort . . . each side of the Diamond is controlled by his thinking effort.

XII. BEHAVIOR (37)

The good poker player aims all his actions to achieve maximum advantage while preventing others from realizing that his behavior is motivated entirely by self-profit. . . . He is a winner acting like a loser.

1. Systemization and Blandness (38)

To prevent opponents from reading his hand or sensing his strategy, the good player systemizes his -

- procedures for observing opponents
- physical movements
- verbal expressions
- vocal tones.

While playing his hand, the good player is seldom an actor. Instead he practices a bland behavior that -

- minimizes readable patterns
- frustrates and confuses opponents
- permits greater concentration.

Until it is his turn to fold, a good player never loses interest in his hand. If opponents can sense his intentions to fold, they will become more defensive when he holds a playable hand, thus decreasing his edge odds.

Improvised acting while playing a hand is usually ineffective because the act does not develop from a well planned basis. When not involved in the action, however, there are many opportunities to act effectively on a carefully planned basis. Occasionally while playing in a hand, the good player deviates from his systemized blandness when he knows a certain behavior will cause an opponent to make a desired move (call, drop, bet or raise).

"What's John doing now?" Scotty Nichols whines. He rubs his wiskered face while wondering if he should call John's $50 raise. ". . . Can't ever read him."

"That's 'cause he sits like a tree stump," Quintin Merck explains. "Gives you nothing to grab. You guys that act are easy to read."

John Finn will act, however, when he is reasonably certain of his opponents' reaction. Consider this hand where he is supposedly sitting like the tree stump:

Wanting Scotty to call, John lets his fingers creep into the pot and spread out the money. He pulls out the big bills and lays them on top. Scotty stares at the money; he is a loser, and winning that pot would make him even . . . he licks his lips and calls.

Poor Scotty never should have called. His Kings-up two-pair were no match for John's full house. Was John acting? Yes, because Scotty was undecided and John varied his own behavior to make him call. John also did some long range acting toward Quintin Merck. How was this? Quintin observed John's maneuver to make Scotty call. John heard Quintin snort when Scotty fell into the trap.

The following week, John and Quintin are battling for a large pot. John raises . . . Quintin scratches his head and then starts to call. John's fingers creep into the pot and spread out the money. He pulls out the big bills and lays them on top. Quintin smiles and shows his three Deuces to everyone before folding. His smile snaps into a frown when John throws his hand face-up on the table. His hand this time? . . . a four flush.

Why does Quintin fall into this trap? He forgets that John would not apply the same tactics toward a poor player (like Scotty) and a sound player (like Quintin). John plays against the individual as well as the situation.

2. Personality (39)

The good player varies his personality to obtain the best advantage. Typical poker personalities he adopts are described below:

a. Unfriendly (40)

In a game consisting of professional gamblers or strangers,

a tough (or unfriendly) behavior may be best. Tough behavior keeps opponents on the defense . . . and defensive players are easier to control. Unfriendly behavior irritates opponents, causing them to act more emotionally and to play poorer poker.

The following unfriendly behavior borders on being unethical, but is advantageously practiced by the good player:

- Throw bets and raises into the pot without saying a word. Give an unpleasant reply when asked about a bet or raise. Make disagreeable remarks when a subsequent player errs because of a silent move.
- At the conclusion of a hand, throw cards face-up on the table without comment. Make opponents figure out the hand.
- Provide planned displays of bad temper.
- Delay anteing and making good on lights (money owed to the pot).
- When dealing, give an inadequate description of the game. When asked for more explanation, give details begrudgingly.
- Push rules and ethics to the limit. For example, fake moves to make the next man believe you have dropped, called, or raised . . . then when he makes his move (a drop, bet or raise), remake your play accordingly.

Planned unfriendly behavior can be effective for increasing edge odds and for controlling other players. The good player, however, uses caution in being unfriendly. He analyzes the game to determine if such behavior is advantageous on both a short and long term basis.

In some games, unfriendly behavior is tolerated if a little humor or congenial behavior is blended in. Also, the good player may adopt a split personality by being unfriendly to certain players and congenial to others.

b. Congenial (41)

In most friendly or regular games, tough behavior is undesirable. It could break up the game, result in expulsion from the game, or cause valuable players to quit. Congenial behavior is often necessary in such games . . . but most friendly traditions are disadvantageous to the good player, such as -

- no betting when only two remain in a hand
- no betting a lock hand (a sure winner)
- no squeeze raising when only three players are in a split pot game.

Only an occasional but obvious display of these friendly traditions, however, will usually satisfy the other players.

Sometimes John Finn is the most congenial player in the game. In other games, he is not so congenial. He behaves in a way that offers the greatest profit.

How can John switch his personality to fit the game? He keeps himself free from emotional ties with the game and players. This lets him think objectively and define what behavior offers the most advantage. For example, he will drive a good player out of the game with unfriendly behavior (see page 161). Why will he do this? Another good player would increase the financial strain on the losers and, thus, cost John more money to keep these losers in the game. In other words, another good player would cost John money . . . so why let him play?

c. Introvert and Extrovert (42)

The good player usually behaves oppositely to the general behavior of his opponents. For example, in a quiet game with serious players, an extrovert personality is often desirable. In a wild or a loud game, an introvert personality is usually advantageous.

The extent of introvert or extrovert behavior that John Finn assumes depends on the game as shown below:

Game	*Players' Behavior*	*Advantageous Behavior (John Finn's Behavior)*
Monday	**Mixed**	**Ambivert**
Tuesday	**Introvert**	**Extrovert**
Thursday	**Intermediate**	**Ambivert**
Friday	**Extrovert**	**Introvert**

3. Practicing Deceit (43)

Only in a poker game can a man lie and practice any form of deceit, except cheating, and still remain a gentleman. The good player makes extensive use of his right to deceive. He conceals facts and lies about anything that offers him an advantage.

a. Concealing desires (44)

The good player confuses his opponents by concealing his desires in the following ways:

Desire for	*Methods to Conceal*
More weak players	Never discuss weaknesses of players.
Faster betting pace	Increase betting pace without verbally indicating a desire for a faster pace. Occasionally complain about the fast pace and wild modifications.

Desire for	*Methods to Conceal*
Higher stakes	Do not discuss higher stakes unless chances are good for an increase, then suggest higher stakes as a way to give losers a break or to make the betting more equitable.
More games	Never reveal activities in other games. Organize games without showing an eagerness to play.

b. Concealing facts (45)

The good player conceals the following facts to avoid arousing unfavorable suspicions:

Facts	*Methods to Conceal*
Easiness of game	Never mention the poor quality of poker played in any game. Praise skill of opponents.
Winnings	Avoid discussions of winnings. After each game report less than actual winnings or more than actual losses...but exaggerate only to a believable extent. Never reveal long term winnings. Conceal affluence by driving an old car to the game.
Tight play	Fold cards without comment or excuses. Make loose or wild appearing plays whenever investment odds are favorable.
Good play	Never explain the true strategy behind a play. Instead, give erroneous reasoning for strategy. Never brag . . . downgrade own performance.
Control over game	Assume a humble attitude.

To turn attention away from his poker success, the good player talks about the superior playing of other winners. In a verbal smoke screen, he discusses and exaggerates everyone's winnings except his own. When losing, the good player complains about the tough game and exaggerates his losses. But he never mentions the losses of other players.

c. Lying (46)

Lying is an important tool of strategy. For example, when asked about his folded cards, the good player lies about them to create the impression that he plays loosely or poorly. To lie effectively, he must do it carefully to keep others from automatically doubting him.

With careful lying and calculated deceit, John Finn builds his image as a kind-hearted, loose player who is an asset to the game. Here is an example of how he builds this advantageous image:

The game is high ball with a twist. John starts with a pair of Aces, draws three cards and ends up with two pair. During the betting, he notices Ted Fehr put twenty-five dollars too much into the pot. John says nothing and plays his two pair pat on the twist. Sid Bennett misses his flush and folds out-of-turn . . . this is very helpful to John.

Now with only two remaining in the hand, Ted bets $25. John reads him for trips and reasons Ted's bet like this: Ted thinks his three of a kind are beat by John's pat hand. So if he checks, John will bet the maximum of fifty dollars, and he will have to call. By making a smaller bet, he hopes that John will only call, thus saving him twenty-five dollars. But his strategy does not work . . . John raises to $75.

"How many cards you draw in the first round?" Ted questions.

"One," John quickly lies.

"A one card draw then pat on the twist . . . I can't call that," Ted sighs as he folds his cards.

John drops his cards face down next to Sid's dead hand then pulls in the pot.

"What'd you have, the straight or flush?" Ted asks.

John picks up Sid's cards, gives them to Ted and says in a low voice, "Don't show 'em to anyone."

"What!" Ted yells looking at the cards. "You play a four-flush pat to win a three hundred dollar pot?" . . .John smiles and nods . . . Ted slumps in his chair. "That's what I like," Sid says. "His wild playing beats all you tight players. . . . You're great John."

John sticks out his lips and shrugs his shoulders then throws twenty-five dollars to Ted.

"What's this for?" Ted asks.

"Your last bet," John says. "I don't feel right about taking it."

"Merciful guy," Ted smiles. Then counting the money he continues, "You might win all my money, but you're still a gentleman."

"That's no gift," Quintin Merck mumbles, "Ted put. . ."

"Whose deal?" John interrupts. . . .So besides winning a three hundred dollar pot, he did a lot of image building with that hand.

4. *Creating an Atmosphere (47)*

A carefree, relaxed, and pleasant poker atmosphere is advantageous to the good player. He creates these atmospheres in the following ways:

a. *Carefree (48)*

A carefree atmosphere stimulates a careless attitude about money and causes opponents to play poorer poker. A carefree atmosphere is developed by -

- increasing the betting pace
- complicating the game
- using poker chips instead of money
- appearing careless with money.

The good player himself is never carefree about poker or

careless with money . . . he always retains his respect for money. His careless behavior is only a planned act.

b. Relaxed (49)

A relaxed atmosphere lulls opponents into decreased concentration, which diminishes their playing ability and increases the readability of their hands. Contributing to a relaxed atmosphere are -

- a suitable location
- good food and beverages
- a comfortable setting with proper table, chairs, and lighting.

The good player denies himself the effects of comfort and relaxation in order to maintain concentration.

c. Pleasant (50)

A pleasant atmosphere holds weak players in the game and attracts new players. The good player creates a pleasant atmosphere by -

- being congenial (when advantageous)
- preventing unpleasant remarks and unfriendliness among players
- displaying a sympathetic attitude toward losers.

Most players gain pleasure from feeling accepted or belonging to the group. The good player, however, gains pleasure from his ability to cope with the realities of the game.

Whenever the Monday night game gets serious, the players think more clearly and make fewer mistakes. When serious, everyone plays tighter and is less prone to John Finn's influence. So he keeps the game carefree and careless by behavior such as described below:

A newcomer, playing in the high stake Monday game for the first time, is nervous and is playing very tight. He shuffles . . . the cards spray from his trembling hands and scatter all over the floor. Finally he deals five card stud. John gets a pair of Aces on his first two up-cards. Everyone drops out, except big loser, Scotty Nichols. "Haven't won a pot all night. I . . . I gotta win one," he chokes. . . .John makes a few small bets. Scotty stays to the end and loses with his wired pair of Queens. The pot is small; it contains perhaps thirty-five dollars.

With quivering lips, Scotty slowly turns his cards over. Suddenly John shoves the whole pot into Scotty's lap while laughing, "Don't be so miserable. It's only money. . . .Take it all."

The newcomer's mouth snaps open. "What a crazy game!" he exclaims. "I've never seen anything like that!"

Scotty grins and mumbles something about John's generous act.

"Help thy neighbor, helps thy luck," John reminds everyone, . . ." nothing is cheaper than money."

The newcomer relaxes and seems less concerned about money. The game perks up as everyone, except John, gets more careless with his money.

That move will be remembered and discussed for a long time. The cost to John, about thirty-five dollars. The return to John, certainly many times that.

5. Observation (51)

The good player depends on observations to formulate his strategy. Observation of opponents requires an analytical technique. Observation of the cards requires a sharp eye. Knowing what his opponents observe also affects his strategy.

a. Reading opponents (52)

All players have repeating habits and nervous patterns that give away their hands. Readable patterns in poker players are usually found in their -

- initial reactions to looking at their cards (freshly dealt hands, draw cards, hole cards, or up-cards)
- reactions when calling, betting, or raising
- methods of handling and looking at cards
- ways of handling money before and during each bet
- extents and directions of interest during the action
- behaviors and remarks during each phase of action
- reactions when other players open, call, bet, raise or drop
- mumblings and spoken thoughts
- tones of voice
- reactions to comments
- responses to questions.

Questions are particularly useful in reading opponents' hands. Often players reveal their hand by impulsive responses to innocuous questions as -

- how many cards did you draw?
- who made the last bet?
- how much was the last bet?
- is it your bet? (when it really is not)
- did you call the last bet?
- are you light?

The good player controls the position of his head and eyes to avoid a direct stare at those opponents who become cautious and less readable when feeling observed. He will, however, stare directly at those players who get nervous and more readable when feeling observed.

When involved in action, the good player reads his opponents and then makes his play accordingly. When not involved in the action, he analyzes the players for readable patterns. At the conclusion of each pot, he correlates all revealed hands to his observations. By this technique, he discovers many readable patterns in each opponent.

The most valuable pages in John's black leather notebook describe the readable patterns of his opponents. For example, consider his notes about Scotty Nichols:

Readable Patterns of Scotty Nichols (February, 1963)

Before hand - When winning, breaking even, or losing slightly . . . he plays very tight and never bluffs. Stays to end only when holding a strong hand. Acts dull or sleepy.

When losing heavily . . . he panics, plays loose and tries many bluffs. Once hooked in a hand, he stays to the end. Gets wide-eyed and wildly alert.

Receiving cards - Grabs for each dealt card when a good hand is developing. Casually looks at new cards when holding a hand with poor potential.

Dealing - Usually flashes bottom card when picking up the deck. Often flashes cards he deals to himself.

Looking at cards - When planning to play, he looks to his right. When planning to raise, he looks to his left. When planning to drop, he looks blankly into space.

Handling cards - Leaves cards on table when he intends to fold. If holding a playable pair, two pair, trips or a full house, he arranges his cards then does not disturb them. If holding a low-ball hand, a bobtail straight or a four flush, he continuously ruffles the cards through his fingers.

Before bet - Touches money lightly when going to call. His thumb lifts edge of money when going to raise. Picks up money when going to bluff. Does not touch money when going to fold.

Betting - Puts money in pot with a deliberate motion when not confident, with a flicking motion when confident, and with a hesitation followed by a flicking motion when sandbagging.

Raising - Cheek muscles flex when holding a sure winner. A tenseness develops around his upper lip when worried. Breathes through mouth when bluffing.

Drawing - Inserts draw randomly in hand, then ruffles cards when drawing to a pair or a four flush. Puts cards on one end with no ruffling when drawing to trips or a four straight. Puts card second from the end when drawing to trips with a kicker. Puts card in center of hand when drawing to two pair. With two pair, he looks at draw quickly. With all other hands, he slowly squeezes cards open. Squeezes very slowly when drawing to low-ball, flush, or straight hands. Jerks hand when he misses.

Looking at draw - Exhales when he misses and eyes stare blankly at table. Inhales when he catches and eyes dart around table.

Stud up cards - After catching a good card, he touches it first then reorganizes his cards. Confirms catch by looking several times at his hole cards.

Stud hole cards - When hole cards are good, he keeps them neatly organized and touches them periodically. Does not bother to organize or touch poor cards.

If one fakes a move to grab his hole cards, he impulsively jumps and grabs the cards if they are good . . . does nothing if they are poor.

Last round bet - A quick call means he will call a raise. Picking up all his money when calling means he will not call a raise. Watching the next caller without looking directly at him means he is hoping for a raise.

Questions - "Do you have three tens beat?" he blinks his eyes if his hand does not beat three tens . . . no blink if it does.

"How many cards did you draw?" He hesitates and turns eyes up in thought if he is bluffing. Gives a casual answer if holding a normal hand. Hesitates and stares at the pot if holding a powerful hand.

After hand - He will play carelessly when sulking over losses. He will play extra tight when winning and counting his money.

With so many readable patterns, Scotty has little chance against John Finn. By putting together several of these patterns, John reads him with a high degree of accuracy. And Scotty's low awareness level keeps him from recognizing the habits that reveal his cards and intentions.

John also knows the other players' habits and can usually read them accurately . . . even a sound player like Quintin Merck. Because of Quintin's greater awareness, he occasionally recognizes and eliminates a habit that tips off his hand. John, however, uses several habits to cross-check revealing patterns . . . he quickly knows when anyone changes or eliminates a habit. After each game, John records in his notebook any new or changed habits.

The question type giveaways are quite reliable and particularly useful for pinpointing the exact value of an opponent's hand. For example, if John holds trips and reads his opponent for trips, he might use questions to find out who has the best hand. Excessive use of questions, however, can arouse suspicion and decrease the usefulness of this valuable tool.

b. Remembering exposed cards and ghost hands (53)

By remembering all exposed cards, a player increases his accuracy in estimating investment and card odds. In games with many players (eight or more), discarded and folded cards are often redealt. Knowledge of these cards can be crucial for estimating meaningful investment odds. In some large-sized games, discarded and folded cards are placed on the bottom of the deck without shuffling. This benefits the good player; if these cards are redealt during the late rounds, he will know what cards are to be dealt to whom . . . a huge advantage for the latter rounds of big bets.

With disciplined concentration and practice, any player can memorize all exposed cards. From the discipline value alone, remembering exposed cards is always a worthwhile effort. But many players excuse themselves from this chore by feeling that memorizing cards dissipates their concentration on the other aspects of the game. This may be true when a player first trys to memorize cards, but a continuous effort in training one's discipline to memorize exposed cards will ultimately increase his concentration on all aspects of the game.

Remembering draw hands or the order of exposed stud cards from the previous deal can bring financial rewards. Old hands often reappear on the next deal (ghost hands), especially when the shuffling is incomplete (the good player encourages sloppy and incomplete shuffling). For example, a good player is sitting under the gun (on the dealer's left) and needs a King to fill his straight in stud. Now the last card dealt in that round (the dealer's card) is a King; the good player remembers the previous hand was draw poker where the winner had three Kings. Since the deck had been poorly shuffled, there is a good chance that the next card (his card) will also be a King. Knowing this, he now has a big betting advantage.

John Finn memorizes all exposed and flashed cards. He mentally organizes every exposed stud card into one of the four following categories by saying to himself, for example ... Sid's two of Hearts would help -

- **my hand**
- **his (Sid's) hand**
- **another opponents (ie: Quintin's) hand**
- **no one's hand.**

This association of each card with a definite hand aids his memory.

Now if Sid folds, and his two of Hearts is the first card to go on the bottom of the deck, John would say to himself ... the fifty-third card is the two of Hearts. Then by counting the dealt cards, he will know when and to whom that card will be redealt. By this procedure, he often knows many of the cards that could be redealt. For example, he may know the 53, 54, 57, 60, and 61st card ... the cards he knows depend on how the folded cards are put on the bottom of the deck.

c. Seeing flashed cards (54)

Many important cards are flashed during a game. Players who see flashed cards are not cheating. Cheating occurs only through a deliberate physical action to see unexposed cards. For example, a player who is dealing and purposely looks at the bottom card of the deck is cheating. But a player who sees cards flashed by someone else violates no rules or ethics. To see the maximum number of flashed cards, one must know when and where to expect them. When the mind is alert to flashing cards, the eye can be trained to spot and identify them. Cards often flash when -

- they are dealt
- a player picks up his hand or draw cards
- a player looks at his cards or ruffles them through his fingers
- a kibitzer or peeker picks up the cards of another player (a peeker is often more careless about flashing someone else's cards than his own)
- a player folds his hand or throws in discards
- cards reflect in a player's eyeglasses.

The good player occasionally tells a player to hold back his cards or warns a dealer that he is flashing cards. He does this to create an image of "honesty", which keeps opponents from suspecting his constant use of flashed cards. He knows his warnings have little permanent effect on stopping players from flashing cards. In fact warned players usually become more careless about flashing because of their increased confidence in the "honesty" of the game.

Using data from one hundred games, John Finn compiles the following table, which illustrates the number of flashed cards he sees in the Monday night game.

Flashed by	*Average Number of Unexposed Cards Identified per Hand (adjusted for a seven man game)*	
	Draw	**7-stud**
Dealer*	6	2
Active Players	7	1
Kibitzers and Peekers	2	1
Folded Players	9	3
Total	24	7

**Also, the bottom card of the deck is exposed 75% of the time.*

These data show that in addition to seeing his own cards, John sees over half the deck in an average game of draw poker - just by keeping his eyes open. The limit he goes to see flashed cards is illustrated below:

Mike Bell is a new player. John does not yet know his habits and must rely on other tools to read him . . . such as seeing flashed cards.

The game is low-ball draw with one twist. The betting is heavy, and the pot grows large. John has a fairly good hand (a seven low) and does not twist. Mike bets heavily then draws one card. John figures he is drawing to a very good low hand, perhaps to a six low.

John bets. Ted Fehr pretends to have a good hand, but just calls . . . John reads him for a poor, nine low. Everyone else folds except Mike Bell, who holds his cards close and slowly squeezes them open; John studies Mike's face very closely. Actually he is not looking at his face, but is watching the reflection in his eyeglasses. When Mike opens his hand, John sees the scattered dots of low cards plus the massive design of a black picture card reflecting in the glasses. (You never knew this? . . .Try it, especially if your spectacled victim has a strong light directly over or behind his head. Occasionally, a crucial card can even be identified in a player's bare eyeball.)

Having already put $100 into the pot, Mike tries to bluff with a $50 bet. If John had not seen that picture card reflect in Mike's glasses, he may have folded. Now he not only calls with confidence, but tries a little experiment . . . he raises $1. Ted folds; and Mike, turning pale after his bluff failure, falls into the trap . . . he makes a desperate double bluff by raising $50. His error? . . . he refuses to accept his mistake and throws good money after bad.

John calmly raises another $1. Mike folds by throwing his cards all over the floor. His playing then disintegrates. What a valuable reflection, John says to himself.

d. Intentional flashing (55)

The good player intentionally flashes cards in his hand to cause opponents to drop, call, bet, raise or bluff. But he uses the intentional flash with caution. If suspected, intentional flashes are less effective and can cause resentment among players.

In the last round of a seven card stud game, John Finn holds a partly hidden flush - three Clubs showing with two more in the hole. He also has a pair of Jacks showing and a pair of sevens in the hole. Ted Fehr has the other pair of sevens showing, and John reads him for two pair - Queens over sevens. Sid Bennett has Aces up and makes a $1 feeler bet. Ted, betting strong from the start, raises $25. John just calls.

"I should raise," Sid thinks outloud as he strokes his chin. "John is weak . . . probably has Jacks up. Ted might have three sevens . . . no other sevens are showing."

John picks up his hole cards, shifts his position and crosses his legs. Accidently-on-purpose, he turns his hand so Sid can see two of his hole cards . . . the pair of sevens.

"I'll raise to $50," Sid chuckles. He now knows that Ted cannot have three sevens and John has two pair. Never thinking that John might also have the flush, he looks pleased with his sharpness in spotting John's hole cards.

Ted folds, and John raises back. Sid calls then slaps his hand against his massive forehead when John shows him a flush. He grumbles something about bad luck while never realizing the trap he was sucked into.

e. Peekers (56)

Folded players and spectators often peek at undealt cards or at hands of active players. Most peekers exhibit highly readable behavior patterns that give away the value of the cards they look at. These patterns are found in their -

- levels of and changes in interest toward peeked-at hands

- timing of peeks and re-peeks
- reactions when folding then peeking at hands of ex-opponents
- eye movements and areas of interest immediately after peeking at cards to be dealt.

Players who allow uncontrolled peeking at their hands encounter problems of -

- readable patterns given to opponents
- flashed cards
- upset strategy
- disturbed concentration
- more frequent, unsolicited peeking.

The good player controls the peekers who look at his hand. He permits selective peeking at his cards in order to -

- convey desired information to the peeker or to other players
- advertise plays that encourage loose or poor playing by others
- create a more careless atmosphere
- upset certain players by not allowing them to peek
- encourage peekers to look at hands of other players.

The good player controls peeking by the following methods:

- He never peeks at cards of other players. This avoids any obligation to let other players peek at his cards. After dropping out of a hand, he concentrates on observation and planning strategy rather than wasting his time on peeking.

- He develops a consistent method to hold his cards to prevent unwanted peeking.
- When players ask to look at his cards, he refuses gently by a remark such as, "I'll show you later."
- When possible, he buries his cards without showing them . . . then advantageously lies about them.

New player, Charlie Holland, sits next to John Finn. In his first big stake game, Charlie is nervous and impressionable. John takes advantage of this, and this is how he uses peekers to throw Charlie into permanent confusion:

In a hand of low ball, John discards a King and draws a good seven low while Charlie has a poor nine low. John manages to keep him in for several large bets. In the last round, Sid makes a defensive $25 bet; Charlie calls. John raises to $75 and everyone folds. John throws his cards on top of his discarded King and then pulls in the pot.

"What'd you have?" Charlie asks.

"A fat King," John smiles as he picks up the cards and shows him the King.

Charlie Holland groans. With a drooping face, he stares at the large pot. "I should've called," he sighs as John slowly pulls in the pot while laying the larger bills on top for better viewing.

What does this have to do with peekers? Nothing yet. . . .The next hand is seven card stud, and Charlie drops out early to study John's technique. He stretches his neck to peek at John's hole cards. With an air of friendship, John Finn loops his arm around Charlie's shoulder and shows him the hole cards - he has an Ace, King Diamond flush.

"We'll kill 'em with this Ace, King Diamond flush," John says loudly.

Surprised that John announced his exact hand, Charlie looks at the cards again then replies, "Yeah man!"

But actually, John is not very confident of his flush because he reads both Ted and Quintin for two pair, and all eight of their full house cards are alive. He figures the odds are about 2 to 1 that one of them will get a full house. He also knows that they fear his

flush and will not bet unless they catch the full house.

Scotty Nichols, who folded early, is sitting between Quintin and Ted. With his head bobbing back and forth, he peeks at their hands as they catch new cards. Now, the last hole card is dealt. John watches Scotty closely . . . first his plump head points toward the highest hand - Ted's Queens over Jacks. He peeks at Ted's new hole card; immediately his head snaps over to check Quintin's cards. Obviously Ted's new card is not very interesting . . . he failed to catch his full house, John figures.

Now Scotty looks at Quintin's new card. He looks again and then glances at Quintin's up-cards . . . then checks the hole cards once again. Scotty does not say a word, but he may as well be yelling, "Interesting! A very interesting catch for the full house!" . . .Adjusting his thick glasses, Scotty looks at John's up-cards; his eyes then dart back and forth between Quintin and John . . . he ignores Ted's hand.

What happens? Ted foolishly bets $25. Quintin raises $1. Scotty covers his smiling mouth with his hand. Expecting some lively action, he waits for John to get sucked into Quintin's great trap. . . .Across the table, Charlie Holland smiles; he waits for John to blast Quintin with a big raise. John Finn folds.

Charlie rises from his seat making a gurgling noise. "You . . . you know what you dropped?" he stammers.

"Yeah, a busted hand," John shrugs.

"A busted hand!" Charlie bellows. His arm shoots to the table and picks up John's folded cards. "Look, you had an Ace, King Diamond flush. You even announced it!"

"Oh, no! I thought it was a four flush," John lies.

Quintin glowers at John's flush and then shows his winning full house . . . Charlie sits down talking to himself.

Alert playing not only saves John money, but confuses and sets up Charlie for future psychological control.

6. Non-Game Behavior (57)

The good player behaves in the following ways toward non-game contacts that could influence his poker activities.

Non-Game Contact	*Behavior*
Friend of a player	Flatter performance of the player. Exaggerate merits of the game.
Potential player	Suggest the easiness of winning money in the game. Stress the sociable and pleasant aspects of the game.
Player from another game	Indicate a desire to play in his game. Extend an invitation to own game. Create an image of being a sociable player.
Family of a player	Flatter poker skill of the player. If they complain about his losses, suggest that his bad luck is due to change.
Other acquaintances	Indicate a desire to play poker. Downgrade past performance in poker . . . talk about losses.

Sometimes the good player practices contrasting *game* and *non-game* behavior. For example, if during the game he practices unfriendly behavior toward a certain opponent, he usually finds it advantageous to be congenial toward this same person outside of the game.

Although the poker players in the Monday night game are independent men (as most regular poker players are), their wives have some influence on them. John plans his behavior toward their wives according to the following notations in his notebook:

Wife Summary - January, 1964

Betty Nichols	**Concerned about Scotty's losses. To calm her, recall his past winnings. Potential of becoming angry, but will not make him quit if reminded that game keeps him from drinking.**
Florence Merck	**Fully supports Quintin's playing, especially since he is winning.**

Stephanie Bennett	**Thinks Sid is foolish for playing. Realizes he will never win and wants him to quit, but knows she has no control over him. Also, having plenty of money, she is not too worried about his losses.**
Rita Fehr	**Does not care and makes no attempt to influence Ted, despite his seriously heavy losses.**

XIII. POLICIES (58)

The good player forms policies about money, credit, and the rules. These policies are his guidelines for strategy and are planned to yield both short and long term advantages. Proper policies result in fewer mistakes and better decisions.

1. Money (59)

Money is the rational basis of poker. To win money is the rational reason to invest time in the game.

a. Maintaining proper attitude (60)

Since poker is a game of money management, the proper attitude about money is crucial. What is the good player's attitude about money? Realizing that each dollar represents an irreplaceable segment of life (the time required to earn that dollar), he respects money out of respect for himself.

b. Stimulating poor attitude in opponents (61)

A poor money attitude in opponents increases the edge odds for the good player. Since most players are influenced by opinions of the good player, he uses this influence to stimulate poor money attitudes by advancing *erroneous* ideas such as -

- one must be dealt good cards to win
- luck is required to win

- streaks of luck run hot and cold, and cards should be played accordingly
- betting should depend on how much one is winning or losing.

The good player often encourages the use of poker chips instead of money in order to -

- decrease the sense of value for money
- stimulate looser play and a faster betting pace
- speed up game.

In certain games, however, players will play for higher stakes when cash (rather than chips) is used.

c. Increasing money in game (62)

The good player tries to increase the cash brought to the game because more cash -

- allows the betting pace and stakes to increase more rapidly
- decreases opponents' respect for money
- makes more money available for loans.

An effective way to increase money brought to the game is to increase the money needed by limiting the use of credit.

Ted Fehr has been losing heavily on the horses. His cash position is low; he is borrowing excessively to stay in the action. John is worried because now Ted brings less than a hundred dollars to the game, loses it immediately and then borrows for the rest of the game. John figures that each player should bring at least three hundred dollars to keep the game healthy. This is how he puts pressure on Ted to increase his cash position:

"Lend me a hundred," Ted says turning to John after losing a pot.

"It's only the third hand and you're broke?" John growls and makes no motion to lend him money. "I can't lend my cash right off . . . what'd I play on?" The other players nod in agreement.

"Who'll lend me a hundred?" Ted asks as he looks around the table . . . his mouth smiles. There is no reply . . . his mouth droops.

Watching Ted's forehead break into a sweat, John finally says, "Write out a check and put it in the game. Next time bring five or six hundred like everyone else does. Then if you run out, there'll be enough cash in the game to lend."

Wrinkles spread across Ted's freckled face as he pulls a blank check from his wallet. "I've lost thousands in this game," he chokes. "Can't even borrow a hundred. Isn't my credit good?"

"Sure your credit is good," John explains as he cashes the check. "That's not the point. It's for your own protection. How can you possibly win without money to back you up?" . . .John knows this meaningless platitude will be swallowed as the truth by most players, especially gamblers like Ted.

"Got to have money to make money," Ted mumbles as the other players nod in agreement. "I'll bring plenty next week and overpower everyone."

During that week, Ted wins at the track. Remembering John's advice and blaming his poker losses to a lack of cash, he brings over a thousand dollars to the next game. The excess cash clouds his sense of value for money . . . he tries to overpower everyone. His overpowering play is an exhibition of wild, reckless poker. By two in the morning, Ted is filling out checks; John Finn is a very big winner.

2. *Credit (63)*

Credit policies can determine the health of a poker game. The use of credit allows a faster betting pace and higher stakes. Since the good player is the most consistent winner, he is the prime source of credit and, therefore, exercises a major influence on the credit policies. He applies the following *credit rule* to poker games:

> ALL DEBTS MUST BE PAID BY THE START OF EACH GAME. NO ONE CAN PLAY WHILE OWING MONEY FROM A PREVIOUS GAME.

This policy is effective in preventing bad debts that can damage or destroy a game. This credit policy also prevents a valuable loser from accumulating such large poker debts that he would be tempted to quit the game and never pay his debts. When a loser is temporarily forced out of the game by this policy, he usually recovers financially, repays his debts, and returns for more losses.

The following additional advantages are offered by this credit policy:

- Provides a clear rule that forces prompt payment of poker debts.
- Forces more cash into the game.
- Increases the willingness of players to lend money, which provides more cash for the losers.
- Detects players headed for financial trouble.
- Forces bankrupt players out of the game before serious damage is done.

The good player is flexible and alters any policy when beneficial. For example, he may ignore this credit policy to prevent a wealthy, heavily losing player from quitting the game. But he carefully weighs the advantages against disadvantages before making any exception to this policy.

By not borrowing money himself, the good player avoids obligations that could restrict his influence over the credit policies. If the good player loses his cash, he writes a check. A check puts more money into the game and sets a good example in minimizing the use of credit. If the good player must borrow, he does so from a player who rarely borrows himself and thus would seldom demand a reciprocating loan.

a. Extending credit (64)

The good player extends credit only to obtain financial benefits. He selectively extends credit for the following reasons:

- Available credit allows big losers to continue playing. Credit also prevents the permanent loss of desirable players; for example, if steady losers must beg to borrow, they may quit the game because of injured pride. If losers can borrow gracefully, they usually continue playing for many more losing sessions.
- Opponents often play poorer poker after they have borrowed money.
- The good player can exercise greater influence and control over players who are in debt to him.

To obtain maximum benefits when lending money, the good player creates impressions that he -

- is extending a favor
- gives losers a break
- lends only to his friends
- lends only when winning and then on a limited basis
- expects other players, particularly winners, to lend money also.

b. Refusing credit (65)

Easy credit by a winning player makes him the expected source of loans. Easy credit decreases the money brought to the game, which in turn decreases the betting pace. Ironically, losers often feel ungrateful and suspicious toward an overly willing lender.

Refusal of credit is an important tool for controlling credit policies. The good player selectively refuses credit in order to -

- prod players into bringing more money
- force other players to lend money
- make borrowers feel more obligated and grateful
- avoid being taken for granted as an easy lender
- produce an image of being tough (when advantageous)
- avoid poor credit risks
- upset certain players.

c. Cashing checks (66)

In most poker games, checks are as good as cash. The threat of legal action forces fast payment of any bounced checks. The good player likes to cash losers' checks because -

- money in the game is increased
- his cash position is decreased, which puts pressure on the other winners to supply credit
- losers get cash without using credit
- losers are encouraged to write checks, particularly if resistance is offered to their borrowing while no resistance is offered to cashing their checks.

d. Bad debts (67)

A bad poker debt is rare. Losing poker players are gamblers, and most gamblers maintain good gambling credit above all else. Some players go bankrupt, but almost all eventually pay their poker debts. When a loser stops gambling to recover financially, the best policy is to avoid pressuring him into paying his debts. Such pressure can cause increasing resentment to where he may never pay . . . or even worse, never return to lose more money.

A house rule that allows bad debts to be absorbed by all players (bad debts reimbursed, for example, by cutting the pot) has two advantages:

1. Players are more willing to lend money.
2. A debtor is less likely to welch against all the players than against an individual player.

Establishing a maximum bad debt that will be reimbursed by cutting pots is a wise addition to this house rule. Limiting this bad debt insurance will -

- restrain careless lending
- discourage collusion between a player and a potential welcher
- avoid a large liability against the pots that could keep players away from the game until the debts were paid.

A gambling debt has no legal recourse (except debts represented by bad checks). A welcher will usually pay if threatened with a tattletale campaign. If he still does not pay, a few telephone calls to his wife, friends, and business associates often forces payment before news of his bad debt is spread too far. The good player openly discusses any bad poker debt as a deterrent to others who might consider welching.

Handling credit is an important and delicate matter for John Finn. He must make credit available to keep the game going, but must limit the use of credit to keep cash plentiful. He must appear generous in lending his winnings while appearing tough against players abusing the use of credit. John pressures other winners into lending their money and pressures losers into writing checks. He protects players from getting their feelings hurt while enforcing the *credit rule* (described on page 92). . . .All this requires careful thought and delicate maneuvering.

Sid Bennett is wealthy and loses many thousands of dollars every year. John takes special care of him. Usually Sid brings plenty of cash to the game, maybe five or six hundred dollars. When he loses that, John gently pressures him into writing checks. Occasionally, Sid gets upset and refuses to write any more checks. He then borrows with gusto. Sometimes when he runs out of money, he scans the table for the biggest pile of money. Then smash, his big fist descends without warning . . . he grabs the whole pile of money and peels off a couple hundred dollars. If the victim objects, Sid just grunts and looks the other way, but keeps the money. The players grant him this liberty because they know he is rich and will always repay them.

Occasionally, Sid gets bitter when suffering big consecutive losses and refuses to pay off his debts by the next game. John realizes that Sid might quit the game if the credit rule were enforced against him. So if Sid owes him money under these conditions, John says nothing and lets the debt ride until the following week. If Sid refuses to pay money he owes to another player, John pays off the debt while reminding him that debts cannot be carried over. Sid usually pays John later the same night or the following week. With his tantrums appeased, Sid happily goes on to lose many thousands more.

While lax with Sid, John Finn rigidly enforces the credit rule against the other players. He is particularly tight on extending credit to Ted Fehr because of his poor financial condition; he often refuses him credit and makes him write checks. This tough policy forces Ted to quit when he is broke. Then when he accumulates enough money, he returns to the game, pays off his debts and then loses more.

When Ted quits for several weeks to recover financially, a losing player occasionally complains about holding one of Ted's debts. John offers to buy the debt at a twenty-five percent discount. This keeps everyone happy; it gives the loser more cash to lose, and John picks up a good profit.

At times, John Finn refuses to lend money to anyone . . . this forces others to lend their cash. At other times, he puts on subtle displays of generosity. For example, if players with good credit run low on money, John advantageously reduces his cash position by silently handing them loans before

they even ask for one. Everyone is favorably impressed with this act of fake generosity.

In John's notebook is the following list:

Credit Rating	
Quintin Merck	**Best**
Sid Bennett	↑
Scotty Nichols	|
Ted Fehr	**Worst**

When a player writes a check, John usually makes a quick move to cash it. To him, checks are usually better to hold than money because cash winnings are more obvious targets for loans than are check winnings.

3. Rules (68)

The good player shuns fixed poker rules. He does, however, provide equitable and consistent interpretations of poker situations because such a policy -

- eliminates rule problems
- increases acceptance of complex games and modifications
- increases his control over the game
- improves his image as a fair and desirable player
- increases his invitations to other games
- increases his ability to control the *house* rules.

Poker, unlike other card games, is not subject to rigid rules. Published rules and the various "Hoyles" on poker are merely descriptions of general conventions. Strict adherence to any set of poker rules produces contradictions and inequities. By avoiding reference to Hoyle or fixed rules and by interpreting poker situations on a consistently equitable basis, the good player gains control of the rules.

a. Modified rules (69)

Standard rules are found in numerous poker books. These rules fail to cover many situations, especially in games involving split pots, twists, and other more complex modifications. To cover the many ruleless situations, the good player formulates new rules (actually, he formulates flexible guide lines rather than rules) on an equitable basis . . . even if it costs him money. But why will he formulate a rule that will cost him money? Because in the long run, this policy works to his financial advantage. Periodically he reminds his opponents of the money he lost because of his fairness . . . this strengthens their confidence in him as the controller of the rules.

b. Disputed plays (70)

Because the good player interprets the rules fairly, his opponents trust him and call on him to settle disputed plays and technical problems about poker. Typical approaches he uses in settling some commonly disputed plays are summarized below:

Disputed Play	*Approach*
Misdeal	Cards are never redealt because of a misdeal. Each player is responsible for his own cards. Any misdealt hand having an uncorrectable advantage must be dropped. Any misdealt hand that is correctable or left at a disadvantage can be played.
Exposed card during the deal	An exposed card can never be exchanged for a new one . . . all cards must be accepted.

Disputed	Approach
Exposed card before the deal	All cards must come off in order. No one can ask for a reshuffle, a cut or a different card.
Out of turn betting, calling, raising or checking	Any play made out of turn (except folding) is meaningless and can be remade or changed during the player's proper turn.

These approaches provide clear and consistent solutions to disputes that occur, especially for complex games involving split pots and twists.

c. Inequitable rules (71)

The good player occasionally caters to a loser's whim (about a rule) to keep him in the game. But he interprets a rule inequitably to prevent a loser from quitting only if the value of this loser outweighs the disadvantage of deviating from an equitable rule policy.

d. House rules (72)

House rules are very important to the good player. They concern betting and playing procedures plus any other rules the players wish to adopt. The house rules not only determine the stakes, but also the pace of the game.

Since most players fail to differentiate between the house rules and poker rules, they often let the good player control the *house* rules because of his fairness in interpreting *poker* rules. Important house rules that he controls to his advantage concern -

- stakes and antes
- games permitted

- types of betting (limits, table stake, pot limit)
- styles of betting (such as pick-up checks, check-raising, and other raising rules)
- treatment of discards to be redealt (such as placing unshuffled discards on the bottom of the deck)
- courtesies (such as showing non-called hands and hole cards).

The good player avoids well defined or written house rules. This gives him greater flexibility in changing the rules when advantageous.

In the Monday night game, John Finn verbally insists on adhering to the rules, but he carefully avoids any reference to published rules. He mediates all disputes fairly, even when it costs him the pot. In his black notebook, he records his rule interpretations and dispute settlements. As a book of law, he refers to these entries in settling future rule problems. The entries in which he loses money are marked by big stars and recorded in accurate detail. He remembers these entries, and at every appropriate opportunity he reminds everyone how his honest rule interpretations cost him money. Of course, he never mentions the interpretations that favored him.

With this policy, John wins the confidence of the players. They know he is fair ... they trust his decisions, ask him to settle disputes, and abide by his interpretations. They accept him as the controller of the rules. Failing to realize that the *game* **rules bear no relationship to the** *house* **rules, they let John's influence spill into the house rules thereby giving him a very important tool for controlling the game.**

Using his influence over the rules, John slowly obliterates and then alters the original house rules. In the Monday night game, the original house rules allowed a maximum bet of one dollar and permitted only straight draw and stud games ... fifty dollar winners were rare. Now hundred dollar bets are made in draw. Wild, twist, and split pot games prevail. Thousand dollar winners are common. After six years of applying his rule policy, John increases his edge odds from 35% to 65%, and his profits soar from $2,500 to $42,000 per year.

4. Arguments and Emotional Situations (73)

The good player avoids involvement in emotional situations such as -

- disputes and arguments
- personal problems
- exposing cheaters or players stealing money.

Involvement is avoided by outwardly ignoring the situation. The good player will, however, study any emotional situation in order to gain an advantage from it. He intervenes only in those situations that threaten his financial interests. For example, he steps in to prevent a loser from quitting the game because of an argument.

When the good player himself is confronted with a potential argument, he maintains control over the situation and the respect of his opponents by either yielding quickly or maintaining his position firmly. He avoids making an issue of something and then yielding his position. He takes a firm position* in an argument only when there is a sufficient financial advantage to do so. When in doubt about yielding or holding firm, he will usually yield before the argument starts.

Sid's loud mouth constantly bellows good-natured insults at the players. Professor Merck does not like Sid to tease him about his moustache, his tight playing, or his beret. He tells Sid to stop. But Sid Bennett grins and rides him even harder by calling him a dirty old man. Quintin accuses Sid of running dishonest road paving business and calls him a pasty face crook. Sid shouts back louder insults. Their bickering adversely affects their playing, and John increases his winnings from the upset men.

* *The good player is careful not to burn bridges behind him by taking a firm position on a situation that would offer future advantages by reversing his position.*

After several weeks, their aggravations increase . . . John begins to worry. Blows are nearly exchanged when Quintin threatens to expose Sid's payola on city paving contracts. Sid threatens to sue him for slander and then calls him a queer. Squinting his green eyes, Quintin cracks the edge of his hand on the table and threatens Sid with a Karate blow. Sid vibrates his big fist close to Quintin's nose, calls him a queer again and then storms out of the house while shouting that either he or Quintin must quit the game.

Fearing that Sid may quit, John telephones both men the next day and settles their argument. He explains how their feud is hurting their playing and costing them money. They both agree and thank him for straightening out their problem.

John made money from their emotional problem. When it became serious, however, he stepped in and eliminated their feud in a way that improved his image as a desirable player.

XIV. CHEATERS (74)

In friendly games of poker, most players consider a cheater less honorable than a thief because a thief robs from strangers, but a poker cheat robs from his friends. The normal, emotional impulse is to banish the cheater from the game. The good poker player, however, resists acting on emotional impulses. He views any cheating situation objectively and then acts in his best financial interest. The good player, of course, never cheats . . . he never needs to.

1. Cheating (75)

Cheating involves the following manipulations of cards, money or betting:

- Cards are secretly switched to alter the value of a hand. Cards are purposely flashed to see undealt or unexposed cards. The deck is stacked to change the sequence of cards to be dealt.

- Money is stolen from the pot or from other players. For example, wrong change is purposely taken from the pot, or lights are purposely not paid.

- Mechanical devices such as marked cards, strippers, mirrors, hold-out equipment and techniques to smudge, nick, or mar cards for future identification are used.
- Betting agreements or partnerships are secretly made. For example, a cheater will signal his partner when to make a bet or a raise. Or a cheater will fold his hand, then peek at a hand of another player and signal his partner.

The good player adapts to any situation. He can usually take favorable advantage of a cheater by increasing his bets in winning situations because an opponent will usually call larger bets when cheating.

Honest poker allows any behavior or manipulation, no matter how deceptive or how cynical, except cheating. Cheating is the only illegal or unethical behavior in poker. But where does cynical deception end and cheating begin? Actually, a sharp distinction exists. Cheating is creating an advantage unavailable to others. Poker deception is taking advantage of something that is available to all. For example, all cards are marked. One can find printing imperfections in any honest deck of cards. Some common imperfections are printing-ink spots, inkless dots, and slightly off-centered designs on the back side of the cards. Also, the normal use of cards produces identifying smudges, nicks, scratches and creases on their backs. (Purposely marring cards for identification would, of course, be cheating.) These natural imperfections and markings that identify unexposed cards are available for any player willing to train his eye and discipline his mind. The good player willingly exerts this effort to learn and then use these natural markings. He may even increase this advantage by providing the game with cheaper (but honest) cards with less perfect printing patterns.

Sid Bennett cheats. While it is quite obvious, only John Finn fully realizes that he cheats. Quintin Merck suspects it, but never makes any direct accusations. The other players watch Sid's

cheating, but refuse to suspect him. His crude cheating techniques include -

- **looking through discards then selecting a card to use in his hand**
- **culling or sorting the cards prior to dealing**
- **peeking at cards to be dealt, especially twist cards**
- **stealing money from the pot when going light**
- **slipping a good card into the hand of a losing player (Robin Hood cheating).**

John estimates that Sid cheats about once in every three hands.

2. Accepting Cheaters (76)

The good player accepts cheaters if they are losers. In fact, he often welcomes cheating because players generally lose more money when they cheat, particularly in complex games involving split pots and twists. A player increases his losses when cheating because he -

- dilutes his attention toward the game by worrying about and concentrating on his cheating
- overestimates the benefits of cheating and thus plays looser and poorer poker
- makes his cards more readable.

Why does a player cheat if he increases his losses? Certain players cheat to satisfy an emotional neurosis. Other players cheat out of financial desperation.

Several cheaters, however, can gang up on a good player to reduce his edge odds below a satisfactory level. He quickly detects gang cheating and either eliminates it or quits the game.

Sid's cheating stems from an emotional rather than a financial basis and is costing him thousands of dollars per year as shown by

the following data (which include a three-month period when Sid worried about getting caught and stopped his cheating):

Edge Odds for Sid Bennett

Period	*Cheating Frequency*	*Average Edge Odds, %*
1963	**Seldom**	**-10**
1964-1965	**Regular**	**-23**
Oct.-Dec. 1965	**Seldom**	**-12**
1966	**Regular**	**-25**

These data indicate that Sid doubles his losses when cheating. With his current losses in the Monday night game totaling $20,000 per year, his cheating costs him about $10,000 per year.

3. Rejecting Cheaters (77)

Under certain conditions, cheating can threaten the financial interests of the good player. For example, valuable players might quit the game if they detected cheating. If necessary, cheating problems can be eliminated in one of the following ways:

Time of Action	*Form of Action*	*Results*
Indirectly, during game	Make the cheater feel that he is suspected and is being watched.	Cheating stops.
Privately, outside of game	Tell the cheater that if he cheats again, he will be publicly exposed.	Cheating stops.
Privately, outside of game	Tell other players about the cheater. Point out that he is a loser and the best way to hurt him is to let him play.	Cheating continues, and the players are satisfied.

Time of Action	*Form of Action*	*Results*
Privately, outside of game	Form a conspiracy with other players to cheat collectively in order to bankrupt the cheater.	Cheater is driven from the game.
Publicly, during game	Expose the cheater during the game in front of everyone.	Cheater quits the game.

The best action against a cheater depends on the situation and attitude of the players. If a cheater must be eliminated, the good player assumes an advantageous hero's role while exposing him.

What about stealing money from the pot? If the good player does not win the pot, he keeps quiet when losing players fail to pay their lights (money owed to the pot) or take improper change from the pot. If chronic money stealing upsets other players enough to threaten the good player's financial interests, however, he may take action (such as listed above for cheating) to stop the stealing.

Scotty Nichols beats Ted Fehr in a close finish for a nine hundred dollar pot. With all attention focused on the action, Sid Bennett takes the hundred dollars that he was light and slips it into his shirt pocket for a two hundred dollar profit. Only John notices Sid's trick, but says nothing. With saliva drooling over his lip, Scotty rakes in the huge pot; his breathing deepens as his fingers sort the money . . . he forgets about Sid's lights. Since Sid is a big loser and Scotty is a big winner for the night, the theft has an equalizing effect that is beneficial to John.

Several hands later, Sid pulls the same trick by pocketing his forty dollar lights for an eighty dollar profit. John wins the pot and says nothing. As the next hand is dealt, he gives Sid twenty dollars and says in a low voice, "You owe me another hundred." . . . Sid blushes and then nods.

4. Robin Hood Cheater (78)

Some players cheat for others without benefiting themselves. The beneficiary is usually a poor player or a big loser. This type of Robin Hood cheating is relatively common and benefits the good player by -

- distributing losses more evenly among players
- decreasing losses of big losers
- making the hands of both the cheater and his beneficiary more readable.

Sid Bennett often cheats for big losers like Ted Fehr. For example, Sid folds then looks at Ted Fehr's hand and sees a four-card Heart flush. Quickly he rummages through the discards, finds a Heart and then grabs Ted's draw card . . . it is a Club; Sid switches it with the Heart. . . .Ted smiles and wins the pot with a flush.

While Sid's card switch is crude and obvious, no one except John lets himself realize what happened. Later in the same game, Sid attempts a partnership with John. This is what happens:

The pot is large. Five players are in for the last bet, including John and Sid who are sitting next to each other. Sid bets and then his knee nudges John's leg. John folds his three Queens, and Sid wins with a full house.

"Remember that," Sid whispers to John while pulling in the pot.

A few hands later, Sid Bennett has a pat straight dealt to him. Again he nudges John, who folds immediately. Sid then grins and winks his faded blue eye at John.

Later that night, John draws to a low-ball hand, but misses. He bets the maximum trying to bluff out his two opponents. . . .Ted Fehr folds because Sid is sitting behind him with a pat hand. (Seat positions of Ted, John and Sid are reversed from the normal position shown on page 55.) John nudges Sid, who then shows his eight low to everyone and folds. "Thanks," he whispers to John. Immediately, John Finn spreads his hand

face up on the table . . . he wins the six hundred dollar low-ball pot with a pair of sevens. Sid raises out of his seat, sputtering dirty words.

Instead of simply saying no to Sid's partnership suggestion, John earns a good profit while making his answer clear.

5. Detection (79)

A cheater's technique is usually crude and easily detected. Most players, however, ignore even obvious cheating to avoid arousing unpleasant emotions. When a player detects cheating, he often rationalizes it as a rule violation or a mistake rather than cheating. The good player notices cheating quickly and can detect even highly skilled cheaters without even seeing a dishonest move. How does he do this? Cheaters are betrayed by violations of logic and probability. The good player with his sharply focused understanding of the game and the odds has an acute sense for improbable patterns . . . this enables him to detect any cheating.

Professor Merck subconsciously suspects Sid of cheating. One night, Sid cheats him out of a $700 pot. After sitting in silence for several hands, Quintin suddenly leaves without a word and slams the front door. . . . Knowing that Quintin detected Sid's cheating and fearful that he might tell others, John pursues him out the door. Quintin stops under the streetlamp when he sees John approaching. For a moment, neither say a word.

"You saw it too?" Quintin asks with squinting green eyes.

"I see it every game."

"Why haven't you said something?" Quintin half shouts. "He should've been bounced from the game."

"Who's the biggest loser in the game?" John snaps. "It's Sid. And you're a big winner. In the past couple years, you've taken Sid for thousands of dollars. Sure he's cheated you, me and everyone else out of pots. What if we'd thrown him out two years ago? We'd have done him a forty thousand dollar favor."

Quintin's mouth opens; he scratches his moustache.

"Sid's a cheater and deserves to be punished," John continues.

"The best way to punish him is to let him play. We only hurt ourselves by bouncing him from the game."

"Never thought about it that way," Quintin says. "Maybe you're right. . . .Who else knows about his cheating?"

"No one who'll admit it. Cheating is a strange thing. Most players have strong feelings against it. . . . Everyone subconsciously knows that Sid cheats. But no one wants an unpleasant experience, so no one sees him cheat."

"Someday, someone will accuse him."

"Aroused suspicion occurs first," John continues. "Take yourself . . . he cheated you out of seven hundred dollars tonight. Yet, you still didn't accuse him. You passed it off till next time. The next time you may have accused Sid or may have passed it off again."

"Yeah, but what if someone does accuse him . . . then what?"

"If he's accused outright, we not only lose Sid but other players might quit. The game might even fold. We must convince any seriously suspecting players that the best action is to let him play. If they won't accept this, then we must either stop the cheating or eliminate Sid from the game."

"So for now, we leave everything as is?"

"Right," John nods. "And when Sid steals your pot, just remember he'll pay you back many times."

"But why is he a big loser if he cheats?"

"Only in fiction is the cheater a winner. In reality, he's a loser and usually a big loser. Why? Most cheaters are poor players. The good player never needs to cheat . . . he can win as much money as the game can lose. A cheater, like a thief, is neurotic . . . he's unrealistic. He overestimates the value of cheating and plays a poorer game. And this is Sid's case."

"True, true," Quintin mumbles.

"See you next week," John says as he walks away.

What does John accomplish by this? He keeps the game intact by pacifying Quintin, and Sid continues his cheating and losing.

XV. TAXES AND LAWS (80)

For federal tax purposes, net annual poker winnings must be declared as straight *income.** Poker income can be listed under the heading of "Other Sources" on page two of the Federal Income Tax Form 1040. In most states, net poker gains can also be declared as income. Gambling losses can be deducted from gambling gains, but net gambling losses cannot be deducted from taxable income.

Poker players and their winnings are not subject to the federal *excise* taxes on gambling.** . . .Apparently, the Federal Government does not consider poker players in private games as gamblers.

A 1966 survey reveals that poker games are technically illegal in most states. Many states, however, do not apply their anti-gambling laws to private poker games, but only to house games (where admission is charged or pots are cut for a profit). The district attorney or attorney general's office can provide interpretation and enforcement intentions of local laws to private poker games.

The following table serves as an approximate guideline for the legal and tax status of poker in the various states:

** Carmack v. Commissioner of Internal Revenue, 183 F.2d 1(5th Cir.1950).*

*** According to United States Excise Tax Regulation 4401 (paragraphs 4020-4032), poker winnings are not subject to the ten percent excise wagering tax. And according to Regulation 4411 (paragraphs 4075-4083) poker players, even professional ones, are not required to register and purchase the fifty dollar Wagering Occupational Tax Stamp.*

State Laws about Poker
1966

State	*Is Poker Legal?**	*Source of Information*	*Legal Reference*	*State Income Tax 1970*
Alabama	No	NAACP of Montgomery, Alabama	Alabama State Statutes	Yes
Alaska	No	Bar Association	Section 11.60.140:	Yes
Arizona	No	Bar Association	Revised Statutes 13-431:	Yes
Arkansas	No	Assistant Attorney General	Statutes Annotated 41-2011 and 3809 (Repl. 1964):	Yes
California	No	Deputy Attorney General	Penal Code 330: Refers only to stud poker as illegal.	Yes

Author's opinion for private games (for use as a guideline only).

State Laws about Poker
1966

State	*Is Poker Legal?**	*Source of Information*	*Legal Reference*	*State Income Tax 1970*
Colorado	No	Bar Association	Revised Statutes Section 40-10-9:	Yes
Connecticut	No	State Police	Sections 53-272 to 277:	No
Delaware	Yes	Assistant Attorney General	Title II Code of 1953 Section 665:	Yes
Florida	No	Attorney General	Section 849.08:	No
Georgia	No	Assistant Attorney General	Georgia Code Section 26-6404 and 6401:	Yes
Hawaii	No	Bar Association	No specific reference given	Yes

****Author's opinion for private games (for use as a guideline only).***

State Laws about Poker
1966

State	*Is Poker Legal?**	*Source of Information*	*Legal Reference*	*State Income Tax 1970*
Idaho	No	Assistant Attorney General	Section 18-3801 Idaho Code:	Yes
Illinois	No	Legislative Reference Bureau	Criminal Law, Chapter 38 section 28-1:	Yes
Indiana	No	Bar Association	Act of 1905, Chapter 169 Statute 10-2307:	Yes
Iowa	No	Solicitor General	Chapter 726, 1966 Code:	Yes
Kansas	No	Bar Association	No specific reference given	Yes

****Author's opinion for private games (for use as a guideline only).***

State Laws about Poker
1966

State	*Is Poker Legal?**	*Source of Information*	*Legal Reference*	*State Income Tax 1970*
Kentucky	No	Bar Association	No specific reference given	Yes
Louisiana	Yes	Republican Party of Louisiana	No specific reference given	Yes
Maine	No	Assistant Attorney General	Revised Statute 1964 Title 16, Chapter 61 Section 1803:	Yes
Maryland	No	Assistant Attorney General	Maryland Article 27, Section 237-264	Yes
Massachusetts	No	Bar Association	Section 1, Chapter 37 General Laws:	Yes

Author's opinion for private games (for use as a guideline only).

State Laws about Poker
1966

State	*Is Poker Legal?**	*Source of Information*	*Legal Reference*	*State Income Tax 1970*
Michigan	No	Democratic State Central Committee of Michigan	Penal Code, 1945 Sections 750.314 and 750.315:	Yes
Minnesota	Yes	Attorney	Statutes 609,75:	Yes
Mississippi	No	Bar Association	Code of 1942 Section 2190:	Yes
Missouri	No	Governor	State Statute	Yes
Montana	No	Attorney General	Section 94-2401 R.C.M. 1947:	Yes
Nebraska	Yes	Bar Association	No specific reference given	Yes

**Author's opinion for private games (for use as a guideline only).*

State Laws about Poker
1966

State	*Is Poker Legal?**	*Source of Information*	*Legal Reference*	*State Income Tax 1970*
Nevada	Yes	Bar Association	No specific reference given	No
New Hampshire	No	Bar Association	577.7 Gaming:	No
New Jersey	No	Deputy Attorney General	Statutes 2A:112-a and 218:85-7:	No
New Mexico	No	Assistant Attorney General	Section 40A-19-1 to 3 N.M. Statutes Annotated 1953 Compilation (P.S.):	Yes
New York	No	Assistant Council to Governor	Article 1, Section 9 of N.Y. State Constitution and Sections 970-998 of N.Y. State Penal Law	Yes

****Author's opinion for private games (for use as a guideline only).***

State Laws about Poker
1966

State	*Is Poker Legal?**	*Source of Information*	*Legal Reference*	*State Income Tax 1970*
North Carolina	No	Bar Association	No specific reference given	Yes
North Dakota	No	Bar Association	Chapter 12-23-01:	Yes
Ohio	No	Bar Association	Section 2915.06 Revised Code:	No
Oklahoma	No	Oklahoma State University	Title 21 of Oklahoma Statutes, 1961, Section 941:	Yes
Oregon	No	Attorney General	ORS 167.25 and 167.510:	Yes

****Author's opinion for private games (for use as a guideline only).***

State Laws about Poker
1966

State	*Is Poker Legal?**	*Source of Information*	*Legal Reference*	*State Income Tax 1970*
Pennsylvania	No	Deputy Attorney General	No specific reference given	Yes (1971)
Rhode Island	No	Attorney General's office	No specific reference given	No
South Carolina	No	Research Clerk	Sections 16-804,505:	Yes
South Dakota	No	Bar Association	No specific reference given	No
Tennessee	No	Attorney General	Section 39-2001 Tennessee Code Annotated	No

**Author's opinion for private games (for use as a guideline only).*

State Laws about Poker
1966

State	*Is Poker Legal?**	*Source of Information*	*Legal Reference*	*State Income Tax 1970*
Texas	Yes	Executive Department	Texas Jurisprudence 2nd volume 26	No
Utah	No	Attorney General	Section 76-27-1 to 3, Utah Code Annotated, 1953:	Yes
Vermont	No	Bar Association	Section 2132 and 13 VSA 2133:	Yes
Virginia	No	Attorney General	Section 18.1-316:	Yes
Washington	No	Assistant Attorney General	Revised Code 9.47.010 to 9.47.030:	No

**Author's opinion for private games (for use as a guideline only).*

State Laws about Poker
1966

State	*Is Poker Legal?**	*Source of Information*	*Legal Reference*	*State Income Tax 1970*
West Virginia	No	Bar Association	No specific reference	Yes
Wisconsin	No	Bar Association	Chapter 945:	Yes
Wyoming	No	Attorney	Statute 6-203,1957:	No
District of Columbia	? (not clear)	United States Attorney	Title 22, D.C. Code Section 1501 to 1515:	Yes
Puerto Rico	No	Bar Association	No specific reference given	

**Author's opinion for private games (for use as a guideline only).*

State Laws about Poker
1966

State	*Is Poker Legal?**	*Source of Information*	*Legal Reference*	*State Income Tax 1970*
Virgin Islands	No	Attorney	Sections 1221-1226 Chapter 61 Title 14:	
United States Government	Yes	Deputy Attorney General	Legality is up to individual states. Winnings are income taxable.	

Author's opinion for private games (for use as a guideline only).

This section of the Federal Tax form (page two, form 1040) shows how John Finn declares his $54,000 poker income for 1965:

Form 1040

U.S. Individual Income Tax Return **1965**

for the year January 1–December 31, 1965 or other taxable year beginning................................,
1965, ending................................, 19.........US Treasury Department—Internal Revenue Service

4 Pensions and annuities, rents and royalties, partnerships, & estates or trusts (Schedule B)		
5 Business income (Schedule C)..........................▶		
6 Sale or exchange of property (Schedule D)....	3,450	00
7 Farm income (Schedule F)..................................▶		
8 Other sources (state nature)..........		
Monday Poker Games	42,000	00
Other Poker Games	12,000	00
Total other sources ▶▶▶▶	54,000	00
9 Add lines 2 through 8. Enter here and on page 1 line 6,.......................................▶▶▶▶	57,450	00

PART FOUR

OPPONENT

In poker, all opponents are potential financial assets. The good poker player first gets his opponents involved in the game; he then exploits them to win their money.

XVI. INVOLVEMENT (81)

As players become emotionally and financially involved in a poker game, they become easier to exploit and their chances of quitting the game decrease.

1. Emotional (82)

Emotional involvement can result from gambling impulses . . . and most players are gamblers. To them, poker is gambling*. When a gambler loses, he keeps on playing in an attempt to recover his losses. When a gambler wins, he forgets his losses while believing he has learned how to win. The

---

* *Gambling is defined as: "The wagering of money at unfavorable odds." In poker, the good player with favorable edge odds is not gambling, but players with unfavorable edge odds are gambling. Horse players, casino patrons, and losing poker players are gamblers.*

The above definition of gambling is consistent with the Webster's *definition (Third New International Dictionary, 1961) - "To wager money or stakes on an uncertain outcome." The good player's outcome is certain; therefore, he is not gambling. . . . Also, the above definition is consistent with the* Funk and Wagnalls' *definition (The Standard Dictionary, 1962) - "To lose, squander or dispose of by gaming." By this definition, the good player is not gambling, but losing players are. . . . And the definition is consistent with the* Random House's *definition (The Random House Dictionary, 1966) - "Any matter or thing involving risk or hazardous uncertainty." The good player's situaton is essentially riskless and, therefore, is not a gambling situation.*

A gambling situation yields a statistically minus *return on money wagered, while a non-gambling (investment) situation yields a* statistically plus *return on money invested. . . . The intensity of the situation (rate of return) is determined by both the time span of the wager (or investment) and the percent return. The intensity of and the differentiation between gambling and non-gambling (investment) situations are illustrated by the tables on pages 125 and 126. Notice the situations of the Monday night poker players relative to other investment and gambling situations.*

Intensity of Investment Situations

Investment Situation	*Monday Night Poker Player*	*Estimated per Investment*		*Investment Intensity**
		Average Return, %/$	*Time Span*	
Good Poker Player	John Finn	+25	6 minutes	+2,000,000
Sound Poker Player	Quintin Merck	+ 5	6 minutes	+400,000
Business		+10	1 year	+10
Bonds		+ 6	1 year	+6
Banks		+ 5	1 year	+5
Stocks		+ 4	1 year	+4

**Intensity values are the Average Return values approximated on an annual basis.*

Intensity of Gambling Situations

Gambling Situation	*Monday Night Poker Player*	*Estimated per Gamble*		*Gambling Intensity**
		Average Return, %/$	*Time Span*	
Lottery		-50	1 month	-600
Numbers		-40	1 day	-15,000
Average Poker Player	Scotty Nichols	- 1	6 minutes	-90,000
Casino Poker**		(Varies at the whim of the house dealer)		
Crap Shooting		- 1	1 minute	-500,000
Horse Racing		-15	12 minutes	-700,000
Poor Poker Player	Sid Bennett	-10	6 minutes	-900,000
Poor Poker Player	Ted Fehr	-10	6 minutes	-900,000
Roulette		- 3	30 seconds	-3,300,000
Slot Machines		--20	5 seconds	-130,000,000

**Intensity values are the Average Return values approximated on an annual basis.*

***Poker played in gambling casinos is normally a gambling situation even for the good player because the pots are heavily cut by the house dealer. This large, arbitrary cut will greatly reduce or even eliminate the profitable return to the good player. And while the good player will have a great advantage over the other players in a casino poker game, he cannot control the game or the transient players as he can in the private game.*

gambler's subconscious desire to punish himself emerges in his consciousness as irrational optimism.

Many players use poker as a diversion to escape reality. Also, many players develop friendships with other players. These involvements are emotional and can compensate for heavy losses.

2. Financial (83)

For a losing player, financial involvement is a form of emotional involvement. When his losses force him to use his savings or to borrow money, he keeps playing in a vain attempt to recover those losses. An occasional win gives him encouragement to continue playing.

A winning player can get financially involved if he becomes too dependent on his poker income. He can even turn into a continuous loser when a series of losses disrupts this income. How does this happen? If a loss of objectivity occurs when he temporarily loses his poker income, his quality of play will deteriorate. If this decreased-objectivity/increased-deterioration cycle continues, his future losses are assured. Memories of past winnings will then sustain him through heavy losses.

John Finn and Quintin Merck normally bet only when the odds favor them; they are not gamblers. All the other players in the Monday night game are gamblers. . . . Each player is involved emotionally and financially as shown in the following table:

	Reasons for Involvement	
	Emotional	*Financial*
John Finn	**(minimum involvement)**	**Receives substantial income**
Quintin Merck	**Soothes ego Finds companionship Relieves boredom**	**Receives moderate income useful for bragging about his poker skill**
Scotty Nichols	**Avoids drinking problems Escapes business disappointments**	**Tries to regain his past winning form**

Reasons for Involvement

	Emotional	*Financial*
Sid Bennett	**Hides insecurities** **Finds companionship** **Releases tensions**	**Seeks hot streak to recover past losses**
Ted Fehr	**Satisfies gambling compulsion** **Escapes domestic problems**	**Hopes for big win to parley on the horses**

XVII. EXPLOITATION (84)

Once players are involved in the game, the good player can take greater advantage of them in areas of –

- personal weaknesses
- play of cards
- betting and raising
- position
- agreements.

1. Personal Weaknesses, Favors, and Bribes (85)

People can be exploited through their weaknesses . . . especially poker players who are involved and motivated through their weaknesses (except the good player . . . he is motivated by money). One or more of the following weaknesses exist in most players:

altruism
carelessness
compulsiveness
dishonesty
exhibitionism
faith
fear
greed
ignorance
impulsiveness
inattentiveness
inexperience

instability	stubbornness
laziness	subjectiveness
mysticism	superstitiousness
nervousness	timidness
preoccupation	whimfulness
self-pity	worry

These weaknesses grow from the player's refusal to think or to act rationally.

The good player determines and then records the weaknesses of each opponent in his notebook; he uses their weaknesses to influence their playing, to read their hands and to lead them into a faster betting pace and higher stakes. His notes on their weaknesses help him to –

- refresh his memory
- see new ways to use their weaknesses
- better understand each opponent
- detect changes in an opponent more quickly.

The weaknesses of each poker player are catalogued in John Finn's notebook as shown below:

Weaknesses

Quintin Merck	Sid Bennett
greed	carelessness
stubbornness	dishonesty
superstitiousness	exhibitionism
	impulsiveness
	inattentiveness
	stubbornness
	whimfulness

Weaknesses

Scotty Nichols	Ted Fehr
carelessness	compulsiveness
faith	faith
fear	fear
greed	impulsiveness
inattentiveness	instability
laziness	preoccupation
mysticism	self-pity
preoccupation	subjectiveness
self-pity	superstitiousness
subjectiveness	whimfulness
timidness	worry
worry	

The following incidents show how John uses his opponents' weaknesses to win their money:

Missing his flush in draw poker, John finds himself in a good position to bluff, so he bets $50. Scotty and Sid fold immediately. Ted Fehr holds two pair and thinks he should drop, but is desperate and considers calling. Now, John must prevent him from calling.

Everyone knows that Ted is superstitious about pennies and never keeps any . . . especially when gambling. So when Ted leans over and shows Sid his hand, John takes a penny from his pocket and slips the coin under the edge of Ted's money.

"Call!" Sid bellows as he gazes blankly at Ted's cards. "He's got nothing."

"Yeah," Ted grins as he picks up his pile of money to call. "What!" his grin fades as the penny tumbles from his money. "No wonder I'm losing!" he yells while picking up the coin and throwing it across the room. As the penny bounces off the wall and rolls around the floor, Ted folds his hand and says, "At least it made me fold. I saved fifty bucks . . ." His voice fades when John shows his winning hand . . . a four flush. Ted's eyes water . . . his superstition costs him a two hundred dollar pot.

* * *

Consider another example of John exploiting an opponent's weakness:

Sid Bennett injures his foot and cannot leave his house. At the last moment, John switches the game to Sid's house so the injured man can play. Knowing there will not be the usual supply of food, John stops at a delicatessen and invests a dollar in a gigantic Italian submarine sandwich nicely wrapped in cellophane.

At three in the morning, Scotty Nichols grips his stomach. He rummages through Sid's skimpily stocked kitchen and devours handfuls of dry cereal; he even gulps down a quarter-filled bottle of ketchup.

The next hand is seven card stud, high-low with two twists. John's hole cards are the Ace and the bug*; he has another Ace face up . . . a beautiful start for both high and low. He wants the maximum number of callers. Now is the time to use his dollar investment . . . he reaches under his chair and pulls the huge sandwich from a brown paper bag. All eyes turn toward the juicy submarine. Scotty moans as his tongue laps around his puffy lips.

John lays the elongated sandwich across the pot, "The winners split it," he declares. Now Scotty's face is sweating and his stomach is growling.

With eyes fixed on the sandwich, everyone calls the first bet. John aggressively bets his strong hand . . . many players keep calling. The final bets are large . . . Scotty keeps calling with a poor hand. "Should fold," he pants. "But that sub . . . Hmm." . . .The red faced man spends over a hundred dollars on calls. Other players also call with their eyes focused on the sandwich. The pot is the largest of the night . . . over seven hundred dollars. John wins both high and low with an Ace high full house and a six-five low. He also wins back his food, which he later uses to build another pot.

With a dollar investment, John Finn exploits his opponents' lack of discipline to win many extra dollars.

** The bug is the Joker counting as an Ace for high and as a wild card for low . . . and good for filling straights and flushes. In high-low games, the bug can be used as both a high and a low card in the same hand.*

The good player takes profitable advantage of man's greatest weakness – laziness. . . . Laziness causes the desire to get something for nothing and expands into desires for unearned approval, respect, and money. The good player manipulates favors that symbolize friendship, respect, and profit. His victims bend to his will in seeking his favors.

Favors that the good player extends and withdraws as the situation dictates are –

- loans
- advice
- compliments
- sympathy
- showing of cards.

Out of the loser's desire for approval from a respected winner, the good player can use his favors as bribes to get, for example, a loser's support for an advantageous change in house rules or for introduction of a new, wild game.

2. Play of Cards and Betting (86)

The good player exploits his opponents during the play of their cards; he tricks them into playing poorer poker than they normally would. With the proper strategy, he causes them to –

- make mistakes
- improperly estimate the value of hands
- play a looser game
- play hands that should be dropped
- drop hands that should be called.

A little exploitation trick that John Finn uses, especially for split pot games, involves the following maneuver to make a hesitant player call a bet:

The game is high-low, five card stud with two twists. John has a lock on low, while Quintin and Ted are battling for high. Quintin bets $20. Ted has a four flush and would like to call, but is afraid that John will raise and Quintin will reraise . . . thus costing him $40 more. He starts to fold. John picks up a twenty dollar bill and holds it over the pot. Now knowing that John will only call and not raise, Ted calls and catches a flush on the twist. After much betting and raising, Ted ends up beating Quintin for high. John wins low and makes an extra fifty dollars by not letting Ted fold.

John seldom fakes this maneuver. So when players see him holding the call money, they know with confidence that he will not raise. He will, however, often fake the reverse maneuver of not holding the call money and then not raising.

The good player also exploits his opponents through betting. When holding a strong hand, he achieves an advantageous betting position by getting other players to do his betting and raising. Successful *indirect* betting requires accurate reading of opponents' hands and knowledge of their betting habits.

Disproportionate betting can trick opponents into desirable betting positions. For example, by making a bet or a raise completely out of proportion with the normal or expected bet, the good player can lure opponents into making the desired bet, raise, call or drop. Disproportionate betting is useful as both an offensive and defensive tool.

Scotty Nichols deals draw poker with one twist. John Finn gets a four-card straight flush. For his best investment odds, he wants the maximum players calling a bet big enough to keep them in for the large, last-round bets. He also wants to avoid raises that would make players fold.

So John opens for $14 instead of the normal $25 . . . noses wrinkle. Players with poor hands smile and then call at this bargain price. Potential raisers, suspicious of the weird bet and

fearing a sandbag, only call. The results are perfect for John . . . everyone calls and no one raises. John's estimated investment odds soar to a highly favorable –

$$\frac{(\$600)\,(.4)}{\$80} = 3.0$$

Suppose John bets the normal \$25 and only two players call. His estimated investment odds tumble to –

$$\frac{(\$250)\,(.5)}{\$75} = 1.7.$$

Now suppose John bets \$25, someone raises to \$50, and everyone else drops. If John calls the raise (which he probably would not), his estimated investment odds fall to an unfavorable –

$$\frac{200\,(.4)}{(100)} = 0.8.$$

By making the disproportionate \$14 bet, John controls the betting and maximizes his financial advantage. Moreover, if he checks his bet on the next round, usually one or more players will feel deprived of a full opening round bet and thus bet aggressively. Then, John can lay back and let them do the betting and raising for him. On the other hand, if John bets on the next round, the other players will probably remain defensive and avoid raising.

With this disproportionate \$14 bet, John increases his investment odds and leaves himself in a favorable, flexible betting position. He can easily turn the betting into either an offensive or defensive tempo, whichever is advantageous to him.

3. Hypnosis (87)

The good player can hypnotize certain players, particularly the dull, emotional or mystical players. He knows his subjects (opponents) well, and with planned experiments he discovers hypnotic responses in them. Typical hypnotic stimuli are –

- staring into the subject's eyes (psychological)
- moving a finger through the pot (visual and motion)
- breathing hard during a tense silence (sound)
- tapping fingers on the table (sound and motion).

While the good player can get certain opponents to bet, call, or fold by hypnosis, he uses this technique cautiously because hypnotizing tricks can give away his own intentions.

The hand is low-ball draw, and John Finn makes the final bet for $100. He has Scotty Nichols beat and wants him to call. Scotty groans. Looking at the huge pot, he sees John's finger slowly stirring the pile of money . . . stirring slowly and smoothly. Ten and twenty dollar bills are moving in circles. Scotty's floating brown eyes start rotating with the money. His chubby hand picks up a hundred dollar bill; he calls John's bet.

Scotty tries to smile as John pulls in the pot. Eventually, he will be wise to this trick, but then John will simply use another hypnotic trick. . . .John estimates his earnings per life of trick range from several hundred to several thousand dollars. He also estimates that in 1965, hypnotic tricks netted him an extra two thousand dollars.

4. Distractions (88)

The good player can take greater advantage of his opponents by distracting them. A radio or television for sporting events has excellent distraction value. A late newspaper is usually good for several hands of distracted play from opponents checking horse race results, the stock market, and the news. Pornographic literature offers an absorbing distraction. Good spreads of food and soft drinks have a steady distraction value.

A faster moving game decreases the quality of poker played by most opponents. The use of poker chips speeds up the betting. Alternating two decks of cards speeds up the dealing.

Availability of beer is sometimes advantageous. One drink takes the sharpness off a player's ability to concentrate. A single beer markedly reduces the edge odds of the better players. This is why the good player never drinks before or during the game. This is why the good player is glad to see the superior players take a drink.

Moderate amounts of alcohol have little effect on poor players because their concentration is already at a reduced level. The poor player must drink enough to become intoxicated before his edge odds are further reduced. The advantages of having a player intoxicated, however, are usually cancelled by disadvantages such as slowing up the game and causing drinking problems that may drive desirable players out of the game.

By encouraging distractions, John Finn keeps the game confused. He also keeps the game moving quickly. In the Monday night game, however, he discovers that the players will play for significantly higher stakes when cash instead of poker chips is used. (This is an exception rather than the rule.) So cash is used because the higher stakes offer more profit to John than would the poorer money attitudes generated with poker chips (see page 91).

By creating distractions, John increases his edge odds by about twenty percent. This means eight thousand dollars additional income per year (at his current winning rate). He estimates his opponents are distracted 35% of the time when involved in the action (playing their hands) . . . and are distracted a much higher percentage of the time when not involved in the action. The table on page 137 estimates the distractions of each player.

Each week, John Finn is a good fellow and brings the late evening paper containing the complete stock market closings and horse race results. Ted and Sid read this paper while playing their hands. Every now and then they lose a pot to John because of this distraction.

These newspapers cost John $5.20 per year; he figures they are worth about one thousand dollars a year in distractions. This is a

Time Distracted, %

(when in-action)

	Eating	*Gossiping*	*Day Dreaming*	*Radio, TV, Newspaper*	*Miscellaneous*	*Total*
Quintin Merck	**2**	**5**	**10**	**5**	**2**	**24**
Scotty Nichols	**10**	**2**	**15**	**2**	**5**	**34**
Sid Bennett	**2**	**25**	**5**	**10**	**5**	**47**
Ted Fehr	**Slight**	**Slight**	**25**	**15**	**2**	**43**
John Finn	**0**	**1**	**Slight**	**Slight**	**2**	**4**

200:1 return on his investment or about twenty-dollars per newspaper.

5. Agreements (89)

The good player finds opportunities to make profitable agreements with other players. For instance, he can sometimes make an agreement with a loose player that each time either one wins a pot they will pay the other, for example, five dollars. Such an agreement will bring the good player a steady side income. Even when the loose player is a big loser, he will usually win more pots than the good player. Most poor players will gladly make such an agreement because they erroneously believe that a winner must win more pots than a loser. Also, most losers desire an association with a winner (the good player); such an association helps the loser feel on the same level with the winner. Often a loose player happily maintains such an agreement indefinitely without ever realizing that he is providing the good player with a steady, side income.

Compared to John Finn, Sid Bennett plays in twice as many hands, wins about fifty percent more pots, but loses nearly three times as often. He jumps at John's suggestion to pay each other five dollars every time one of them wins a pot. Two years later, Sid is still pleased with this arrangement as indicated by his comments:

"At least I keep collecting these side bets," he smiles as John wins a huge pot and gives him five dollars. "Don't understand why you made such a stupid bet."

"Ha!" Quintin Merck snorts; he knows John makes money from that agreement. John knows it too, and his notebook data prove it:

The Sid Bennett Agreement

	#+Weeks, Average	*#-Weeks, Average*	*Net Income*
1964	**40, $30**	**10, $10**	**+ $1100**
1965	**40, $35**	**8, $10**	**+ $1320**

So far, Sid has lost $2,420 on John's stupid bet and is very happy about it . . . sort of an ideal arrangement for John.

XVIII. MONEY EXTRACTION (90)

The good poker player is involved in a long-term process of extracting money from the game as well as from each individual player.

1. Winning Too Fast (91)

Extraction of money at the maximum rate is not always in the best, long-term financial interest of the good player. Uncontrolled money extraction can cause the following problems:

- Players who would be long-term sources of important income may quit the game.
- Stakes or rules may be disadvantageously changed.
- Unfavorable attitudes may develop.
- Game may break up.

These problems suggest that the good player can win too fast. To extract the maximum money, he often decreases his winning rate in order to control the flow of money. In other words, maximum money extraction may require a slower winning rate.

2. Uncontrolled Money Flow (92)

Over a period of many games, uncontrolled money flows in a pattern similar to that illustrated by the *top* figure on page 141. As the good player accumulates performance data on each player, these money movement patterns become evident.

Data for a game with an uncontrolled money flow are tabulated on page 142. Notice the heavy losses absorbed by poor players A and B compared to players C and D. In this game, the good player E is extracting winnings through normal, uncontrolled money flow. But poor player A may quit, for example, because continuous losses hurt his pride. And poor player B may insist on lower stakes because his sharp losses cause an acute financial strain. The good player may be risking his future earnings unless he alters the money flow to a controlled pattern similar to that illustrated by the *bottom* figure on page 141.

The ideal money flow pattern for the good player occurs when he wins at the maximum rate that each player can tolerate. . . .This usually means winning less from the poorest players and more from the better players.

3. Controlled Money Flow (93)

The good player evaluates the money extraction patterns on both a short and long term basis. If a controlled pattern seems desirable, he then determines how the money flow should be altered (extent and direction). In a controlled pattern, he usually extracts money more evenly from his opponents. In other words, he extracts less from the poorer players and more from the better players. Controlled money flow shifts everyone's performance as shown on page 143.

MONEY FLOW PATTERNS

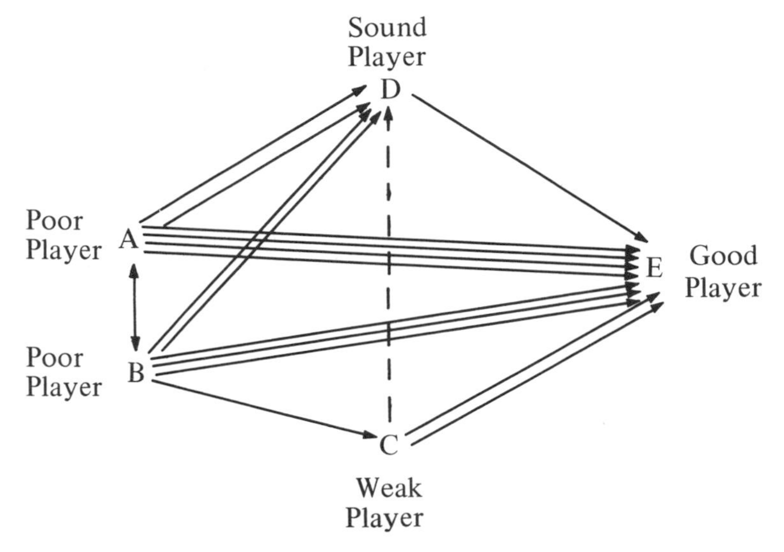

Normal, uncontrolled money flow

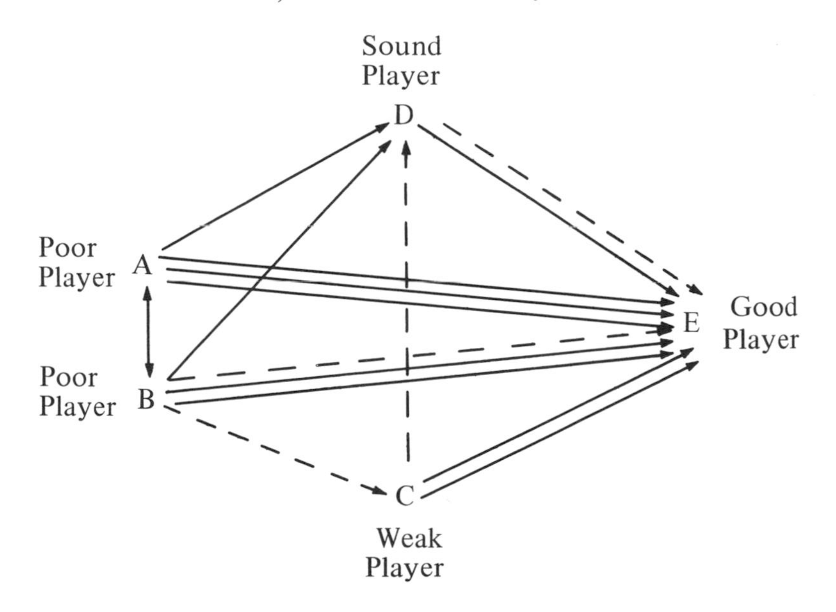

Controlled money flow

** Broken arrow represents half the money flow of a solid arrow.*

PERFORMANCE DATA

Ten Games

(Uncontrolled Money Flow)

Players	*A*		*B*		*C*		*D*		*E*		*Irregular*	
Rating	*Poor*		*Poor*		*Weak*		*Sound*		*Good*		*Players****	
Performance, $	+	-	+	-	+	-	+	-	+	-	+	-
1961-1962												
12/4/61	200			200	100		200			220		100
12/11		200	300			100	50			80	50	
12/18		100		200		150	50		440			50
1/8/62		150		400		200		250	860		100	
1/15		350	Absent		Absent		200		260			100
1/22		400		100	550		0	0		100	50	
1/29	Absent			300	250		150		240			350
2/5		200	100			250		150	680			200
2/12	400		50			200	100		20			350
2/19		100	Absent			100	100		520			400
Totals	600	1500	450	1200	900	1000	850	400	3020	400	200	1550
Average*		-100		-95		-10	+45		+262			-135
Edge Odds,%**	-22		-21		-2		+10		+59		-30	

**Averages are calculated by dividing the number of games attended into the net winnings or losses of each player.*

***The big winner for these ten games averages plus $445 per game. Edge odds of the good player, for example, are then calculated as $262/$445 x 100 = 59%.*

****These are average values for the irregular players. In this set of data, their relative losses are heavier than usual.*

PERFORMANCE DATA
(Average of 100 Games)

Player-Rating-	*A Poor*	*B Poor*	*C Weak*	*D Sound*	*E Good*	*Irregular Players**
Uncontrolled money flow, $/game	-102	-85	-22	+54	+196	-41
Controlled money flow, $/game	- 58	-52	-35	+ 6	+174	-35

**Average values for the irregular players.*

This controlled pattern costs the good player an average of $22 per game. But if the money flow were not controlled, the continued heavy losses of poor players A and B could have destroyed the game and cost him the $17,400 that he won over these hundred sessions. This $22 per session is his insurance premium for keeping the game at favorable conditions. He keeps accurate performance records to determine the cost, value, and effectiveness of his control over the money flow. This control normally costs him 10-15% of his net winnings.

The good player usually takes control of the money flow during the early rounds when his betting influence is the greatest at a mimimum cost. He alters the money flow patterns by the following methods:

- Helps and favors the poorest players at the expense of the better players whenever practical.
- Drives the poor player out with first round bets when a better player holds a good hand. And conversely, he uses first round bets to keep the better players in when a poor player holds a good hand.

- Avoids playing alone against poor players; this decreases his advantage over them at a minimum cost. When betting against poor players, he makes image building and long term strategy plays at less favorable investment odds.

John Finn spends some of his winnings to hold big losers like Sid Bennett and Ted Fehr in the game. Data from John's records for 1965 indicate that this is a profitable expenditure:

Breakdown of 1965 Poker Income and Insurance Costs

Source of income	*Estimated net income,$*	*Estimated insurance costs,$ (on-purpose losses)*
Quintin Merck	2,500	100
Scotty Nichols	5,500	500
Sid Bennett	13,000	2,000
Ted Fehr	9,000	700
Others	12,000	1,200
Total:	$42,000	$4,500

Without paying this insurance, he theoretically could have won $4500 more in 1965. By not paying the insurance, however, the greater psychological and financial pressures on the big losers may have forced them to quit . . . and each big loser is worth much more than this $4500 per year insurance cost. The Poker game could even end if several big losers quit. John, therefore, considers this insurance cost as an important investment.

How does he spend this $4500? This money buys him the valve that controls the money flow. He watches the losers closely. When they are in psychological or financial trouble and on the verge of quitting, he opens the valve and feeds them morale boosting money until they are steady again.

Winning players are of little use to John. There is no need to help them or boost their morale; he keeps the valve closed tight on them. He may even spend money to drive them out of the game if they hurt his financial interests.

John Finn never spends money on any player except to gain an eventual profit.

PART FIVE

GAME

More players and more games mean more income to the good player. He increases his poker activity by -

- finding other games
- organizing games
- expanding games
- maintaining games
- starting new games.

XIX. OTHER GAMES (94)

Other poker games offer new sources of income. Even if the stakes are not worthwhile, the good player enters new games in order to -

- take control then increase the pace and stakes to worthwhile levels
- evaluate the players . . . some may be good candidates for larger stake games
- make contacts with new players that may lead to still other poker games and other new players.

John Finn first enters the Monday night game on June 6, 1960; the stakes are not worth the effort required to play poker. He takes control of the game, reorganizes it then steadily increases the pace and stakes. The table on page 63 tabulates his progress during the next five years as his profits for Monday nights climb to $42,000 in 1965.

1. Finding Game (95)

Practically every regular poker game needs, at times, an additional player. Most games need more permanent players.

When a desirable player spreads word of his poker interest, he usually gets invitations to other games. Most poker players consider a player desirable if he -

- plays a clean game
- arrives on time
- is cooperative and congenial
- acts respectful toward other players
- plays to the end regardless of his winnings or losses
- keeps the game organized.

The good player by design has these desirable traits, but does not consider them as important traits in his opponents. Since he is interested only in extracting maximum money from the game, desirable opponents -

- are poor players
- are steady players
- have sufficient money
- do not harm the game.

Ironically, most players will invite the expensive, good poker player to their game in preference to a profitable, poor player.

The players in the Monday night game consider John Finn a desirable player and an asset to the game. They refuse to realize that he is their biggest liability . . . a staggering liability of $42,000 per year. They are glad John is in the game because he is cooperative, congenial and respectful. He plays a clean game, always arrives on time and plays until the end. They are grateful that he keeps the game organized. He is a pleasant, soothing, comfortable player. Everyone appreciates him.

John knows this; he works hard to keep them satisfied and happy. His fee for the effort is $42,000 per year.

2. Becoming a Permanent Player (96)

Once in a game, the good player gets a repeat invitation by making the other players feel favorable and obligated toward him. He does this with thoughtful gestures such as -

- lending money at the first opportunity
- offering his own cigars, candy and gum to the players
- helping to pick up the cards between deals
- sympathizing with losers
- praising winners
- complimenting good plays of his opponents
- helping to clean up after the game
- offering to bring refreshments to the next game.

If the new game is financially worthwhile, the good player plans his behavior to get a permanent invitation by -

- avoiding the image of being a tight or a tough player
- keeping quiet about his activities in other poker games.

The good player will not press for maximum edge odds until he becomes a permanent player. Once a permanent player, he concentrates on taking control of the game. He builds the ego of a key player (one with important influence over the game) in order to win his friendship and confidence. With the support of a key player, he is in a better position to take control of the game.

The first time John Finn plays in the Monday night game, he is a swell fellow - humble, quiet, even timid...but very considerate in passing out all his cigars and admiring everyone's poker skill. Best of all, he loses money and plays loose. And he never slows down the game or irritates anyone.

A fish, an ideal player, a nice guy . . . so everyone thinks. How about those nutty plays he makes? Raising then drawing four or five cards. Loosest player I've ever seen. Did you see how he lent Sid fifty dollars? Sid never even asked him for it. He even offered to pick up the refreshments for the next game. Sure hope be becomes a regular player. At least he'll come back next week to collect Sid's loan.

Over the next few sessions, John puts zest into the game. He plays wild, exciting poker. Everyone knows he is bound to be a big loser. His popularity grows; his friendships deepen. He establishes his supporters, and no one has an excuse to get rid of him. Soon John becomes a permanent player . . . he then takes control of the game.

Five years later, he has taken $90,000 from the game, but he is just as popular. . . . John Finn never gives anyone a reason to dislike him.

In one-shot games, especially those with strangers, the good player will press for immediate advantage over his opponents. Many of his tactics are opposite to those he would use in regular games. . . .His behavior may be tough and aggressive. He concentrates on extracting money at a maximum rate from the weakest players. He is not concerned about being a nice fellow if his opponents have no future value to him.

3. Quitting Game (97)

The good player quits a game that is not financially worthwhile or that conflicts with a more profitable game. He quits under the best possible circumstances and retains good relationships with everyone. Even after quitting, he may occasionally play in this game to renew his contacts and to recruit players for bigger games.

John Finn quits the Thursday night game because it is not profitable enough to consume another weekday night on poker. He quits under congenial circumstances and occasionally returns to play and recruit new players for the bigger games. In the past two

years, he recruits four of these players into the Monday and Friday night games. He estimates that these four players were worth $10,000 to him in 1965.

4. Breaking up Game (98)

The good player sometimes breaks up a game to free its players for more profitable games. If he controls and keeps the game organized, he can destroy this game simply by not organizing it and then putting its players into other games.

Besides the Monday night game, John Finn regularly plays in a Friday night game and occasionally in Tuesday and Thursday night games. The Tuesday night game has the least profit potential, but one of its players would be a good addition to the Monday game. John estimates his entire income from the Tuesday game is less than the money he could win from this player on Monday nights. So he breaks up the game by hurting its two worst players with consecutive, morale damaging losses. In three weeks, they quit and the game collapses.

By destroying this game, John gains a free night along with a new source of income for the big Monday game. He also gains other free players for the Friday and Thursday games.

XX. ORGANIZATION (99)

The financial potential of a game depends on how well it is organized. The good player organizes a game by -

- scheduling it on a regular basis at a time and place most suitable for maximum attendance
- establishing a firm starting time
- contacting players before each game to get commitments to play.

1. Regular Game (100)

Compared to the occasional game, the regularly scheduled, weekly game is easier to organize because players can plan for it in advance. And a regular game provides more opportunities for money extraction. Also, players get more involved in games that are regular and frequent.

If a game is about to collapse because players are losing at rates beyond their financial limits, the good player may temporarily re-schedule the game on a less frequent bi-weekly or monthly basis instead of reducing the stakes or the betting pace. More often, however, he will reduce the stakes temporarily.

In keeping the Monday night game going on a weekly basis, John Finn increases the stakes until some players are losing at rates beyond their financial limits, he then drops the stakes. He may raise and drop the stakes several times before permanently establishing them at a higher level.

In going to higher stakes, the losing tolerances of players increase as they get accustomed to their greater losses. When John drops the stakes, it is usually the big losers who insist on returning to the higher stakes.

Sometimes, John stabilizes a shaky game by bringing in new players. These new players supplement his income and help hold the game at the higher stakes. By controlling the stakes and adding new players, John has kept the high stake Monday game going on a regular, weekly basis for the past six years.

2. Starting Time (101)

An indefinite starting time can destroy a game. If players must wait for others to arrive before starting the game, then these early arriving players may come later the following week to avoid waiting . . . thus causing progressively later starting times and a subsequent loss of players. The following methods encourage players to arrive on time:

- Make a firm starting time clear to all players.
- Emphasize the importance of being on time.

- Admonish late arrivals.
- Establish fines or penalties for late arrivals.
- Fill the game so late arrivals will not get a seat.

The Monday night game is supposed to start at eight o'clock. As more and more players arrive late, the game starts later and later. Eventually, players start arriving at ten and eleven o'clock. Attendance begins to suffer, so John Finn takes action. He suggests a five dollar fine for anyone arriving after the game starts. The players, disgusted with the late starting times, all agree.

The next week, six players arrive by eight o'clock and the game starts at eight-fifteen. . .the earliest start in months. At nine o'clock, Quintin Merck wanders in.

"Get it up!" Sid roars.

"Uh, what ya mean?" Quintin grumbles as he sits at the table.

"You're late," Sid grins. "Five buck fine, buddy."

"Ah, don't give me that kid stuff. Deal the cards," Quintin says puffing hard on his cigarette.

Sid deals Quintin out.

"Hey!" Quintin slaps his hand on the table. "What about me?"

"You ain't playing till you pay your fine," Sid says. The other players nod in agreement.

"We play for thousands of dollars and you boy scouts hound me for five bucks," Quintin grumbles while throwing a five dollar bill at Sid.

The following week, all the players are at Scotty's house by eight o'clock. Since the fine was put into effect, the game never starts later than eight fifteen.

It's amazing, John thinks, they'll casually lose thousands, but make a big effort to avoid a five dollar fine.

3. Quitting Time (102)

As a game continues into the night, most players tire and their ability to concentrate and play poker decreases. The good player, therefore, encourages an indefinite or late quitting time. If, however, players start avoiding the game because the late hours are hurting their jobs or health, the good player may enforce an early quitting time (at least temporarily) to keep them playing. He will also quit early in small games not worth staying up all night for. The good player usually breaks up these smaller games when he leaves in order to save the losers' money for himself the following week.

Making players quit early is easier when the last round is played at higher stakes. Higher stakes serve as a psychological climax to the game. If the good player wants to enforce an agreed upon quitting time, he plans the final round so the last deal ends with him. He then gathers the cards after the last hand, cashes his chips, and leaves before someone starts a new deal.

Also, by letting any player (winner or loser) leave whenever he wishes, the need for a definite quitting time decreases, and the game is more pleasant for most players.

John Finn plays all night on Mondays because the game is worth it. In 1965, he plays about four hundred hours of Monday night poker and wins $42,000. Of this amount, $23,000 is won after midnight at the rate of $115 per hour while $19,000 is made before midnight at the rate of $95 per hour. Another important reason why John plays all night is shown in the following data:

Estimated Edge Odds, %

	PM *8:00 - 12:00*	*AM* *12:00 - 4:00*	*Change*
John Finn	**+56**	**+62**	**+ 6**
Quintin Merck	**+15**	**+ 5**	**-10**
Scotty Nichols	**- 2**	**- 8**	**- 6**
Sid Bennett	**-24**	**-16**	**+ 8**
Ted Fehr	**-24**	**-18**	**+ 6**
Others	**-27**	**-31**	**- 4**

These data show that John gets an extra 6% edge odds after

midnight. Also important is the decreased losing rate of the poorer players (Sid and Ted) at the expense of the better players (Quintin and Scotty); this advantageous shift in money flow is accomplished without costing John money. In other words, John controls the money flow more cheaply during the late hours.

In determining the value of playing all night, John considers the effects on his job, health, and personal life. He evaluates each game, and then enforces an earlier quitting time in games of lesser value as shown below:

Game	*Quitting Time*	*1965 Income (# games)*	*Estimated Income for 50 Games Played to 4:00 AM*
Monday	**None (4-5 AM)**	**$42,000 (50)**	**$42,000 (△ = 0)**
Tuesday } Thursday }	**12:30 AM**	**$ 2,500 (17)**	**$17,600 (△ = +$15,100)**
Friday	**1:00 AM**	**$ 9,500 (48)**	**$22,400 (△ = +$12,900)**
Total		**$54,000**	**$82,000 (△ = +$28,000)**

Δ = The difference between columns 3 and 4.

These data indicate that personal factors outweigh the additional $28,000 that John could earn by playing as late and as often in the smaller games as he does in the big Monday night game.

4. Contacting Players (103)

Two important tools for organizing a game are a list of players and a telephone. The good player usually asks another player to help him organize the game . . . eager players and recent winners will normally help. He often has someone else call the big losers, thus avoiding the impression that he is anxious for losers to play. If unfavorable feelings develop about his organizing efforts, he simply stops calling anyone for a few games. This quickly makes the players appreciate his organizing efforts.

The best time for telephoning players is late in the afternoon before the game. This is early enough so they can plan for the game and late enough so those available will seldom have a subsequent excuse for not playing. The exact number of players that will show up is, therefore, usually known.

Mimeographed forms with the players' names and telephone numbers, along with a column for their responses (as shown on page 155) are convenient. By filling out these forms and periodically reviewing them, the good player obtains valuable information about the -

- health of the game
- attendance patterns
- character of his opponents and their motives for playing
- players with declining attendance who may need special treatment to bring them back as regular players
- ways to keep the game organized and players interested.

In some games, players do not expect telephone calls. The game is played on a regular basis, and everyone just shows up. While such a game is convenient, the good player generally prefers to organize each game because his telephone calls provide opportunities to -

- get information
- increase his control over the game
- propagandize players and talk to them about their problems
- obtain definite commitments, which make the game less vulnerable to collapse from a lack of players.

John Finn telephones the players each Monday afternoon and fills out the mimeographed form as shown on page 156.

MONDAY GAME *DATE* ___________

Player	*Phone # (*)*	*Called by (Time)*	*Response*	*Comments*
Quintin Merck	LM 8-7295 (O) LM 4-1467 (H)			
Scotty Nichols	YO 6-3460 (O) TF 7-0446 (H)			
Sid Bennett	YO 4-8391 (O) KI 8-7382 (H)			
Ted Fehr	EV 9-5267 (O) 732-8793 (H)			
Charlie Holland	YO 4-9006 (O) KI 8-3388 (H)			
Aaron Smith	YO 4-1147 (O) 732-5493 (H)			
Others				
Mike Bell	?			

*** (O) = office phone, (H) = home phone***

MONDAY GAME — *DATE* <u>*Monday 6/4/62*</u>

Player	*Phone # (*)*	*Called by (Time)*	*Response*	*Comments*
Quintin Merck	LM 8-7295 (O) LM 4-1467 (H)	*John (3:30)*	*Yes*	*Quintin will call Sid and Charlie.*
Scotty Nichols	YO 6-3460 (O) TF 7-0446 (H)	*John (3:40)*	*Yes*	*Seems shaky and upset, but eager to play. Must be a personal problem.*
Sid Bennett	YO 4-8391 (O) KI 8-7382 (H)	*Quintin (5:30)*	-	*Check - not contacted.*
		(6:30)	*Yes*	*Check - OK*
Ted Fehr	EV 9-5267 (O) 732-8793 (H)	*John (3:45)*	-	*Not contacted. Must be at the races.*
		(5:30)	-	*Not contacted.*
		(7:00)	*Yes*	*OK, 30 minute discussion about the game, finances and credit. Sounds like he's in bad shape.*
Charlie Holland	YO 4-9006 (O) KI 8-3388 (H)	*Quintin (5:30)*	*No*	*Stunned and disgusted by heavy loss last week . . . probably will play next week.*
Aaron Smith	YO 4-1147 (O) 732-5493 (H)	*John (3:35)*	*Yes*	*Check – OK, excited about winning last week.*
Others				
Mike Bell	?	*Scotty (5:40)*	*Yes*	*Check – OK, concerned about recent losses.*

* *(O) = office phone, (H) = home phone*

5. A Place to Play (104)

A game kept in one location is usually desirable for the good player. Normally, at least one player is willing to establish the game at his house. The good player seldom plays in his own house in order to avoid the impression that it is "his game". If necessary, a player is induced to keep the game permanently at his house by, for example, cutting the pot for a weekly cleaning woman. . . .A game played at one location offers the following advantages:

- Game is more stable.
- Burden of locating suitable places to play is eliminated.
- Players not contacted always know where the game is.

A game played in different locations each week, however, offers advantages such as -

- closer control over who is invited
- more flexibility because the game can be changed to locations offering the greatest advantage
- decreased possibility of a robbery (particularly in a high stake game).

Every Monday night the game is played at Scotty Nichols' house; this is advantageous to John. Then Scotty leaves town on a vacation for six weeks. The game shifts to Sid Bennett's house, and the danger for any high stake game is revealed . . . the danger of an armed robbery:

Sid loves to brag about the game to everyone. Now that the game is in his house, he makes his wife watch him play. Then to the shocked disapproval of the players, Sid invites his street paving crew to watch the action. When the players arrive, they find the poker table ringed with a gallery of seats occupied by a dozen cigar smoking, beer drinking laborers wearing bib overalls;

the tar-covered men laugh and joke while waiting for the show to start.

John frowns as he sees the spectators' eyes bulge when the big money comes on the table; the crew is fascinated by the game. Two of the men remain until the game ends at four in the morning. . . . "You playing here next Monday?" one of them asks.

"Yeah," Sid chuckles, "You can count on that." . . .Now John frowns severely.

After the game, the players harshly criticize Sid for bringing the spectators. . . .The following week there are no spectators. But at three in the morning, Sid's kitchen door opens. A man with a nylon stocking stretched over his head rushes to the game room. He pulls a revolver from a shopping bag and levels it at the players.

"Stand up," he orders. Obedience is swift and silent. "Empty your pockets," he says while walking around the table and grabbing the money already in front of each player. . . . Quickly throwing the money into his shopping bag, the thief leaves without a word. John steps to the window and sees two men drive away with their lights off.

"I'll call the police," Sid says lifting the telephone.

"No," Quintin Merck replies. "We'll get bad publicity."

"I can keep it out of the papers," Sid replies. "Think that guy is someone from my paving crew." . . .When the police arrive, they discuss the hold-up and estimate that four thousand dollars were stolen. They all agree that the big money in their game is a strong incentive for a robbery. A lot of cash can be stolen at low risk, certainly at less risk than a bank hold-up. The players make future security plans that include locked doors, covered windows, keeping the police informed of the game, prohibiting spectators, and not discussing the game with non-players.

The following week, they shift the game to Quintin Merck's house. . . . John realizes this hazzard is greater when the game is played regularly at the same house, but he figures the advantage of a stable game location outweighs the probability of another robbery.

XXI. EXPANSION (105)

The good player finds the following advantages in expanding a poker game:

- Game becomes more stable.
- More sources of income are provided.
- Choices for selecting desirable opponents increase.
- Losses are spread more evenly among losers.
- Confusion increases.
- Greater control over the game is possible.
- Betting pace and stakes are easier to increase.
- If relatively tight play offers the best edge odds, tight play is less obvious and less resented in a full game.

A poker game is expanded by adding new players and by improving attendance of the present players.

1. New Players (106)

The good player mentions poker to potential players. He gauges his comments to bring out their poker interests. The more he mentions poker, the more potential players are revealed. He hunts for losers, and evaluates all potential players with respect to the possible income that could be extracted from them.

John Finn tries to fill the Monday night game with at least eight players. He has a nucleus of five players (Sid, Ted, Scotty, Quintin and himself) who have played regularly over the years. There is a circulation of two or three other regular players who last from six months to a year and sometimes longer. Then there are eight or nine men who play only sporadically or when coaxed. These irregular players provide important income and are valuable for filling out the game.

About half of the new players are introduced to the Monday game by John. His major source of new players (about eighty percent) is the other, smaller poker games. Mentioning poker to social and business contacts generates a few players, especially for the smaller games. Some of these players later graduate to the big game.

a. Keeping players (107)

If a new player is a financial asset, the good player keeps him in the game by -

- being congenial and helpful to him (especially if the new player is timid or nervous)
- making him feel that the game is relaxed and enjoyable
- warding off remarks and actions by other players that may upset him (Probably more players quit poker because of hurt feelings than because of hurt finances.)
- avoiding overpowering or scaring him
- not taking full advantage of his weaknesses
- making him feel that he is welcome to the game
- favoring him whenever possible
- flattering him when he wins and offering him sympathy when he loses
- giving him encouragement and advice about the game.

John Finn brings a new player, Aaron Smith, to the big Monday night game. Although Aaron plays in the smaller Friday night game, he is timid and nervous. Knowing that Aaron will lose many thousands of dollars if he becomes a permanent player, John sits next to him and helps him whenever possible. He

protects Aaron from upsetting losses that could scare him out of the game. He shields him from embarrassing remarks that could insult him out of the game. Once Aaron gets accustomed to the game and acquainted with the players, he will absorb financial losses and take insults gracefully.

Whenever John folds, he studies Aaron's hand and gives him good advice; he helps him to a winning night. Aaron is excited . . . his confidence increases and fear decreases. Whenever Sid throws an insulting remark at him, John counters with an ego building comment. By his third game, Aaron Smith is hooked; he loves the Monday night game and its players. At this point, John withdraws his help and Aaron is on his own.

When Aaron Smith, or any big loser gets discouraged and contemplates quitting, John Finn extends his protection to hold them in the game through their crisis.

b. Rejecting players (108)

If a new player is a financial liability, the good player gets him out of the game. The simplest way to eliminate an undesirable player is not to invite him to the next game. If this is not possible, the good player forces him out by -

- encouraging unpleasant and unfriendly incidents toward him
- irritating him and hurting his feelings
- refusing him credit
- telling him not to play again.

Scotty Nichols brings a new player, Boris Klien, to the Monday night game. John Finn quickly realizes that Boris is a winning player who will increase the financial strain on the losers . . . this would force John to reduce his winnings in order to keep these losers in the game. Boris is a financial liability and, therefore, an undesirable player. John wants him out of the game quickly and permanently.

"High-ball draw with a twist," Quintin Merck announces. John

notices how Boris carefully watches the deck for flashed cards during the deal.

John checks, and Boris opens for $5.

"Five bucks? . . . we ain't playing penny-ante," Sid laughs and then raises to $30. "You've gotta bet something in this game."

"I'll just call; now you can re-raise to fifty," Quintin says winking at Boris.

"I'll raise . . . fifty-five dollars," Boris barks.

"Hey, he knows what he's doing," Sid chokes. "He laid back and sandbagged us."

On the draw, Boris wraps his knuckles on the table. "Pat!" he says sharply and then bets $50. Sid folds and Quintin calls.

On the twist, Quintin draws one card. Boris again plays pat and then holds a fifty dollar bill over the pot.

"Put it in if you're betting," John Finn frowns then turns to Quintin and says, "That's an old bluff trick . . . "

Boris scowls at John.

"Forget it," Quintin says folding his hand without realizing what John is telling him. "I just had two little pair."

Boris grabs the pot and barks, "Look here!" as he flips his cards face up on the table.

"He's got nothing!" Ted Fehr shouts. "He pulls a pat bluff on his first hand and wins a three hundred dollar pot!"

"Wise guy," Quintin grunts as his blinking green eyes gaze at Boris' worthless cards. . . . The other players sit in frowning silence.

Over the next hour, Boris Klien plays very tight. He avoids all action until a low-ball hand with John Finn. The pot is large; and after the last bet, only Boris and John remain. Boris declares his hand. John says nothing, so Boris starts pulling in the pot.

"Get your hands off my money," John snarls.

"Uh? What do ya mean?" Boris asks. "I won, didn't I?"

"Can't you read?" John says pointing to his winning hand turned up on the table. He then snatches the pot from

under Boris' stiffened fingers.

"Why didn't you declare your hand?" Boris half shouts.

"Why didn't you look at my cards?" John growls out the twisted corner of his mouth. "This is a poker game, buddy boy. Cards speak for themselves, remember?"

"Wish I hadn't come to this game," Boris mumbles to Scotty Nichols. "I'm not only losing, but I'm getting a bad time."

"Wish I hadn't come myself," Scotty whines. "Lost all the money I won last week."

"Yeah, but I . . . "

"Listen," John says pointing a stiff finger at Boris. "No one made you play. If you don't like our game . . . get out!"

Three hours later Boris Klien is winning over four hundred dollars.

"He's taking all our money," Sid Bennett remarks.

"I started out losing four hundred," Boris grunts. "I'm still stuck a hundred."

"Liar!" John snaps. "You're up four hundred bucks . . . Where'd you dig up this jerk, Scotty?"

"At this point, I don't know or care," Scotty mutters. "I'm losing plenty, and Boris took most of it."

"This is my last round," Boris says. "I've . . . "

"The bore is even a hit and run artist!" John shouts. "Plan on this permanently being your last round."

Boris frowns. He then looks at his pile of money; his frown disappears.

"Seven card stud high-low with qualifiers and one twist," John announces as he deals. "Trips - eight*," he adds in a whispering voice.

After the sixth card, John raises on his low hand and drives out the other low hands. By the last card, only Boris remains; he calls John's final $30 bet. . . . John wins low.

** Three of a kind are needed to qualify for high. Eight low is needed to qualify for low.*

"Split the pot," Boris says showing his two pair. "I've got high."

"Look at that hand!" John hoots as he points to Boris' cards. "The sucker calls all my big bets and can't even qualify. I get the whole pot!"

"What do you mean?" Boris sputters. "I got two pair."

"Three of a kind qualifies for high, you creep," John says as he shoves Boris' cards into the deck.

"Trips for qualifiers!" Boris shouts. "They've been two pair all night."

"I announced trips - eight," John laughs. " . . . Clean your ears."

"I heard him announce it," Ted Fehr says weakly.

"Yeah? . . . Well, then it'd be impossible for me to call," Boris says reaching toward the pot. "I'm taking back my last bet."

"It stays in the pot," John says slapping his hand over the money. "When you make a stupid play, you pay for it."

"I've had enough," Boris scowls while getting up to leave.

"You're winning," Scotty says. "Sit down and play a while."

"Let the clod go. We'll play longer without him bothering us," John says. Then turning to Boris, he makes a sharp hitch-hiking motion toward the door, "So long jerk, hope we never see you again."

"I won't be back," Boris huffs.

"Good!" John yells. Boris grabs his coat and leaves slamming the front door.

"He'll never come back," Scotty Nichols says scratching his head. "Why so rough on him? He's an honest player."

"He's a milker," John explains in a soft voice. "He lays back and waits for a big hand to kill you with. Look how he hurt you tonight. . . . Why should a stranger come to our game and leech money from the regular players? Not only that, he cries when he wins, tries to take back bets, lies about his winnings and leaves early when he's ahead."

"Don't understand it," Scotty says. "Seemed like a nice guy outside of the game. Maybe we should give him another chance."

"He'd ruin our game," John adds. "Don't ask him back."

"I won't," Scotty shakes his head.

"Besides he's a good player," Sid Bennett adds. "We need more fish with lots of money."

"More players like Sid," Quintin chirps as his leathery face breaks into a smile.

c. Women players (109)

The good poker player considers opponents only from a financial viewpoint. If a woman player is an over-all financial asset, she is a welcome player. A woman player can cause men to be less objective, thereby increasing the good player's edge odds. However, control over men players and attempts to increase the betting stakes are often more difficult when a woman is present. For this reason, the good player usually keeps women out of the game.

Since intellect and character are neuter, women players can function identically to men players. A woman can, therefore, be as good a player as a man. But the good female player will probably experience greater difficulty in controlling men players and in getting invitations to high-stake poker games.

As the game starts, Scotty informs the players that Sid is bringing his wife, Stephanie Bennett, to play poker. All object to having a woman, particularly the wife of a player, in the game. Quintin even threatens to quit if she plays.

"I don't want her playing either," John says. "But she's already expecting to play. . . . Let her play tonight; we'll keep her from playing again."

. . . When the players finish their first hand, Sid and Stephanie arrive. All the players stand up to greet her. She is wearing a tight dress with a hemline well above the knees.

"Just treat me as one of the boys," says the woman touching her hair that sweeps up in a high French twist with curls on top; she sits down crossing her long, curving legs.

"Impossible," Quintin rasps.

The game becomes erratic; eyes keep focusing on the woman. When Stephanie is in a hand, the betting becomes subdued; the players are reluctant to bet into her. When she is not in a hand, the betting and raising become heavier than usual as the men show off in front of the perfumed woman. John Finn takes full advantage of their poor betting.

After two hours, Stephanie is about even and Sid is losing three hundred dollars. The players begin to fidget and grumble under the strain of her presence. John gets involved with Stephanie in a game of five card stud with two twists. On the third up card, she has a pair of Aces showing and bets $15. Sid raises to $30 with his pair of Kings showing; Stephanie raises back. Quintin folds while grumbling that Sid is raising to build the pot for his wife.

"Aye," Sid snorts, "Greed is a many splendored thing." . . . Then John raises to $60; Sid emits a gagging cough. . . . After the next card, John has a King, Queen, Jack and ten of Diamonds showing - a four card straight flush. On the twist, Stephanie pairs her fives to give her two pair showing - Aces up. . . . John stays pat.

"Pat!" Sid exclaims. "He's got to have the flush or straight."

John bets $25, and Sid folds. Stephanie calls and then twists her hole card. John plays pat again and bets $30. . . . Sid advises his wife to drop.

"He might be bluffing," she says while starting to call.

"Naw!" Sid shouts. "Not after staying pat with all that betting and raising."

"I can't take your money," John says waving his hand. "I've got the Diamond flush."

"Thanks for saving me money," Stephanie smiles as she folds her hand.

John Finn peeks at his hole card, the Jack of Clubs, and then mixes it into the deck. Handing Stephanie twenty-five dollars, he says, "Here's your last bet. . . . Guess I'm not a good gambler. Can't take money from a woman. So I'll quit while you're playing."

"Oh, no," Stephanie says handing the money back and standing up. "I lost it fairly. And you already lost money by not letting me call that last bet. . . . You keep on playing. I'm tired and going home now. . . . I've had my fling at poker."

Sid Bennett drives his wife home then hurries back to the game.

"Stephanie should play instead of you," Quintin says when he returns. "She'd win if you'd . . . "

"That lovely woman doesn't belong in this tough game," John interrupts. "Don't let her play again."

"You're right," Sid frowns as he slumps in his chair. "I'll never let her play again."

2. Improving Attendance (110)

Players are attracted to a full game. In fact, they become eager to play in games that are completely filled. An effective way to expand a game, therefore, is to fill it. For example, if eight players are the maximum for a game, the good player makes sufficient telephone contacts to get nine or ten players. When the game is so crowded that some players cannot be seated, an interesting phenomenon occurs . . . irregular players become regular players, and the scheduled starting time becomes rigidly adhered to. Good attendance is also encouraged by keeping the game well organized and by maintaining the proper atmosphere.

Efforts to improve attendance can result in excess players, who can be used in other games.

John tries to keep the Monday night game filled. The full game helps draw the big losers back every week. The crowded table and fast action excite poor players like Sid and Ted . . . they feel they are missing something if they do not play.

A packed game increases John's flexibility. With excess players, he can increase the stakes and pace more quickly because the loss of one or two players would not seriously hurt the game. Excess players also lessen the need for him to reduce his earnings to keep losers from quitting.

XXII. MAINTENANCE (111)

Maintenance of a poker game determines its health. The good player keeps losers in the game by protecting them, helping them, holding up their morale, and by making the game attractive.

1. Making Game Attractive (112)

A player often tolerates great financial losses if he enjoys the game. Also, an attractive game will draw new players. . . . The good player makes the game more attractive by -

- encouraging a carefree and relaxed atmosphere
- keeping players out of arguments
- preventing complaints about the game
- selecting the more pleasant and weaker players for the game, especially when available players are abundant
- keeping the game well organized
- preventing the action from getting dull
- providing good refreshments and new cards.

John Finn makes certain that at least a dozen new decks of cards are available for every Monday night game. Although the pots are cut to pay for these cards, the players appreciate this luxury. Losers like Sid feel important when they can call for a new deck of cards at their whim. . . . This makes them feel like big gamblers in a big game. And big gamblers in a big game bet more money.

Other small deeds by John also help make this high stake game attractive. For example, he spends six dollars and buys a dozen green plastic eyeshades. At three in the morning as most players are glumly reflecting their losses, John opens a bag and hands each player an eyeshade. Everyone appreciates this sudden,

thoughtful gift. When Scotty suggests they cut the pot for the eyeshades, John refuses with a shaking head and a waving hand. All players smile as they don their green shades and laughingly make remarks about gambling at Vegas and on the Mississippi river boats. John Finn smiles too.

2. Helping Losers (113)

Heavy losers are valuable assets to the good player. He keeps them in the game by shielding them from -

- personal comments that could hurt their feelings
- arguments
- unpleasant players
- personal problems of others
- bad credit.

Big losers are usually grateful for the good player's protection. As a result, they forget that he is responsible for their continuous heavy losses.

If big losers never win, they will lose interest and quit the game. If necessary, the good player helps them win occasionally. He can help poor players (relative to the better players) by -

- increasing the ante
- increasing the betting pace for early bets
- decreasing the betting pace for late bets
- interpreting the rules to favor the big losers
- assisting the weakest players whenever possible.

The good player helps others only to the extent that he can profit.

Big losers Ted Fehr and Sid Bennett think that John is helping them when indeed he is financially hurting them. Consider this incident with Ted Fehr:

Ted is losing over a thousand dollars. It is four in the morning; Quintin and Scotty get up to leave.

"Hey! Play a little longer," Ted says in a shaky voice. "Don't quit now. I'm stuck a fortune. . . . I never quit when you're hooked."

"You never quit, 'cause you never win," Sid laughs.

"I'm going," Quintin grumbles. "You can win it back next week."

Ted turns his sweaty face toward John and says, "We can't quit now."

"Look," John says raising his hand, "Ted is way down. Give him a chance for a comeback. Everyone play another hour at double stakes. We'll all quit at five o'clock sharp."

"Yeah," Ted smiles, "everyone play another hour at double stakes."

Scotty Nichols objects to the higher stakes, and Quintin Merck objects to playing another hour . . . but they both sit down to resume playing.

"Thanks," Ted says leaning over and patting John on the shoulder. "You're the one guy who gives losers a break."

At five o'clock the game ends. In that extra hour, Ted loses another eight hundred dollars . . . he is pale and staggers around the room with unfocused eyes. In that extra hour, John wins another thousand dollars . . . he leaves quietly.

After a few days, Ted always forgets his losses; but he remembers the favors his friend John does for him . . . such as keeping the game going when he is losing.

3. Raising the Morale of Losers (114)

The good player raises the morale of the losers. Sympathy and understanding properly offered can keep losers in the game indefinitely. After suffering sharp losses, some players develop harmful attitudes . . . such as demanding lower stakes. A good player can often change their attitudes by privately talking to them about their troubles . . . this has a therapeutic effect.

New player, Mike Bell, is a valuable financial asset to John Finn. After losing several weeks in a row, Mike becomes discouraged. Fearful that he may quit, John moves to boost his morale. By leading him into several winning pots, he carries Mike to a winning night. Then with the following dialog, he further boosts Mike's morale:

"The way you're winning, you'll break the game," John says. "How much you ahead?"

"A few big bills," Mike grins as he splits a high-low pot with Quintin. "I've been lucky."

"Lucky? The way you caught that full house - I call that skill," John remarks adjusting his voice to a deep tone. "Why'd you throw your Ace and keep the ten kicker?"

"The other three players drew one and two cards," Mike gloats. "They probably had low hands . . . so they'd hold Aces rather than tens. My chances were best for drawing another ten." Mike Bell then glances around. Bored expressions cover all faces except John's; he listens with an opened mouth while slowly shaking his head. Mike leans toward him and says in a low voice, "I drew the ten to catch the full house, didn't I?"

"Right," John replies. "Pretty smart thinking."

"Ban Mike from the game," Sid snorts. "He thinks . . . that gives him too much advantage over us."

"Don't listen to him," John says as he puts his hand on Mike's shoulder and shapes his lips into an oval. "We respect a man that plays good poker."

"Look who's talking about good poker!" Sid yells. "You win low ball games with full houses. You hear about that one, Mike?"

"Sure did. Scotty told me all about it," Mike says. He then shakes his finger at John. "Don't ever pull that on me. I'd call you out of my grave."

"At least John plays more than two hands a night," Sid says.

"If we all played tight like Quintin, the game would fold from boredom."

Mike Bell counts his winnings and then smiles at John, "Guess I'll be playing permanently in this game."

4. Off-Days (115)

When a good player has an off-day (emotional problems or feeling ill), he may skip the game to avoid a breakdown in his discipline. Or he may play on an off-day (knowing he will not play his best) in order to -

- alter the consistency of his play
- make money with decreased but still favorable edge odds
- maintain the continuity of the game. (Even when he misses a game, he helps organize it when possible.)

John Finn seldom misses the Monday night game. If feeling below par, he may play just to add another variable to his poker style. Consider the following Monday night game:

"Where's John?" Mike Bell asks.

"Recovering from the flu," Scotty says.

"But he called me this afternoon about playing," Mike replies with a wrinkled forehead.

"He'll organize the game even if he's sick."

"Mighty thoughtful guy."

"He's also mighty thoughtful about taking your money," Quintin adds. "He's won a fortune in this game."

"He takes your money pleasantly . . . hardly mind losing to him," Mike says. "He's always fair."

"But he's tough on anyone who's wrong," Sid adds. "Remember how he tore apart Boris Klien?"

. . .About midnight, John walks in and says with a weak smile, "I'm never too sick for a poker game."

"Good!" Sid cheers. "We need your money."

"I took a nap after dinner," John replies as he sits next to Sid. "Woke up about eleven feeling pretty good. I'm ready for action."

. . .After two hours, John Finn is losing over six hundred dollars.

"You're playing a lousy game," Sid remarks. "You're losing almost as much as me."

"When my luck turns bad, I lose big," John groans while shaking his head. "Losing over a thousand dollars. . . .I'm going for the all time record loss."

"Great act," Quintin Merck mumbles, "Great act."

5. *Leaving Game Early (116)*

When a good player leaves a game early, he minimizes the disturbance and resentment among players by -

- announcing before the game starts that he must leave early
- announcing his last round before going, then silently leaving without breaking up the game.

The Monday night game usually breaks up around four or five in the morning. Occasionally it continues into the next day . . . John Finn seldom leaves before the end. The longest Monday night game on record is twenty-seven hours (from eight-thirty Monday night until eleven-thirty Tuesday night). This is how John leaves after twenty-two hours:

At seven in the morning, Scotty's wife chases the players from the house. Heavy loser Ted Fehr is playing with money from the second mortgage on his restaurant. He has a thousand dollars left and begs everyone to continue playing at his apartment. The five players eat breakfast at a diner and then go to Ted's place.

Ted continues to lose . . . slowly at first, then at an increasing pace. By eleven in the morning, most of his cash is gone. He plays carelessly and is involved in nearly every hand. He no longer seems to care . . . he even smiles when he loses a pot.

John Finn is a big winner, but avoids getting in hands with Ted. . . . Sid and Scotty, however, continue to beat Ted and win most of his money. By now, all of Ted's cash is gone; he asks John for a loan.

"They've won all your money," John says nodding toward Sid and Scotty. "They'll lend it back."

By two in the afternoon, Sid and Scotty are reluctant to lend Ted more money. They are still beating him consistently, however, and feel obligated to furnish him cash.

By five in the afternoon, Ted's bloodshot eyes gaze into space . . . he has lost all his cash and borrowed over two thousand dollars. Now Sid and Scotty are running out of money.

"We broke the record - over twenty hours of poker," John announces. "You guys keep playing, I'm leaving at six."

After another round and in the middle of a big hand, John Finn silently leaves. He has most of the cash and escapes without lending money to Ted.

. . . At six-thirty, Ted asks for another loan, but Sid and Scotty are out of money. The only person with cash is Quintin, and he refuses to lend him money. Then with trembling fingers, Ted writes a check. When Quintin refuses to cash it, the freckled faced man sits in a stupor and stares blankly at him. After a moment of eerie silence, Quintin stands up and says, "I'm going home."

"You took all my money!" Ted suddenly screams; the players start rushing toward the door. "No! . . . please don't quit! I'm due for a comeback! Please, give me a break like John always does!"

. . . No one ever saw Ted Fehr again.

XIII. MAJOR AND MINOR LEAGUE GAMES (117)

For continuous and expanding income, the good player organizes several regular games at significantly different stakes. He runs these games as major and minor league games with a sort of a baseball farm system relationship between them.

1. Major League (118)

A major league game is the highest stake game. It has the most financial value to the good player and consists of players with the most money, the better players, compulsive gamblers, and players, "trying their luck" in the big game. In this game, the good player continually pushes the pace and stakes to the maximum. The size and health of the big game depend on the availability of players. . . . The minor league (smaller stake) games are a valuable source of these players.

2. Minor League (119)

The good player can gain worthwhile income from smaller stake games. More important, however, he uses the minor league game as -

- a place to break-in new players (Many potential players would never consider playing the big game. After they become accustomed to a smaller game, however, they will often move up to a bigger game.)
- a proving ground to test and develop new plays, concepts, and modifications before introducing them to the big game
- a pool for selecting new players for the big game
- a game where poor players who will never play in the big game can lose their money
- a resting place for players dropping out of the big game. (Smaller games provide a place to hold valuable losers who are driven out of the big game. Without a smaller game to fall back on, they might quit poker completely and never return. In a small game, these players still play poker. In time, they usually recover their confidence and finances then return to the big game.)

When playing in several different games, however, the good player must carefully budget his time.

3. Farm System (120)

The good player controls both the major and minor league games ... and he promotes advantageous transitions of players from one game to another. This system allows him to make the best use of his resources (poker players). He promotes players to the big game when they appear ready to move up. Conditions that indicate when a player is ready for the big game are -

- an increase in his financial resources
- a winning streak to provide him with capital and courage
- development of experience and confidence
- personal situations that make him want to play in the big game.

An obvious sign that a player is ready to drop back to a smaller game occurs when he quits playing poker. Approaching him about a smaller game must be tactful to avoid injuring his pride. The proper approach depends on his reason for quitting. Reasons that a player quits a big game include -

- discouragement from a losing streak
- loss of too much money
- hurt feelings or pride
- personality conflicts
- personal problems
- time conflict
- health reasons.

If the approach is proper, most players welcome an opportunity to continue in a smaller game rather than to quit poker altogether.

The following chart summarizes John Finn's system of poker games.

Weekly Poker Games
(Games Attended in 1965)

Game	*League, Purpose*	*Earnings (Average $ per game)*	*Nucleus Players, #*	*Irregular Players, #*	*Potential Major League Players, #*
Monday	**Major, Income**	**50 $42,000 (840)**	**5**	**12**	-
Tuesday	**Minor, New Contacts**	**7 $ 1,100 (160)**	**4**	**7**	**1**
Thursday	**Minor, New Contacts**	**10 $ 1,400 (140)**	**6**	**8**	**2**
Friday	**Intermediate, Farm Team, Income**	**48 $ 9,500 (200)**	**6**	**8**	**4**
Totals		**115 $54,000 (470)**	**21**	**35**	**7**

John Finn gains a large income by applying the "Advanced Concepts of Poker". By maintaining the above system of games, he will earn over $1,000,000 from poker in the next twenty years.

CONCLUSION

The good poker player functions rationally. He views all situations realistically. With objective thinking, he directs his actions toward winning maximum money. He pits the full use of his mind against the unwillingness of his opponents to think. . . .The good player cannot lose.

Poker is a game of money and deception; poker exposes man's character, and the consequences are always deserving. The rewards go to the strong, and the penalties to the weak. The loser dissipates his time and money. The winner earns money and satisfaction. . . .But what is the net result of poker? Is it merely time consumed and money exchanged with nothing positive produced? Is the net result a negative activity? . . .Poker is a character catalyst that forces players to reality. Those willing to work and use their minds are rewarded; those who evade thinking and act on whims cannot escape the penalties. The results are clear and true; the lazy evader fails and can never fake success; the thinking performer is always rewarded.

In poker, man is on his own; he must act as an individual. No one will help him. Success depends on the rational use of his mind; success depends on exercising his positive qualities and overcoming his negative qualities; success depends on him alone. In poker, man can function entirely for his own sake. The results are his own. The winner has made himself a winner; the loser has made himself a loser.

Poker is sheer justice.

APPENDIX A

HISTORY

The memoirs of an English actor (Joseph Cowell) touring America in 1829 described a game being played in New Orleans in which each player received five cards, made bets, then whoever held the highest combination of cards won all bets. Mr. Cowell was probably describing the earliest form of poker or its immediate predecessor, the game of Âs.

The first direct reference to poker (found in Jonathan H. Green's book, "An Exposure of the Arts and Miseries of Gambling", G.B. Zieber, Philadelphia, 1843) described poker games on a steamer running between New Orleans and Louisville. This book indicated that poker began in New Orleans about 1830.

A detailed examination of the original game (on page 180) revealed that poker descended directly from the Persian game of Âs Nâs and not, as commonly believed, from the French game of Poque, the German game of Pochen, or the English game of Bragg. But these and other European games quickly exerted their influence on the original game of poker as shown on pages 180 and 181.

Sailors from Persia taught the French settlers in New Orleans the gambling game called Âs, which was derived from the ancient Persian game of Âs Nâs. The Frenchmen would bet by saying, for example, "I poque for a dollar," . . . and would call by saying, "I poque against you for two dollars." These were the betting expressions used in their game of Poque, a three-card game first played by commoners in France and then by Frenchmen in America as early as 1803. Poque was similar to Bouillotte, a card game popular with the aristocrats in France just prior to the French Revolution.

Combining the words "As" and "Poque", the game became known as "Poqas". Then influenced by the German bluff game of Pochen and the southern accent, the pronunciation of "Poqas" became "Pokah". Under Yankee

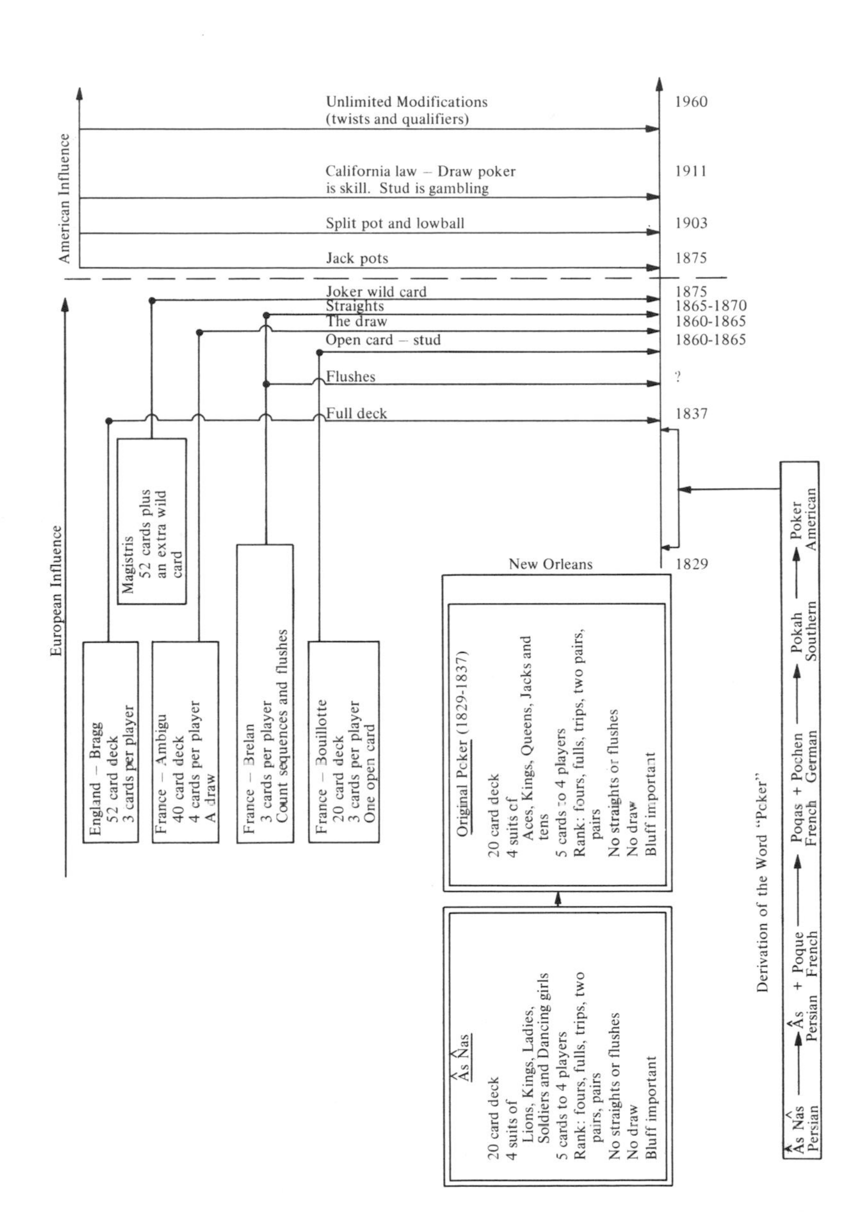
American Influence
Unlimited Modifications (twists and qualifiers)
1960
California law – Draw poker is skill. Stud is gambling
1911
Split pot and lowball
1903
Jack pots
1875
European Influence
Joker wild card
1875
Straights
1865-1870
The draw
1860-1865
Open card – stud
1860-1865
Flushes
?
Full deck
1837
New Orleans
1829
Magistris
52 cards plus an extra wild card
England – Bragg
52 card deck
3 cards per player
France – Ambigu
40 card deck
4 cards per player
A draw
France – Brelan
3 cards per player
Count sequences and flushes
France – Bouillotte
20 card deck
3 cards per player
One open card
Original Poker (1829-1837)
20 card deck
4 suits of
Aces, Kings, Queens, Jacks and tens
5 cards to 4 players
Rank: fours, fulls, trips, two pairs, pairs
No straights or flushes
No draw
Bluff important
Âs Nâs
20 card deck
4 suits of
Lions, Kings, Ladies, Soldiers and Dancing girls
5 cards to 4 players
Rank: fours, fulls, trips, two pairs, pairs
No straights or flushes
No draw
Bluff important
Âs Nâs Persian → Âs Persian + Poque French → Poqas + Pochen French German → Pokah Southern → Poker American
Derivation of the Word "Poker"

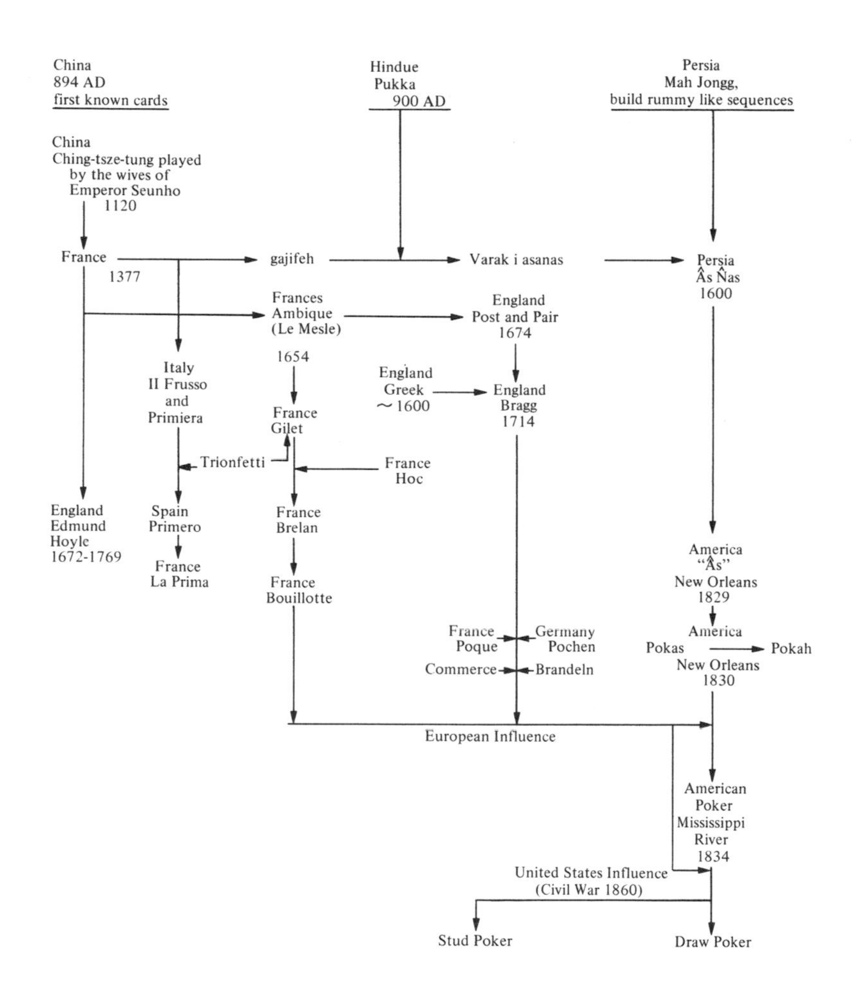
China
894 AD
first known cards
Hindue
Pukka
900 AD
Persia
Mah Jongg,
build rummy like sequences
China
Ching-tsze-tung played
by the wives of
Emperor Seunho
1120
France
1377
gajifeh
Varak i asanas
Persia
Âs Ñas
1600
Frances
Ambique
(Le Mesle)
1654
England
Post and Pair
1674
Italy
Il Frusso
and
Primiera
England
Greek
~1600
England
Bragg
1714
France
Gilet
Trionfetti
France
Hoc
England
Edmund
Hoyle
1672-1769
Spain
Primero
France
Brelan
France
La Prima
France
Bouillotte
America
"Âs"
New Orleans
1829
France
Poque
Germany
Pochen
America
Pokas
Pokah
New Orleans
1830
Commerce
Brandeln
European Influence
American
Poker
Mississippi
River
1834
United States Influence
(Civil War 1860)
Stud Poker
Draw Poker

influence, the pronunciation finally became "Poker".

Poker moved from New Orleans by steam boat up the Mississippi and Ohio rivers. From the river towns, the game spread East by the new railroad and West by the covered wagons. Between 1834 and 1837, the full fifty-two card deck replaced the original twenty card deck. Soon after this, the flush was introduced. During the Civil War, modifications such as open cards (stud poker), the draw, and the straight became popular. When the Joker was introduced as a wild card in 1875, the European influence on poker ended. Further development of the game was essentially American.

Jack pot poker (an ante with a pair of Jacks required to open) began about 1875. Split pot and low ball poker started around 1903. Two Missouri assemblymen (Coran and Lyles) introduced a bill to the state legislature in 1909 to control and license poker players in order to prevent, "millions of dollars lost annually by incompetent and foolish persons who do not know the value of a poker hand". In 1911, California's Attorney General (Harold Sigel Webb) ruled that closed poker (draw poker) was skill and beyond anti-gambling laws.... but open poker (stud poker) was luck and, therefore, illegal. This stimulated the development of new draw games and the use of wild cards. The variety of poker games grew steadily, particularly during the first and second world wars. In the 1960's poker expanded into unlimited variations with modifications such as the twist (extra draw) and qualifiers (minimum hands to win).

APPENDIX B

BIBLIOGRAPHY

Early poker literature tried to establish firm rules for the game. But being a uniquely dynamic game, poker could never be bound in rigid rules as other card games could. Continuously changing within a loose framework of traditions, poker remained a versatile, living game always subject to infinite modifications and variations. The literature has described over one hundred and fifty varieties of poker.

As early as 1674, "Cotton's Complete Gamester's" (published in England) described a card game called "Post and Pair", a predecessor to "Bragg", which in turn was a predecessor to poker with a full deck. Bragg and the art of bluffing were first described in Cotton's 1721 edition. "Poque", a French card game that influenced the development of poker, was described in the eighteenth century editions of "Acadence Universelle des Jeux".

Until 1850, there were no printed rules for poker.* Neither of the two American Hoyles then in print (George Long, New York, 1825, and G. Cowperthwait, Philadelphia, 1838) mentioned poker. The English Hoyles ("Bohn's Handbook of Games") made no reference to poker in the 1850 or 1887 editions. But the 1850 American reprint of Bohn's book mentioned poker in a tacked-on addendum. Also in 1850, "Hoyles' Games", H.F. Anners, Philadelphia, had a brief note about poker that described a full deck, ten players (therefore, no draw) and a bonus paid for any hand of trips or better. In 1857, Thomas Frere's "Hoyle", T.W. Story, New York, described poker without referring to a draw.

** The history of poker rules is as vague as the rules themselves. The common reference, "Poker according to Hoyle", is interesting because the English writer and lawyer, Edmund Hoyle (1672-1769) never heard of poker; he died sixty years before the game was born. Hoyle was a famous Whist player, and his original book described three card games - Whist, Piquet, and Quadrille. His authority for card game rules grew, however, until all card and board game rules became known as "Hoyles". Since many different "Hoyles" now exist, "Poker according to Hoyle" depends on who published it.*

The first mention of draw poker appeared in the 1867 edition of "Hoyles", Dick and Fitzgerald, New York. Also, this edition was the first to mention an ante, a straight (which beat two pair, but not trips), and the straight flush (which beat four of a kind). The 1875 edition of Dick and Fitzgerald's "Hoyles" mentioned jackpot poker and the Joker used as a wild card.

The first printed poker rules in England were written by General Robert E. Schenck, the United States' minister to England. He introduced poker to the guests at a country house in Somersetshire. The hostess, a prominent duchess, persuaded him to write down the rules. In 1872, the duchess privately printed these rules for her court. The game caught Queen Victoria's fancy, and the popularity of poker quickly spread through Great Britain. Soon, poker in England became known as "Schenck poker".

Several years later, a description of poker appeared in Cavendish's "Round Games of Cards", De La Rue & Co. (1875).

After 1875, books about poker appeared regularly in America, England and Europe. Data on poker books published in the ninety years between 1875 and 1965 have been tabulated on pages 185 and 186.

Number of Poker Books Published Every Ten Years
(Data for 107 books whose publishing dates are known)

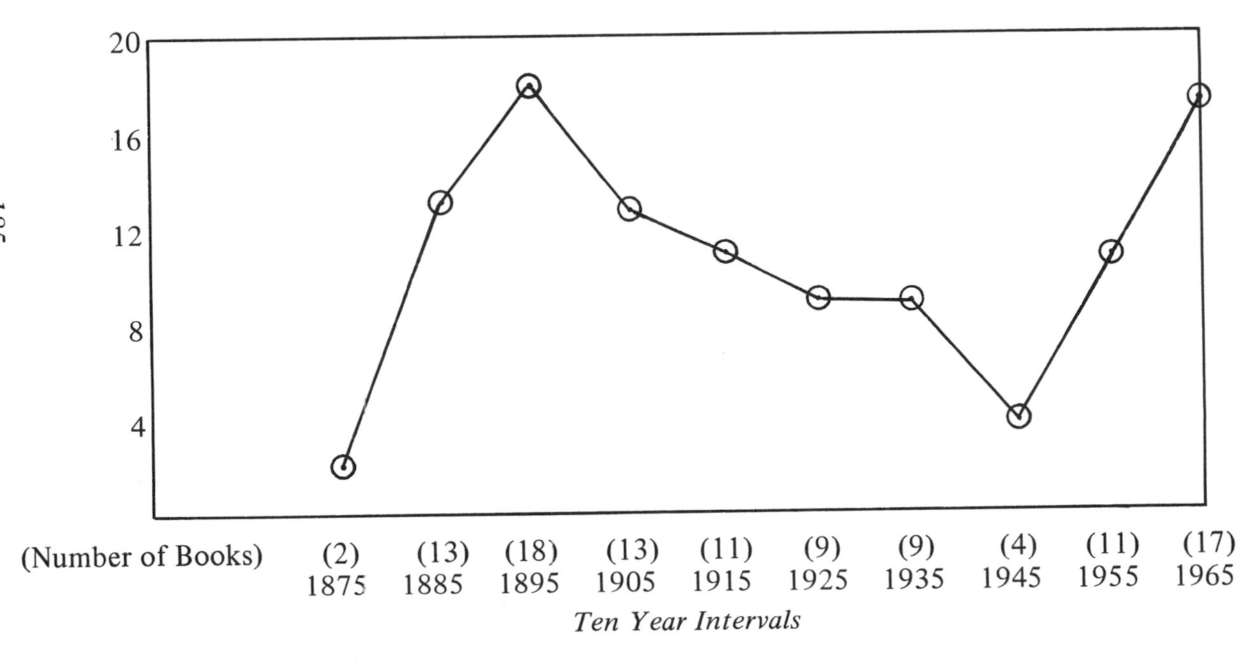

Poker Books Published From 1875 to 1965
(Date for 128 books whose publishing locations are known)

	# Books	%	Country Published
	93	72.6	United States
	22	17.2	England
	8	6.2	France
	2	1.6	Italy
	1	0.8	Germany
	1	0.8	Holland
	1	0.8	India
Total	128	100.0	

A bibliography of 133 poker books are tabulated below:

Books on Poker in The Library of Congress

Subject Heading "Poker" Catalog Number	*Author*	*Library of Congress Card Information**
1. GV1251 A15	Abbott, Jack. A treatise on Jack pot poker, with the game of sancho pedro, when played for stakes. New Orleans, Clark & Hofeline, printers, 1881. 64 pages	
2. GV1258 A43	Allen, George W. Poker rules in rhyme, with chances to improve the hand by drawing. St. Louis, Mo., 1895. 74 pages	
3. GV1251 B6 (other editions)	Blackbridge, John. The complete poker player. A practical guide book to the American national game: containing mathematical and experimental analysis of the probabilities at draw poker. New York, Dick & Fitzgerald, 1880. 142 pages	
4. GV1253 B8 1916 (other editions)	Brown, Garrett. The autocrat of the poker table, or, How to play the game to win. 3rd ed., Boston, R.G. Badger, 1916. 105 pages	
5. GV1251 C15	Cady, Alice Howard. Poker: the modern game. With passing description of its origin. New York, American sports publishing company, 1895. 37 pages	

* *Verbatim card information.*

Subject Heading "Poker", Catalog Number	*Author*	*Library of Congress Card Information**
6. GV1251 C65	Coffin, George Sturgis. Fortune poker; a world-wide round-up of the traditional American game. Complete with new laws according to Hoyle. With a forward by Ely Culbertson, Philadelphia, D. McKay Co., 1949. 198 pages	
7. GV1251 C67	Coffin, George Sturgis. The official laws of poker. Baltimore, Ottenheimer, 1956. 64 pages	
8. GV1251 C68	Coffin, George Sturgis. Pocket guide to the play of poker. Baltimore, Ottenheimer, 1956. 64 pages	
9. GV1251 C95	Curtis, David A. The science of draw poker; a treatise comprising the analysis of principles, calculation of chances, codification of rules, study of situations, glossary of poker terms necessary to a complete understanding of the great American game. New York, D.A. Curtis, 1901. 216 pages	
10. GV1253 D62	Dowling, Allen Nicholas. Confessions of a poker player by Jack King (pseud.) New York, I. Washburn, Inc., 1940. 209 pages	
11. GV1253 D62	Dowling, Allen Nicholas. Under the round table by Jack King (pseud.). Philadelphia, Dorrance, 1960. 219 pages	

* *Verbatim card information.*

Subject Heading "Poker", Catalog Number	*Author*	*Library of Congress Card Information**
12. ?	Edel, Edmund. Poker ein spieler - roman. Charlottenburg, E. Beyer, 1912. 176 pages	
13. GV1253 E26	Edwards, Eugene. Jack pots; stories of the great American game. With over fifty original pen and ink illustrations. Chicago, Jamieson - Higgins Co., 1900. 342 pages	
14. GV1251 F5	Fisher, George Henry. How to win at stud poker ... instruction for the novice, principles of strategy, problem hands, hand valuation, card probabilities, complete set of rules, history of the game, etc. Los Angeles, The Stud Poker Press, 1933. 111 pages	
15. GV1251 F63	Florence, William Jermyn. The gentleman's handbook on poker. New York, London, G. Routledge & Sons, Ltd., 1892. 195 pages	
16. GV1251	Foster, Robert Frederick. Practical poker. New York, Brentano's 1905. 253 pages	
17. GV1251 G47	Gilkie, Robert J. Experimental drawing at poker from five thousand hands. Dorchester, Mass., 1886. 13 pages	
18. GV1251 G5	Girardet, Philippe. Philosophie et mathematique du poker. Paris, M. Senac, 1929. 160 pages	

* *Verbatim card information.*

Subject Heading "Poker", Catalog Number	*Author*	*Library of Congress Card Information**
19. GV1251 G77 (other editions)	Gray, E. Archer. Hints on poker. Washington, D.C., 1886. 16 pages	
20. GV1251 H2	Hardison, Theodore. Poker; a work exposing the various methods of shuffling up hands, as well as other ways of cheating that are resorted to by professional gamblers, also embracing the cardinal principles by which every sleight-of-hand trick known with cards may be played. St. Louis, Hardison Publishing Co., 1914. 120 pages	
21. GV1251 H4	Heineman, Walter Raleigh. Draw poker; a compilation of rules governing the game of "Jack pots", by Jack Pot (pseud.). New York, Chrisholm Printing Co., 1923. 48 pages	
22. GV1251 H52 (other editions)	Henry, R.J. Poker boiled down. . .the latest authentic rules. . .on the great national game. . . 1st edition. Boston, Massachusetts, Tourist Publishing Company, 1890. 13 pages	
23. GV1233 H6 (Temporary entry)	History and anecdotes of card games (especially poker). 43 cuttings from newspapers, etc ... bibliographical notes in ms ... Gift of Prof. Brander Matthews.	
24. GV1251 J2 1947 (other editions)	Jacoby, Oswald. Oswald Jacoby on poker, with a forward by Grantland Rice, and an introduction by William E. McKenney. Rev. ed. Garden City, New York, Doubleday & Company, Inc., 1947. 175 pages	

* *Verbatim card information*

Subject Heading "Poker", Catalog Number	*Author*	*Library of Congress Card Information**
25. GV1251 J22	Jacoby, Oswald. Winning poker. New York, Permabooks, 1949. 189 pages	
26. GV1251 K59	Keller, John Wiliam. The game of draw poker. Including the treatise by R.C. Schenck and rules for the new game of progressive poker . . . New York, White, Stokes & Allen, 1887. 84 pages	
27. GV1251 M15	MacKenzie, Collin. Jack pots. A collection of poker stories. By A. Pair (pseud.). Chicago, the Illustrated Publishing Co., 1887. 160 pages	
28. GV1251 P32	Patton, F. Jarvis. How to win at draw poker. Showing all the chances of the game. New York, Dick & Fitzgerald, 1896. 45 pages	
29. GV1253 P6 (Office)	Unknown. Poker as it was played in Deadwood in the fifties. Palo Alto, California, Wheatstalk Press, 1928. 5 pages (A reprint from an article in Hutching's California magazine in August, 1858 - Vol. III, pg. 85)	
30. GV1253 P77 (Houdini Collection) (other editions)	Poker; how to play it. A sketch of the great American game with its laws and rules, and some of its amusing incidents. By one of its victims. London, Griffith & Farran, 1882. 109 pages	

* *Verbatim card information*

Subject Heading "Poker", Catalog Number	*Author*	*Library of Congress Card Information**
31. QA/273 P96	Proctor, Richard Anthony. Chance and luck: a discussion of the laws of luck, coincidences, wagers, lotteries, and fallacies of gambling; with notes on poker and martingales. London, Longmans, Green & Co., 1887. 263 pages	
32. GV1251 R3 (other editions)	Radner, Sidney H. The key to playing poker and winning. Owings Mills, Maryland, Ottenheimer Publishers, 1964. 189 pages	
33. GV1251 R37	Reese, Terence. Secrets of modern poker. New York, Sterling Publishing Co., 1964. 148 pages	
34: GV1251 R4	Renaudet, G. Le poker; regles completes et commentaires, l'art de gagner au poker; poker a 52 cartes; a 48, 44, 40, 36 et 32 cartes; freeze out; la partie a la cave; calud des probabilities; le blugg, physiologie du jeu. Paris, S. Bornemann, 1922. 31 pages	
35. GV1253 R47	Rhoads, William Morston. Poker, smoke, and other things; fun and pictures. Rules of poker, recipes, toasts, mixed drinks. Chicago, the Reilly & Britton Co., 1907. 69 pages	

* *Verbatim card information.*

Subject Heading "Poker", Catalog Number	*Author*	*Library of Congress Card Information**
36. BF21 A7 (other editions)	Riddle, Ethel Marie. Aggressive behavior in a small social group; bluffing, risking and the desire to beat . . . studied by the use of a poker game as an experimental technique. New York, 1925. 196 pages (Also published as a Ph.D. thesis in psychology, Columbia University)	
37. GV1251 R65	Rottenberg, Irving. Friday night poker, or, Penny poker to millions, by Irv Roddy (pseud.). New York, Simon & Schuster, 1961. 222 pages	
38. GV1251 S32	Schenick, Robert Cummings. Rules for playing poker. Brooklyn, New York, Private printing, 1880. 17 pages (1st edition, 1872)	
39. GV1251 S32 1881 (Toner Collection, Office)	Schenick, Robert Cummings. Draw poker. Published for the trade, 1880. 8 pages	
40. GV1251 S5	Smith, Russell, A. Poker to win. El Paso, Texas, 1925. 110 pages	
41. GV1251 S68	Steig, Irwin. Common sense in poker. New York, Cornerstone Library, 1963. 188 pages	
42. GV1251 7	Steig, Irwin, Poker for fun and profit. New York, McDowell, Obolensky, 1959. 181 pages	

* *Verbatim card information.*

Subject Heading "Poker", Catalog Number	*Author*	*Library of Congress Card Information**
43. GV1251 T2	Talk of Uncle George (pseud.) to his nephew about draw poker. Containing valuable suggestions in connection with this great American game. New York, Dick & Fitzgerald, 1883. 50 pages	
44. GV1251 U55	United States Playing Card Co. Poker; official rules and suggestions, endorsed by Association of American playing card manufacturers. Cincinnati, Ohio, the United States Playing Card Company, 1941. 64 pages	
45. GV1251 W3	Walter & Philip (pseud.) Il poker familiare, come si giuoca in Italia. 2nd edition, Milano, U. Hoepli, 1945. 81 pages	
46. GV1253 W4	Webster, Harold Tucker. Webster's poker book glorifying America's favorite game; a handy volume for the hearthside consisting of fifty portraits; informative and diverting text on the joys, rules, love and pitfalls of poker; sideline suggestions and interpolations; authoritative data on the history and technique of poker; including hints from Hoyle and a forward by George Ade; together with a compartment containing a set of poker chips and a pad of I.O.U. forms ready for instant use. New York, Simon & Schuster, 1925. 126 pages	

* *Verbatim card information*

Subject Heading "Poker", Catalog Number	*Author*	*Library of Congress Card Information**
47. GV1251 W5 1944 (other editions)	Wickstead, James M.	How to win at stud poker. Louisville, Kentucky, Stud Poker Publishing Co., 1944. 115 pages
48. GV1251 W55	Winterblossom, Henry T.	The game of draw poker, mathematically illustrated; being a complete treatise of the game, giving the prospective value of each hand before and after the draw, and the true method of discarding and drawing, with a thorough analysis and insight of the game as played at the present day by gentlemen. New York, W.H. Murphy, 1875. 72 pages
49. GV1251 X3	Xavier, Francois.	Le poker, sa technique, sa psychologie, suivi d'une etude sur le stud poker. Paris, B. Grasset, 1955. 222 pages
50. GV1251 Y3	Yardley, Herbert Osborn.	The education of a poker player, including where and when and how one learns to win. New York, Simon & Schuster, 1957. 129 pages

Subject Headings other than "Poker", Catalog Number	*Author*	*Library of Congress Card Information**
51. GV1243 C8	Clubertson, Ely. Morehead, Albert H. and Geoffrey, Matt-Smith.	Culbertson's Hoyle: the new encyclopedia of games, with official rules. New York, Graystone Press, 1950. 656 pages

* *Verbatim card information.*

Subject Headings other than "Poker", Catalog Number	*Author*	*Library of Congress Card Information**
52. Reference	Encyclopedia Britannica. Poker. Volume 10, page 128, Chicago, William Benton, 1965. 4 pages	
53. GV1251 F79 (temporary entry)	Fox, Richard K., Poker, how to win, together with the official rules. New York 1905. 90 pages	
54. GV1243 F85	Frey, Richard L., pd. The new complete Hoyle; an encyclopedia of rules, procedures, manners and strategy of games played with cards, dice, counters, boards, words, and numbers. Philadelphia, D. McKay Co., 1947. 740 pages	
55. GV1239 J3	Jacoby, O., et el. The fireside book of cards. New York, Simon & Schuster, 1957. 364 pages	
56. PZ3 L628P	Lillard, John F.B., ed. Poker stories, as told by statesmen, soldiers, lawyers, commercial travelers, bankers, actors, editors, millionnaires, members of the Ananias club and the talent, embracing the most remarkable games 1845-95. New York, F.P. Harper, 1896. 251 pages	
57. GV1243 D8	Ostrow, A.A., The complete card player. New York, McGraw-Hill Book Company, Inc., 1945. 771 pages	
58. GV1291 P6P6	Poker-bridge; een nieuw kaartspel. Amsterdam, A.J.G. Strengholt, 1954. 32 pages	

* *Verbatim card information.*

Subject Headings other than "Poker", Catalog Number	*Author*	*Library of Congress Card Information**
59. AP2 W64		Poker chips, a monthly magazine devoted to stories of the great American game. New York, F. Tousey, June -Nov. 1896. 243 pages (continued as the White Elephant magazine)
60. GV1247 S37		Scarne, John. Scarne on cards. Including a photographic section on cheating at cards. Revised, New York, Crown Publishers, 1965. 435 pages

The Library of Congress does not catalog books about poker under the subject of "Gambling". The three hundred and seventy-five books under "Gambling" include books on-

blackjack
boule
cards
cardsharping
craps
fero
horse race betting
pari-mutuel betting
probabilities
raffles
roulette
speculation
trente-et-quarante
wagers

.. but none on poker. Apparently, the Library of Congress does not classify poker as gambling.

---

* *Verbatim card information.*

Seventy-two other poker books not found in the Library of Congress are listed below:

61. Allan, L. The Laws of Poker. Mudie, 1929. 41 pages

62. Ankeny, Nesmith. Scientific Poker. Harper, 1967

63. Ante - I Raise You Ten. 75c, Jamieson - Higgans

64. Arnold, F. and Johnston, H. Poker, 3s 6d, Routledge, 1929

65. Bergholt, E.G.B. Poker. 9d, De La Rue

66. Browning, H.S. Royal Auction Bridge and Poker. Routledge, 1920. 64 pages

67. Carcini, Nick. A Course in Professional Poker Playing. $1.49, Memphis, Tennessee, Edall Publishing Co., Box 12403, 1966. 84 pages

68. Carleton, Henery Guy. Thompson Street Poker Club. 25¢, Dick & Fitzgerald, 1888

69. Coffin, G.S. Poker Game Complete. 12s 6d, Faber and Faber, 1950

70. Coffin, G.S. Complete Poker Game. $3.95, Wehman

71. Crafton, A. Poker: Its Laws and Principles, $1, Wyeil, 1915

72. Crawford, John R. How to be a Consistent Winner in Most Popular Card Games, New York, $2.95, Doubleday, 1953. 256 pages

73. Curtis, D.H. Queer Luck. New York, Brentanos, 1900

74. Dalton, W. Pocket Guide to Poker Patience. De La Rue, 1909

75. Davis, A.D. An Analysis of Five and Seven Card Poker. Philadelphia, 1959. 101 pages (Mimeographed Master's Thesis)

76. Debebian, D. Game of Poker. New York, 1889. 25 pages

77. Decisions on Moot Points of Draw Poker. New York

78. Diehl, Charles Vidol. Poker Patience and Progressive Poker Patience. London, The Advanced Publishing Co., 1909. 16 pages

79. Draw Poker. 15¢, Dick

80. Draw Poker. 15¢, Fitzgerald Publishing Corporation

81. Draw Poker. London, 1884. 63 pages

82. Draw Poker and Spoil Five. London, Routledge & Sons, 1884

83. Ellinger, M. Poker. Faber, 1934

84. Endnase, S.W. The Expert at the Card Table. London, Stationers' Hall, 1902

85. Fisher, G.H. Stud Poker Blue Book. $1, Los Angeles, California, Stud Poker Press, Box 900, 1934

86. Football Poker. 25¢, Brentano's

87. Foster, J.H. Traite du jeu de Poker. Paris, 1889. 73 pages

88. Foster, R.F. Pocket Laws of Poker. De La Rue, 1910

89. Gilbert, Kenneth. Alaskan Poker Stories. Seattle, R.D. Seal, 1958. 46 pages

90. Guerndale, Richard. Draw Poker Without a Master. 25¢, Dillingham

91. Guerndale, Richard. The Poker Book. London, I. Upcott Gill, 1889. 80 pages

92. Habeythe. Jeu de Poker. Paris, 1886

93. Hirst, E. deF. Poker as Played by Skilled Professional Gamblers. 2nd ed., $1, 1902

94. Hoffman, W. Draw Poker, the Standard game. $1, Dutton, 1913

95. How To Play Poker. 10¢, Wehman Bros.

96. How To Win At Draw Poker. 25¢, Dick

97. How To Win At Draw Poker. 25¢, Westbrook

98. Hoyle (pseud.), How To Play Poker. 10¢, Ogilvie, 1916

99. Jackpot, Poker-Patience. International Card Co., 1909. 20 pages

100. Lamenti, C.E. Il Poker. Milano, A. Corticelli, 1929. 59 pages

101. La Shelle, Kirbe. Poker Rubaiyat. Phoenix, Arizona, Bunder Log Press, 1903. 28 pages

102. Laugher,A.B. Poker. C. Goodall, 1913. 28 pages

103. Laugher, A.B. Poker. London, 1889. 28 pages

104. Laun. Jeu de Poker. Paris, Watilliaux, 1897

105. Major. The Poker Primer. New York, 1886. 31 pages

106. Matthews,J.B. Poker Talk (p. 187 of "Penn and Ink"). New York, Longmans, Green & Co., 1888

107. Meehan, C.H.W. The Rules for Playing Draw Poker (Game of Euchre). Philadelphia, T.B. Peterson, 1877

108. Morehead, Albert Hodges. New Complete Hoyle. Toronto, $4.75, Doubleday, 1956. 740 pages

109. Morehead, Albert Hodges. My Secret: How to Play Winning Poker. Los Angeles, W.R. Mathews and Sons, 1957

110. Morehead, Albert Hodges. The Complete Guide to Winning Poker. New York, Simon and Schuster, 1967

111. Moss, John (Pseud. for Jack Potter). How To Win at Poker. pap. $1.50, Doubleday, 1955

112. Mott. Street Poker Club. 25¢, Dick

113. Nabot. Jew de Poker. Paris, Henri Gautier, 1893 (contains many probability tables)

114. Pardon, C. F. (Raudon Crawley). Poker. London, Chas. Goodhall & Sons, 1889

115. Percy, Alfred. Poker: Its Laws and Practice. Allahabad, India, Pioner Press, 1879

116. Phillips, Hubert. Profitable Poker. 18s. Arco Publications, 1960

117. Philpots, E.P. A Treatise on Poker. London, 1904. 93 pages

118. Poker: The Nation's Most Fascinating Card Game. Cincinnati, United States Playing Card Company, 1950

119. Poker. Heines Publishing Co., Inc., Minneapolis, Minnesota, 33 pages

120. Poker. How To Play It. London, 1882, 109 pages

121. Poker Primer. 25¢, Platt & Nourse

122. Potter, Jack. How To Win At Poker. pap.$1, Garden City Books, 1955.

123. Primer. 10¢, Excelsior

124. Proctor, R.A. Poker Principles and Chance Laws. New York, Dick & Fitzgerald, 1883

125. Rander, S. H. How To Play Poker and Win. pap. $1 (Key), Assoc. Booksellers, 1965

126. Reese, Terrence and Watkins, Anthony. Poker Game of Skill. $3.95, Wehman, 1962

127. Reynolds, A. Poker Probabilities Calculated. Sheffield, 1901. 40 pages

128. Rules of Poker. London, 1882. 16 pages

129. Sinclair, E. Poker. 18s, Arco Publications, $3.75, Ambassador, 1964

130. Strong, Julian. How To Play Poker. London, New York, W. Foulsham, 1928. 61 pages

131. "Templar", Poker Manual. $1.25, Warne

132. Welsh, Charles. Poker: How To Play It. London, Griffith & Farren, 1882

133. Virt, L.H. Traite Complet du Jeu de Poker. Paris, 1913 (contains only rules)

Addendum
(Poker books published since 1968)

134. Castle, J. L. How Not to Lose at Poker, $4.50, Boston, Little, Brown and Company, 1970. Perpetuates many of the erroneous clichés about poker. Goes deep into probability mathematics. 150 pages

135. Dowling, A.N., The Great American Pastime, New York, $5.95, A.S. Barnes and Company, 1970. Contains interesting history and anecdotes about poker. 244 pages

136. Livingston, A.D., Poker Strategy and Winning Play, Philadelphia, $5.95, J.B. Lippincott Company, 1971. Little new except two tables of odds for widow games such as Hold Me. Heavy on calculations of odds and descriptions of stud, lowball and widow variations of poker. 227 pages

137. Rubins, J. Win at Poker, New York, $1.50 paperback, Funk & Wagnalls, 1968. Well written, but based on many of the fallacious concepts advanced by other poker books. 218 pages

138. Wallace, F.R., Poker, A Guaranteed Income for Life by using the Advanced Concepts of Poker, Wilmington, Delaware, $12.50, I & O Publishing Company, 1972 (revised). The only definitive and valid treatment of poker available. 279 pages

APPENDIX C

GLOSSARY

Over eight hundred and fifty words and phrases used in poker literature and heard in poker games are defined below:

Action – The betting.

Active Player – A player competing for a pot.

Add Them Up Low Ball – Draw poker where the hand with the lowest point total wins.

"Advanced Concepts of Poker" – The concepts used by the good poker player to win maximum money from a poker game.

Advertise – To have a bluff called in order to mislead opponents.

A-game – The highest stake game in the house.

Age – First position to the left of the dealer. (A, Able, or Edge)

Alien Card – A card not belonging to the deck in play.

Alive Card – See Live Card.

All Blue, or All Pink – A flush.

All The Way - Cincinnati with a progressive bet.

Alternate Straight – A sequence of every other card, such as 2, 4, 6, 8, 10. (Dutch Straight, Skipper, Skip Straight)

Ambique – A French card game that influenced the draw variation of poker.

American Brag – A game where the raiser shows the first caller his hand and then the worst hand folds.

Anaconda – A seven-card game with bets made on five rolled-up cards.

Announce – To declare high, low, or the moon in high-low poker.

Announced Bet – A verbal bet made by a player before putting his money in the pot.

Ante – Money put in the pot before dealing.

A Priori Odds – The probability that an event will occur.

Arkansas Flush – A four flush.

Around the Corner Straight – A sequence running from the highest to the lowest values, such as Q, K, A, 2, 3.

Âs Nâs – A Persian card game from which poker was directly derived.

Assigned Bettor – The player who bets first.

Australian Poker – Draw poker with a blind opening.

Automatic Bluff – A lowball situation that always requires a bluff.

Back-in – To win by default or unexpectedly.

Backer – A non-player who finances an active player.

Backraise – A re-raise. To make a minimum raise to avoid a larger raise.

Back-to-back – A pair on the first two cards dealt in stud. (Backed Up)

Bait – A small bet that encourages a raise.

Bank – Where the money from purchased chips is kept.

Banker – The person responsible for selling and cashing chips.

Bank Night – High-low five-card stud with two twists.

Barn – A full house.

Baseball – A stud game involving 9's and 3's as wild cards.

Beans – Chips.

Bear – A tight player.

Beat the Board (Table) – To have a hand better than all others showing.

Beat Your Neighbor – A five-card game that requires each player in turn to expose his cards until his hand beats the board.

Bedsprings – Similar to Cincinnati except ten cards are dealt face up for use in everyone's hand.

Belly Hit – When a draw fills an inside straight. (Gut Shot)

Belly Strippers – Cards with slightly trimmed edges that taper from a wider center to the ends. (Humps)

Best Flush – A game where only flushes win the pot.

Bet – Money wagered and put in the pot.

Bet Into – To bet before another player who apparently has a better hand.

Bet or Get – A rule that one must either bet or fold with no checking allowed. (Bet or Drop, Pass-out)

Bet the Limit – To bet the maximum amount allowed.

Bet the Pot – To bet the same amount as is in the pot.

Bet the Raise – When the maximum bet is twice that of the previous bet or raise.

Betting Interval – The period from the first bet to the last call in any given round.

Betting Pace – The degree, extent, and aggressiveness of bets and raises.

Betting Stakes – The maximum bet and raise permitted.

Betty Hutton – Seven-card stud with nines and fives wild.

Bicycle – A straight to the five . . . A, 2, 3, 4, 5. (Wheel)

Bid – To declare for high or low in split-pot poker.

Big Bill – A hundred dollars or a thousand dollars.

Big Bobtail – A four-card straight flush.

Big Cat – Five unpaired cards from the King to the eight.

Big Dog – Five unpaired cards from the Ace to the nine.

Big Squeeze – Six-card high-low stud with one twist.

Big Tiger – See Big Cat.

Bill – A dollar or a hundred dollars.

Bird Dog – One who gets players for a game.

Blaze – A five-card hand containing five picture cards.

Blaze Full – A full house in picture cards.

Bleed – To slowly drain money from a game or a player.

Bleeder – A tight, winning player.

Blind – A bet by the Age before the deal.

Blind Bet – To bet before looking at one's hand.

Blind Low – Five-card low stud bet blind all the way to the last bet.

Blind Open – An opening bet made without looking at one's cards.

Blind Tiger – Draw poker where the Age opens blind. (Open Blind and Straddle)

Block System – An ante, open, and first raise automatically done in the blind by the dealer.

Blood Poker – A higher stake poker game played primarily for money rather than for social reasons.

Blow Back – A raise after previously calling or checking.

Bluff – The attempt to win a pot by making better hands fold.

Board – The poker table.
All exposed cards in stud.

Bobtail Flush or Straight – A four-card flush or a four-card open end straight.

Bolt – To fold.

Bone – A white chip, the lowest denomination chip.

Bonus – A fixed sum established by house rules that is paid by each player to the holder of a very high value hand such as a straight flush. (Premium, Royalty, Penalties)

Book – A three-card draw.

Boost – To raise.

Border Work – Markings added by cheaters to the printed borderlines of cards to identify their value.

Bottom Deal – To deal cards off the bottom of the deck when cheating.

Bouillotte – A French card game that influenced the open card, stud variation in poker.

Boxed Card – A card turned the wrong way in a deck.

Boy – A Jack.

Brag – The betting expression in the English game of Bragg.

Bragg – An English three-card game that influenced the use of the full fifty-two card deck in poker.

Braggers – Jacks and nines, which are wild. Or the Ace of Diamonds, the Jack of Clubs, and the nine of Diamonds, which are wild.

Brandeln – A card game similar to Commerce.

Breakers – Openers.

Breathe – To pass the first opportunities to bet.

Brelen – A French card game that influenced the use of straights and flushes in poker.
Three of a kind.

Brelen Carre – Four of a kind.

Brief – A single stripper card in a deck used to facilitate illegal cuts.

Buck – A marker or a knife used to designate the player permitted to deal a special hand, usually a hand with a dealer advantage such as draw.
A dollar.

Buddy Poker – To avoid betting against a friend or partner.

Buffalo – To fool opponents.

Bug – The Joker used as an Ace or a wild card for filling straights and flushes. A wild card in lowball. In high-low, it can be used as both high and low in the same hand.
A device fastened beneath the poker table by a cheater to hold out a card or cards.

Bull or Bullet – An Ace.

Bull Montana – Five-card stud with betting, then Jacks required to open the final bet.

Bull the Game – To bluff or bet aggressively.

Bump – A raise.

Buried Card – A card randomly inserted in the deck.

Burn – A full house.
To lose a hand.

Burnt Card – An exposed card put face up on the bottom of the deck.

Busted Hand – A worthless hand. (Bust)

Busy Card – Any card that completes a hand.

Butcher Boy – An open hand form of poker where four of a kind is needed to win.

Buy – To call bets in order to draw cards.
To bluff someone out.

Buy In – The stack of chips that a player buys at the start of a game.

By Me – An expression meaning to pass.

California Lowball – Lowball.

Call – Money put in the pot to match a bet or raise.

Carding – Noting exposed cards during a hand.

Card Odds – The probabilities of being dealt or drawing to various hands.

Card Sharper – See Sharper.

Cards Speak – A rule that the value of a hand is based on what the cards are rather than on what a player thinks he has.

Case Card – The last available card of a particular value or suit.

Cash In – To exchange poker chips for cash and then quit. (Cash Out)

Cat – Any big or little tiger or cat hand.

Catbird Seat – A position where the player declaring last can assure himself half of the pot.

Catch – To be dealt or draw a certain card or hand. . .usually a desirable card or hand.

Chalk Hand – An almost certain winner.

Chase – To stay against a better hand.

Cheater – A player who intentionally violates the rules to gain an advantage.

Check – When no money is bet.

Check Blind (Check in the Dark) – To check without looking at one's own cards.

Check Cop – A paste palmed in a cheater's hand and used to steal poker chips or to hold out cards.

Check Raise – To check then subsequently raise in the same round of betting.

Chicago – Seven-card stud where the hand with the highest spade wins half the pot.

Chicago Pelter – A kilter.

Chicken Picken – An eleven-card game, two cards in hand and nine on the table in rows of three.

Chink Ink – A special ink used by cheaters to mark the edge of cards.

Chip – Money represented by a disc.

Chip Along – To bet the smallest amount possible.

Chip Declaration – To use chips in declaring for high or low.

Chip In – To call a small bet.

Chipping – Betting.

Choice Pots – Dealer's choice.

Cinch Hand – A certain winner. (a Lock, an Immortal)

Cincinnati – A ten-card game with five in each hand and five face up for everyone's use. (Lame Brains)

Cincinnati Liz – Like Cincinnati except the lowest face up card is wild.

Clam – A dollar.

Class – Rank of a poker hand.

Closed Card – A concealed card in one's hand.

Closed Game – A game barred to newcomers.

Closed Hand – The concealed cards in one's hand as in draw poker.

Closed Poker – Any form of poker where all cards are dealt face down.

Close to the Chest – To play tight. (Close to the Belly)

C-Note – A hundred dollar bill.

Coffee Housing – To act oppositely to one's emotions.

Cold Deck – A deck from which poor hands are being dealt.
A stacked deck.

Cold Feet – A description for a player wanting to quit the game early.

Cold Hands – Showdown hands.
A run of poor hands.

Cold Turkey – A pair of Kings, back to back, on the first two cards in five card stud.

Come – See On The Come.

Come In – To call.

Come Off – To break up a lower value hand to draw for a higher value one.

Commerce – A three-card game with three cards in the widow.

Common Card (Communal Card) – An exposed card good in every player's hand.

Consecutive Declaration – A rule for declaring high-low hands in consecutive order.

Contract – To declare for high or low at the conclusion of split-pot poker.

Contract Poker – High-low, split-pot poker with oral declarations.

Corner Card – An eight-card game, five cards in hand and three on the table, with last card up and all like it as wild.

Cosmetics – Preparations such as ashes, waxes, abrasives, aniline pencils, luminous inks used by cheaters for marking cards. (Daub)

Counter – One chip.
A player who continuously counts his chips.

Count Cards – The Jack, King and Queen. (Court Cards, Face Cards, Picture Cards)

Coup – A brilliant play.

Cowboy – A King.

Crank – To deal.

Crazy Otto – Five-card stud with low card as wild.

Crimp (Bridge) – To bend and hump the upper or lower section of the deck to make a false or an illegal cut. (See Debone)

Criss Cross – Same as Southern Cross except five cards are laid out with the center one wild.

Crooked-Honest System (C-H System) – The system of two cheaters in partnership. When one catches a strong hand, he signals the other to raise thus squeezing all callers. (Cross Lift)

Cross (The Cross) – Like Cincinnati but the five table cards are in a cross formation with the center card and all like it as wild.

Crosscards – A ten-hand poker solitaire game. (Patience Poker)

Cross Lift – See Crooked-Honest System.

Crossover – A combination of draw and stud poker involving wild cards.

Cull – To arrange or cluster good cards together before shuffling.

Curfew – The agreed upon quitting time.

Curse of Mexico – The deuce of Spades.

Curse of Scotland – The nine of Diamonds.

Customer – An opponent who calls.

Cut the Cards – Putting the bottom cards of a deck on top of the deck.

Cut the Pot – Money withdrawn from pots for a purpose such as to pay for refreshments.

Dame – A Queen.

Daub – See Cosmetics.

Dark Bet – A blind bet.

Dead Cards – Discarded or folded cards.

Dead Hand – A foul hand that cannot be played.

Dead Man's Hand – Usually Aces and eights, two pair. Sometimes Aces and eights full house or Jacks and eights, two pair.

Deadwood – Dead cards.

Deal – To distribute cards to the players.

Dealer-Advantage Game – Any game where the dealer has an advantage.

Dealer's Choice – When the dealer can play the poker game of his choice.

Dealer's Percentage – Any game offering the dealer a significant advantage. (Dealer's Game, Dealer's Advantage)

Deal Off – To deal the final hand of the game.

Deal Out – To omit a player from a hand.

Debone – A card or portion of a deck that has been crimped both lengthwise and crosswise.

Deception – An important and accepted tool of poker.

Deck – All the cards used in the game. (Pack)

Declare – To announce if going for high or low.

Deep Low – The lowest hand for any card . . . for example, a deep seven is an A, 2,3,4,7.

Defensive Bet – A bet designed to decrease one's potential loss.

Deuce – A two.

Deuces Wild – When all deuces are wild.

Devil's Bed Posts – A four of Clubs.

Dig – To replenish one's stake while playing a hand.

Discard – When cards are exchanged for new cards during the draw or twist.

Disproportionate Bet – A peculiar bet or a bet much larger or smaller than the normal bet.

Doctor Pepper – Seven-card stud with deuces, fours and tens wild.

Dog – Any big or little dog hand.

Doghouse Cut – Any cut that divides the deck into more than two stacks.

Double – To raise.

Double Barreled Shotgun – High-low draw with four rounds of betting after the draw as each card is turned face up. (Texas Tech)

Double Bluff – A bluff made by making a bluff bet on the final round and then re-raising a subsequent raise.

Double-End Straight – See Bobtail.

Double Header – A pot not won that passes to the next deal. A second game that follows an earlier one.

Doubling Up – Betting twice as much as the previous bet.

Down and Dirty – The final, hole card dealt in seven-card stud.

Down Cards – Cards dealt face down.

Down the Chute – To take a heavy loss.

Down the River – Seven-card stud.

Drag (Snatch) – When money is separated from a pot to signify the amount owed by a player. (Light)

Draw – The exchange of a card or cards for new ones.

Draw Out – To catch the winning hand with the last card or cards drawn.

Draw Poker – One of the two basic forms of poker (the other is stud) and is played as a closed five-card hand with a closed draw.

Drib – An inferior player.

Driller – A loose player. A player who bets and raises frequently.

Driver's Seat – The position holding the best hand.

Drop or Drop-out – To retire from a hand by not calling a bet or raise. (Fold)
The last card dealt to a player.

Drum – To play tight.

Drummer or Drummer Boy – A tight player.

Dry – To be out of money.

DTC Method – The technique of good poker . . . Discipline, Thought and Control.

Duck – A deuce.

Duffer – An inexperienced or poor player.

Duke – A hand of cards.

Dutch Straight – See Alternate Straight.

Dynamite – A two-card poker game.

Eagles – The cards of a fifth suit in a sixty-five card deck.

Early Bet – A small bet after the first card in stud or the first two cards in draw.

Edge – An advantageous position.
The dealer or sometimes the Age.

Edge Odds – The advantage or disadvantage of a player relative to the other players.

Edge Shot – A bet made from an advantageous position.

Eldest Hand – The first player to the dealer's left.

Elimination – Like Cincinnati, but cards matched with table cards are discarded. (Weary Willie)

End Bet – The last bet of an interval.

End Bets – Last round bets.

End Strippers – Cards tapered along the ends for cheating.

English Poker – Draw played with a blind opening.

English Stud – A stud game with a draw.

Ethics or Etiquette – The understandings and courtesies of which violations do not constitute cheating.

Exposed Cards – Cards purposely dealt face up, as in stud.

Face Card – Any picture card.

Faced – A card lying face up.
To receive a face card.

Fall of the Cards – The order that cards are dealt.

False Cut, False Deal, False Shuffle – Illegal cut, deal or shuffle.

False Openers – A hand that has opened improperly.

Family Pot – A pot where everyone calls the bet.

Farm System – Several different size poker games under control of a good player.

Fast Game – A game with a fast betting pace.

Fatten – To increase the money in the pot. (Sweeten)

Feeble Phoebe – Like Hollywood, except table cards are turned over two at a time and played for high and low.

Fed the Pot – To foolishly bet or raise.

Feeler Bet – A small or nominal bet made to seek out strength or raising tendencies of opponents.

Fever – A five.

Filling – Drawing and then catching a full house.

Fin – Five dollars.

Finger Poker – A game run on credit.

First Jack Deals – A method to determine who has the first deal in a poker game.

First Hand – The first player allowed to bet a hand.

Fish – An easy or a poor player.

Fish Hook – A seven or a Jack.

Five and Dime – A hand containing a five and a ten with three unpaired cards in between.

Five Card Stud – Stud poker played with one hole card and four exposed cards.

Five of a Kind – Five cards of the same value.

Fixed Limit – The maximum betting stakes allowed.

Flash – Five cards, one of each suit plus the Joker.
When concealed cards are exposed.
To expose a common card for everyone's use when there are not enough cards to complete a stud game.

Flat Poker – Poker with a blind open.

Flicker, Flicker – Five-card stud high-low.

Flinger – A wild or crazy player.

Flip Stud – Five-card stud where the optional hole card and matching hole cards are wild.

Flush – Five cards of the same suit.

Fluss (Flux) – A flush.

Flying – An expression for a full house.

Fold – To drop out of a hand by not calling the bet or raise. (Drop)

Football – A stud game similar to baseball involving 6's and 3's as wild cards.

Foul Hand – A hand containing the wrong number of cards.

Four Flush – Four cards of the same suit.

Four-flusher – A cheater, particularly one who tries to win pots by purposely miscalling his hand.

Four Forty-Four – Eight-card stud with fours wild.

Four of a Kind – Four cards of the same value. (Fours)

Freak – A Joker or a wild card.

Freak Hands – Non-standard poker hands such as Blazes, Dutch Straights, Kilters and Skeets.

Free Ride – Playing without paying.

Free Wheeler – A bankrupt player allowed to play free until he wins a pot.

Freeze-Out – When a player is required to leave after losing a certain amount of cash.

Freezer – A call for less than the amount of the bet in table stakes. (Short Call)

Friend – A card that improves a hand.

Full House, Full Barn or Full Tub – Three of a kind with another pair. (Full Hand)

Fundamental Position – The value of a player's hand relative to the other players' hands.

Fuzzing – Mixing the cards by continuously stripping off the top and bottom cards. (Milking, Snowing Cards)

Gaff – A cheater's device or technique.

Gallery – Non-playing spectators.

Gambler – A player who wagers money at unfavorable edge odds.

Gambler's Last Charge – Played with five hand cards and five table cards with last card turned up being wild when matched in one's hand.

Game behavior – Artificial behavior used in a poker game.

Game Pace – Betting done on various hands compared to betting normally done on these hands.

Gang Cheating – When several players cheat in collusion.

Gap – The missing space (card) required to fill a straight.

Garbage – The discards.

Ge – A pair.

Ghost Hand – A hand that reappears on the next deal because of incomplete shuffling.

Giant Twist – A twist allowing the exchange of up to all of one's cards.

Gilet (Gillet or Gile) – An old French card game that was the predecessor of Brelan.

Gimmick – See Gaff.

Girl – A Queen.

Gi-Til-Satisfy – An unlimited giant twist with progressively increasing costs for new cards.

Gleek – Three of a kind.
An early English card game.

Go – To start dealing.

Go All In – To bet all one's money in table stakes.

Going Better – A raise.

Going In – A call.

Golden Chairs – Played with four hand cards and three table cards with one's low hand card sometimes played as wild.

Good Hand – A winning hand.

Good Player – A player who extracts maximum possible money from the poker game.

Go Out – To drop.

Grand – A thousand dollars.

Gravy – One's winnings.

Greek – A card sharper. (Grec)

Greek Bottom – The second card from the bottom dealt by a dishonest player.

Grifter – A cheater.

Gut Shot – See Belly Hit.

Guts to Open – When any value hand can open.

Half Pot Limit – Where the betting limit is half the size of the pot.

Hand – The cards dealt to a player.

Hand Cards – Concealed cards that are dealt face down.

Hand Pace – The extent of betting, calling, raising and bluffing compared to the size of the pot.

Head to Head – When only two players are playing.

Heavy – When too much is in the pot.

Hedge Bet – A side bet to limit possible losses.

Heeler – A kicker.

Heinz – Seven-card stud with fives and sevens wild and also penalty cards.

Help – To improve a hand on the draw or with additional cards in stud.

Hidden Declarations – A rule for declaring high-low hands by concealing different color chips in one's hand.

Highball – Poker where the highest hand wins.

High-Low – A game where the highest and lowest hands split the pot.

High Spade in Hole – Seven-card stud with high Spade in the hole dividing the pot with the high hand.

Hilo Pocalo – Five-card stud where the up-cards can be refused and passed to the player on the left. (Take it or Leave it)

Hit – An improving draw or catch.

Hokum – A stud variation providing an option to receive cards face up or down.

Hold Me (Hold Me, Darling) – A seven-card game with two closed cards in each hand and five face up for everyone's use. (Tennessee Hold Me)

Hold Out – When a cheater conceals a card or cards for future use.

Hold Out Device – A mechanical device used by cheaters to hold out a card or cards. (See Bug, Lizard, Spider)

Hole Cards – The cards dealt face down in stud.

Hole Card Stud – Five-card stud where betting starts on the first hole card.

Hollywood – Fifteen-card Cincinnati with five in each hand and ten table cards.

Holy City – A big hand, usually with Aces and picture cards.

Honest Readers – The normal marks or irregularities on any deck of cards.

Honor Card – A ten or higher value card.

Hook – A Jack.

Hot Deck – A deck from which good hands are being dealt.

Hot Hands – A run of high value hands.

Hot Pot – A special pot, usually played for higher stakes. (Pistol Stud)

Hot Streak – A run of good luck or winning hands. (Spinner)

House – The person or organization running a poker game.

House Cut – The amount cut from the pots for the house.

House Game – A poker game where admission is charged or the pots are cut for the host's profit, often an illegal game.

House Rules – Rules, especially about betting, agreed upon by the players.

Hoyles – Any accepted rules for card games.

Humps – See Belly Strippers.

Hurricane – Two-card poker.

Ice – A cold deck.

Ideal Edge Odds – The theoretical maximum edge odds. . . which are impossible to achieve.

Idle Card – A card that adds no value to a hand.

"IF" – See Gambler's Last Charge.

Immortal – The best possible hand.
A sure winner.

Improve – To draw cards that improve one's hand.

In – To remain in the pot.

In Action – The time when a player is involved in playing his hand.

In a Row (Line) – A sequence or a straight.

Index – The number or letter printed on the corners of cards.

Indirect Bet – When an opponent bets or raises for a player sandbagging a strong hand.

Inside Straight – A broken sequence of four cards, such as 3, 5, 6, 7.

Intentional Flash – Closed cards purposely shown to an opponent.

In the Hole – Cards dealt face down in stud poker.

In the Middle – The position of the players calling bets between two raising players. (Middle Man)

Investment Odds – The estimated returns on betting investments.

Iron Duke – An unbeatable hand. (Ironclad Hand)

Jack and Back – Jackpots which reverts to lowball if no one opens. (Jack and Reverse, Jacks Back, Jackson)

Jackpots – Draw poker where a pair of Jacks or better is required to open.

Jacks to Open – When a pair of Jacks or higher is required to open in draw poker.

Jack Up – To raise.

Jake – A Jack.

J-Boy – A Jack.

Jinx – A curse of bad luck.

Jog – An unevenly stacked deck used by a cheater to mark where his partner should cut the deck. (Step)

John – A Jack.

Joker – The 53rd card added to a deck. (See the Bug)

Joker Poker – Poker played with the Joker as wild.

Jonah – An unlucky player.

Kankakee – Seven-card stud with the Joker as wild in everyone's hand.

K-Boy – A King.

Key Card – An important card needed to complete a hand.

Key Player – A player with important influence over the game.

Kibitzer – A commenting spectator.

Kicker – An extra card held with a pair, trips or four of a kind during the draw or twist.

Kick-it – To bump it.

Kilter – A five-card hand starting with the Ace and alternating values to the nine – A, 3, 5, 7, 9.

King without the Moustache – The King of Hearts as wild.

Kitty – Money cut from pots.

Klu Klux Klan – Three Kings.

Knave – A Jack.

Knock – To check or pass by rapping the table.

Knock Poker – Draw poker with rummy drawing.

Laddie – A fellow poker player.

Lady – A Queen.

Lalapolooze – A freak hand allowed to win once a night.

Lame Brain Pete – Same as Cincinnati except the lowest exposed card and all cards like it are wild.

Lame Brains – See Cincinnati.

Lay Down – The show of hands after the last bet.

Lay Odds – To offer a larger bet against a smaller one.

Lead – To make the first bet.

Leader – The player who is betting first.

Lid – The top card or the card of a single card draw.

Light – Money separated from a pot to signify the amount owed by a player.

Limit – The maximum bet or raise allowed.

Limit Stakes – When the maximum bets and raises are limited by the house rules.

Little Bobtail – A three-card straight flush.

Little Cat – Five unpaired cards from the 8 to the 3.

Little Dog – Five unpaired cards from the 7 to the 2.

Little Squeeze – Five-card stud, high-low with a twist.

Little Tiger – See Little Cat.

Little Virginia – Six-card stud with low hole card as wild.

Live Card – A card that has not been dealt or exposed.

Live Hand – A hand with a good chance to improve.

Lizard – A hold-out device that works up and down a cheater's sleeve.

Lock – A hand that cannot lose.

Long Studs – Stud poker with more than five cards dealt to each player.

Look – To call.

Looking Down One's Throat – Having an unbeatable hand

against an opponent.

Lowball – Poker where the lowest hand wins and 5, 4, 3, 2, A is the perfect low.

Low Hole – A stud game where the lowest hole card and all matching cards are wild.

Low Poker – Poker where the lowest hand wins, and 7, 5, 4, 3, 2, is the perfect low.

Luck – An illusion of winning or losing more than one should be.

Luck Out – To outdraw and beat a good hand.

Luminous Readers – Cards marked by cheaters with a special ink that can be seen only through special lenses or glasses. (See Pink Eye)

Ma Ferguson – Five-card stud with low card on board and all like it as wild.

Main Pot – The first pot apart from side pots.

Major Hand – A straight or better.

Major League Game – The largest stake game of several poker games.

Make Good – To pay money owed to the pot.

Make The Pack – To shuffle and prepare the cards for dealing.

Marked Cards – Cards with markings that enable a cheater to read them from the back side.

Marker – See Buck.
A promissory note.

Matching Card – A card of the same value or suit as another in one's hand.

Match It – Five-card stud with hole card becoming wild only if matched by an up card.

Match the Pot – To put in the pot an amount equal to that already there.

Mate – A card that matches or pairs another.

Mechanic – A dishonest dealer.

Mechanic's Grip – A special way to hold a deck for dishonest dealing.

Meet a Bet – To call the full bet.

Mexican Stud – Five-stud where cards are dealt down and the player always has an option to choose his hole card.

Mickey Mouse – A totally worthless hand.

Middle Dealer – A dealer who can deal cards from the middle of the deck.

Middle Man – See In the Middle.

Milker – A tight player.

Milking the Cards – See Fuzzing.

Milking the Game – To slowly drain money from the game by tight playing.

Minnie – The perfect low hand.

Minor League Game – A smaller stake game.

Misdeal – A faulty deal resulting in a re-deal.

Misere – The English name for lowball poker.

Miss – The failure to draw a helpful card.

Mistigris – A wild Joker.

Money Flow – The direction, amount and pattern that money passes among players in a game. The amount of money that can be won or lost per unit of time.

Monkey Flush – A three-card flush.

Monte – A three-card poker game.

Moon – When a player wins both the high and low halves of a split-pot game.
When a player declares both high and low.

Moon Hand – A hand of good high and low value.

Mortgage – Seven-card stud requiring a player to win twice before winning the pot.

Mouth Bet – A bet not substantiated by money.

Murder – A two-card high-low game with several twists.
A six-card high-low game with several twists.

Mystical Attitude – An irrational, unreasoned attitude.

Nailing (Blistering, Indexing, Jagging, Pegging, Punctuating, Pricking) – A cheater's technique to mark cards with his fingernail or a device.

Natural – A hand without wild cards.

New Guinea Stud – Seven-card stud starting with four down cards then roll up any two.

New York Stud – Five-card stud where a four flush beats a pair.

Nickel-Dime – A small stake game.

Nigger Bet An unusual bet such as a nine dollar bet instead of the normal ten dollar bet.

Nigger Mike – Six-card draw with a bet on each dealt card.

Nits and Lice – Two pair or a full house of deuces and threes. (Mites and Lice)
Deuces and threes as wild cards.

No Limit – When any size bet or raise can be made. (Sky's the Limit)

Northern Flight – Seven-card stud with all Hearts wild unless a Spade is in the hand.

Nucleus Players – The dependable, regular players.

Nursing – Fondling cards.

Objective Attitude – A rational, reasoned attitude based on reality.

Odds – The probabilities.

Odds Against – Number of failures per success.

Odds For – Number of attempts per success.

Odds On – Odds at less than even money.

Offensive Bet – A bet designed to maximize the pot.

Office Hours – A straight from the 5 to the 9 or 4 to the 8.

Omaha – Seven-card stud with two cards in hand and five table cards rolled-up one at a time.

One End or One Way Straight – A four-card straight open only on one end, such as J, Q, K, A.

One Eye Jacks – When the Jack of Spades and the Jack of Hearts are wild.

One Eyes – Picture cards with profiles showing only one eye. (Jack of Hearts, Jack of Spades and the King of Diamonds)

On The Come – To bet before one has made his hand.

Open – The first bet of the first round.

Open At Both Ends or Open End – A four-card sequence that can be made a straight by two different value cards. (One End Straight)

Open Blind – To open without looking at one's cards.
To open in Blind Tiger.

Open Cards – Face up cards in stud. (Up Cards)

Opener – The player who opens the pot.

Openers – A hand on which the betting can be started.

Open Game – A game in which any newcomer can play.

Open Pair – An exposed pair in stud.

Open Poker – Stud poker.

Open Seat – A chair available for another player.

Option – Five-card, high-low stud with a twist.

Option Card – A card that may be kept or exchanged. (Twist) A stud card that may be kept in the hole or exposed.

Original Hand – The cards dealt to a player before the draw.

Overcards – Cards that rank higher than a pair.

Overhand Shuffle – To shuffle by sliding cards from the top of the deck into the other hand.

Pace – See Betting Pace and Game Pace.

Pack – The deck of cards.

Packet – A portion of the pack.

Pa Ferguson – Five-card stud with high card on board and all like it as wild.

Paint – A face card in a lowball hand.

Pair – Two cards of the same value.

Palmed Card – A card concealed for future use by a cheater.

Paperwork – Markings added to cards by cheaters.

Pass – To drop out instead of betting.

Passed Pot – When no one opens the pot.

Pass-Out – To drop when a bet or a drop is required.

Pass the Deal – To relinquish one's turn to deal.

Pass the Trash (Garbage) – A high-low stud game involving the exchanging cards among players.

Pasteboard – A card.

Pat Hand – A hand where the player keeps all his cards without drawing or twisting new cards.

Patience Poker – See Crosscards.

Peeker or Peeper – One who looks at an active player's hand.

Peek Poker – Seven-card stud.

Peep and Turn – See Mexican Stud.

Pelter – A five-card hand containing a 2, 5, 9, and one card either a 3 or a 4 and the other card either a 6, 7 or 8. (Skeet)

Penalties – See Bonus.

Penny Ante – A small stake game.

Penultimate Card – The next to the last card in the deck.

Percentage – The house cut.
Probabilities expressed in hundredths.

Perdue – Cards turned down.

Perfect Low – An unbeatable lowball hand, such as 1(A)2345, or 1(A)2346, or 23457 . . . depending on the game.

Philosopher – A card sharper.

Pick-Up Checks – When a player can bet or raise the limit for every check made before his play.

Picture Card – A Jack, Queen or King.

Pigeon – An easy player or a sucker.
A valuable card for a hand.

Pig in the Poke – See Wild Widow.

Pile – A player's money.

Pinch – Five dollars.

Pink Eye (Red Eye) – A pink tinted contact lens worn by a

cheater to identify luminous readers. (See Luminous Readers)

Pips – The spots or marks on the face of a card.

Pirahna – An aggressive bettor.

Pistol Stud – See Hole Card Stud.

Place and Show Tickets Split Pot with Twist Your Neighbor – A game where cards are drawn from hands of other players, and the pot is split between the second and third best hands.

Place Tickets – The second best hand.
Draw poker where the second best hand wins.

Play – To call or stay in.

Play Back – To declare a false stake in table stakes.

Played Card – A card dealt to a hand.

Poch – The best pair, three of a kind, or four of a kind.

Pochen – A German card game from which the name of "poker" was partly derived.

Point – The value of a card.

Poker Dice – Cubical dice, each with a nine, ten, Jack, Queen, King and Ace on its six faces.

Poker Face – A face not showing any emotion or change in expression.

Poker Rules – A loose, flexible framework of laws for playing poker.

Poker Solitaire – See Crosscards.

Pone – The player on the dealer's right.

Pool – A pot.

Poque – A French card game from which the name of "poker" was partly derived.
A French betting expression.

Position – The relative situation of a player to the other

players. (Fundamental Position, Seat Position, Technical Position)

Pot – Where the ante, bets and raises are put.

Pothooks – Nines.

Pot Limit – When the maximum permitted bet is the size of the pot.

Pot Limit Dig – Pot limit poker with no table stake restrictions.

Poverty Poker – A game where a player can lose only a predetermined amount, after which he can play with the winners' money.

Powerhouse – A very strong hand.

Premium – See Bonus.

Primero – An old, betting card game of Spanish origin.

Private Game – A poker game where money is not cut for the host's profit.

Proctor and Gamble – A game with four hand cards to everyone and three rolled table cards with the last one and all like it as wild.

Progression of Bets – The increase in betting limits for each round of betting.

Progressive Poker – Where the ante, bets and opener requirements increase after a passed pot.

Pull Through – A type of false shuffle.

Punters – Those who play against the banker.

Puppy Feet – Clubs.

Puppy Foot – The Ace of Clubs.

Push – Passing unwanted cards to players on one's left.

Put Up – To pay money owed to the pot.

Quadruplets – Four of a kind.

Qualifier – The minimum hand allowed to win.

Quart – A four-card straight flush.

Quint – A straight flush.

Quint Major – A royal straight flush.

Quitting Time – An agreed upon time to end a poker game. (Curfew)

Quorum – The minimum number of players needed to start a poker game.

Rabbit – A weak player.

Rabbit Hunting – Looking through the undealt deck of cards.

Rags – Worthless cards.

Raise – See Bump.

Rake-Off – The money taken from the pot by the house.

Rangdoodles – When the betting limit is increased after a very good hand such as four of a kind.

Rank – The relative value of hands.

Rat Holer – A player who quietly pockets his money or winnings during the game.

Readable Pattern – A behavior pattern that reveals the value of a player's hand.

Readers – Marked cards.

Redeal – A new deal after a misdeal.

Redskin – A face card.

Rembrandt – Any game where all face cards are wild.

Reraise – A raise after having been raised.

Rest Farm – An expression for the whereabouts of a player

driven from a game because of heavy losses.

Restraddle – The third blind betting twice as much as the straddle.

Restricted Pot – When a minimum value hand (or better) is necessary to win the pot. (Qualifier)

Ribbon Clerk – A player unwilling to play poker at higher stakes or a faster pace.

Rickey de Laet – A form of Mexican Stud where the player's hole cards and all like them are wild for him.

Ride Along – To stay in a round where no bets are made.

Ride the Pot – Going light.

Riffle – Flipping the edge of the deck with the thumb.

Right to Bet – When every player has a right to at least one bet or raise per round regardless of the number of raises during that round.

Ring-In – Slipping an unfair deck into play.

Robin Hood Cheater – One who cheats for someone else without benefiting himself.

Roll or Rolled Card – A face down table card or cards turned up one at a time with a round of betting after each exposure.

Roll Your Own Baseball – Same as baseball except one of three original hole cards is turned up and the low hole card and all like it are wild.

Roodles – A round of play at increased stakes. (Wangdoodle)

Rotation – Movement in the direction of the deal . . . clockwise.

Rough – The highest lowball hand of a given value, such as 7, 6, 5, 4, 3.

Round of Betting – When every player is allowed to check, open, bet, raise or drop.

Round of Play – When every player deals a poker hand.

Round the Corner Straight – See Around the Corner Straight.

Round the World – The same as Cincinnati, except four cards are dealt to the players and the widow.

Routine – A straight flush.

Rover – One unable to play because the game is full.

Royal – The best possible lowball hand.

Royal Flush - A straight flush to the Ace.

Royals – See Eagles.

Royalties – See Bonus.

Rub the Spots Off – To excessively shuffle or riffle the cards.

Run – A sequence or a straight.

Run One – An attempt to bluff.

Runt – A hand of mixed suits and no pairs.

Run Up a Hand – To stack a deck during the play, often by arranging discards.

Sandbag – To check then raise the opener.
To check to get more money in the pot.

Sawbuck – Ten dollars.

Say – The turn of a player to declare what to do.

Scarne Cut – To cut by pulling cards from the center of the deck and placing them on top of the deck.

Schenck's Rules – First known rules of poker printed in England in 1872.

Schoolboy Draw – An unsound draw.

Scooping – See Shoot the Moon.

Screwy Louie – Similar to Anaconda except discards are passed to the players on one's left.

Seat Position – The position of a player relative to the other players.

Seat Shot – A bet or raise made from an advantageous seat position.

Second – The second card from the top of the deck being dealt.

Second Best – To hold the best losing hand.

Second Deal – To deal the second card from the top of the deck when cheating.

See – To call in the final round of betting.

Seed – An Ace.

Sequence – Cards of consecutive value as in the straight 4, 5, 6, 7, 8.

Sequential Declaration – High-low poker where the last bettor or raiser declares his hand first.

Serve – To deal.

Session – The period in which a poker game is held.

Seven Card Flip – Seven-card stud where the first four cards are dealt down and then the player turns any two up.

Seven Card Pete – Seven-card stud with all sevens as wild, or low hole or last card and all like it as wild.

Seven Card Stud or Seven Toed Pete – Stud poker played with three hole cards and four exposed cards.

Sevens Rule – A rule in lowball where anyone with seven low or better must bet or forfeit further profits from the pot.

Seven Toed Pete – Seven card stud.

Sharper or Sharker – A cheater.

Sharp Top – An Ace.

Shifting Sands – The same as Mexican stud except hole card and matching cards are wild.

Shill – A house man.
A partner or a cheater.

Shiner – A tiny mirror used by a cheater to see unexposed cards.

Shot the Moon – To declare both high and low in an attempt to win both halves of a high-low pot. (Moon, Scooping, Swinging)

Short – Insufficient money or cards. (Shy)

Short Call – Calling part of a bet with all the money a player has left in table stakes.

Short Pair – A pair lower than openers, such as a pair of tens in Jackpots.

Short Studs – Five-card stud.

Shotgun – Draw poker with extra rounds of betting starting after the third card.

Shove Them Along – Five-card stud where each player has the choice to keep his first up card dealt to him or to pass it to the player on his left. (Take It or Leave It).

Show – To expose one's cards.

Show Cards – The exposed cards in stud.

Showdown – The showing of cards at the end of a hand.
An open hand played for a predetermined amount.

Show Tickets – The third best hand.
Draw poker where the third best hand wins.

Shuffle – To mix the cards prior to dealing.

Shy – See Short.

Side Arms – The second pair of two pair.

Side Bet – Any bet not made in the pot.

Side Cards – Cards that do not influence the value rank of a hand.

Side Money or Side Pot – The amount set aside from the main pot in table stakes.

Side Strippers – Cards tapered along the sides for cheating.

Sight – Calling for a show of hands after tapping out.

Silent Partner – An innocent player used by a cheater as an unwitting partner.

Simultaneous Declaration – High-low poker where everyone declares his hand at the same time.

Sixty-Six – Six card stud with sixes wild.

Skeet – See Pelter.

Skeet Flush – A skeet in one suit.

Skin – A dollar.

Skin Game – A game having two or more cheaters or partners.

Skinning the Hand – A cheater's technique to get rid of extra cards.

Skipper – See Alternate Straight.

Skip Straight – See Alternate Straight.

Skoon – A dollar.

Sky's The Limit – A game in which no maximum is placed on any bets or raises.

Smooth – The lowest lowball hand of a given value, such as 7, 4, 3, 2, A.

Snarker – A player who wins a pot then ridicules the loser.

Snow – To fake or bluff.

Snowing Cards – See Fuzzing.

Sorts – A deck of cards made up of irregular or imperfect cards sorted from many normal decks of cards.

Southern Cross – A variation of Cincinnati with nine up cards arranged in a cross.

Spider – A hold-out device attached to the cheater's coat or vest.

Spike – An Ace.
A pair in lowball.

Spinner – A winning streak. (Hot Streak)

Spit Card – A card turned up which is used in every player's hand.

Spit in the Ocean – A draw game where an exposed card and all matching cards are wild.

Split Openers – To break up the hand required to open.

Split Pair – A pair in stud with one card in the hole and the other exposed.

Split Pot – A pot equally divided between two winners.

Spot – An Ace.

Spot Card – Any card from the deuce to the ten.

Spots – The printed marks on the face side of a card.

Spread – A hand.

Squared Deck – An evenly stacked deck ready for cutting or dealing.

Squeeze – To look at cards by slowly spreading them apart. (Sweat)

Squeeze Bet or Raise – To bet or raise against another strong hand to draw more money from a third player holding a weaker hand.

Squeezed Player – A caller who is being bet into and raised by players on both sides of him. (Whipsaw)

Squeezers – Cards with suit and value indicators printed at the corners.

Stack – A pile of chips.
Twenty chips.

Stacked Deck – A deck with pre-arranged cards for a dishonest deal.

Stake – The money with which a player enters a game.

Stand – To decline a draw.

Standing Pat – To play the original hand without drawing.

Stand-off – A tie.

Stay – To remain in the hand by calling the bet or raise.

Stenographers – Four Queens.

Step – See Job.

Still Pack – The deck not in play when two decks are used.

Stinger – A sequence.

Stock – The cards remaining in the deck after dealing.
The stacked portion of a deck.

Stonewall – One who calls to the end with a poor hand.

Stormy Weather – Similar to Spit in the Ocean except three cards are dealt in the center.

Straddle – A compulsory blind raise such as played in Blind Tiger.

Straight – Five cards in sequence, such as 3, 4, 5, 6, 7.

Straight Draw – Draw poker not requiring openers.

Straight Flush – Five cards of the same suit in sequence.

Stranger – A new or unfamiliar card in a hand after the draw.

Streak – A run of good or bad luck.

Stringer – A straight.

Stripped Deck – A deck used with certain cards purposely removed such as the deuces.

Stripper Deck – A dishonest deck with slightly wedge-shaped cards (usually a thirty-second of an inch trimmed off the edge or side of a card or cards) that the cheater can pull out of the deck. (See Belly Strippers, Side Strippers, End Strippers, Brief)

Strip Poker – Poker played where the loser of a pot must remove an article of clothing.

Stud Poker – One of the two basic forms of poker (the other is draw) and is played with up or exposed cards and one or more concealed, hole cards.

Substitution – An exchange of a card for one from the deck. (Twist)

Suck – To call when the proper play is to fold.

Sudden Death – High-low five-card stud.

Suicide King – The King of Hearts . . . the king with a sword pointed at its head.

Suit – Any of the four sets (Clubs, Diamonds, Hearts and Spades) in a deck of cards.

Super Seven Card Stud – A game starting with five cards to each player; then after discarding two, the game proceeds as seven-card stud.

Sweeten – To add more money to a pot such as an extra ante.

Swinging – See Shoot the Moon.

Table – See Board.

Table Cards – Cards turned face up on the table for use in everyone's hand, such as used in Cincinnati.

Table Stakes – When the betting and raising is limited only to the amount of money a player has in front of him.

Take It or Leave It – See Shove Them Along.

Take-Out – The number of chips a player starts with in table stakes.

Take the Lead – To make a bet or raise.

Talon – The remainder of the deck after the deal.

Tap – To bet all one's money in table stakes.

Tap Out – To bet and lose all one's cash forcing him to leave the game.

Tape You – When a player bets an amount equal to all the money his opponent has on the table in table stakes.
A raise.

Technical Position – The strategic and psychological advantage of a player relative to the other players.

Tennessee – Draw poker where a bet is made after each round of cards is dealt.

Tennessee Hold Me – See Hold Me.

Tens High – Poker where no hand higher than a pair of tens can win.

Ten-Ten – High-low, five-card stud with ten for low and a pair of tens for high as qualifiers; usually played with two twists.

Texas Special or Texas Tech – See Double-Barreled Shotgun.

The Diamond – A way to measure the idealness of a poker game for the good player.

Thirty Days or Thirty Miles – Three tens.

Thirty-Three – Six-card stud with threes wild.

Three Card Monte – Three-card poker similar to Bragg.

Three of a Kind – Three cards of the same value. (Triplets, Trips)

Three Toed Pete – Three-card poker.

Throat Shot – When a player barely loses a big pot.

Throw Off – To discard.

Throw Up A Hand – To fold.

Ticket – A card.

Tie – When two hands of equal value win a pot. The pot is then divided between tied hands.

Tierce – A three-card straight flush.

Tiger – A low hand from the 2 to the 7.

Tight Player – A player who seldom bets unless he has a strong hand.

Top – To beat an opponent.

Trey – A three.

Tricon – Three of a kind.

Trio, Triplets, or Trips – Three of a kind.

Trips Eight – Stud, or draw, split-pot poker with an eight for low and trips for high as qualifiers, usually played with one or two twists.

Tulsa – See Omaha.

Turn – A player's chance to deal, receive cards, or bet.

Turn Down – To fold.

Turnie-Turnie – See Mexican Stud.

Twenty Deck Poker – When poker is played with twenty cards. All cards lower than the ten are thrown out.

Twin Beds – A high-low game involving five cards in each hand and ten turned up on the table.

Twist – A draw in stud or an extra draw in draw poker.

Twisting Your Neighbor – Drawing cards from the hands of other players.

Two Card Poker – Any poker game where the best two cards win.

Two Pair – Two pairs of different values in a hand, such as 99 and 33.

Two Pair Nine – Stud or draw split-pot poker with a nine for low and two pair for high as qualifiers; usually played with one or two twists.

Two Way Hand – A hand having possibilities of winning both the high and low half of a split-pot game.

Uncle Doc – Five-card stud with a single spit or table card and all like it as wild.

Undercut – When the final down card is the lowest hole card in low-hole stud games.

Under the Gun – The position of the first bettor.

Unlimited Poker – Poker in which no limit is on the bet or raise.

Up – The act of anteing.
The higher of two pair such as Queens-up.

Up-Cards – The face-up cards in stud. (Open Cards)

Up the Creek – When split whiskered Kings are wild.

Utah – See Cincinnati.

Valet – A Jack.

V8 Ford Special – Thirteen-card stud with five cards to each player and eight table cards in a V formation with one side of the V played for high and the other side played for low.

Vigorish – The amount paid to the house for running the game.

Walk the Table – The automatic winning of the entire pot with a certain specific card or hand.

Wash – To shuffle.

Waving – Coiling or crimping cards by a cheater so the wavey card can be spotted in an opponent's hand or in the deck.

Weary Willie – See Elimination.

Wedges – Certain cards that are strippers, which can be pulled from a deck when needed by the cheater.

Welcher – A player who fails to pay a debt.

Whangedoodle – A round of Jackpots played after a big hand such as four of a kind.

Wheel – See Bicycle.

Whipsaw – Aggressive betting and raising action on both sides of a calling player. (Squeezed Player)

Whiskey Poker – Draw poker with widow cards that can be exchanged from one's hand.

Whore – A Queen.

Widow – The money cut from pots. (Kitty)
A card or cards common to all hands. (Spit Card)

Wild Annie – See Double-Barreled Shotgun.

Wild Card – A card changeable to any value or suit desired by its holder.

Wild Game – A game using wild cards.
A highly spirited game.

Wild Widow – A card turned up for use as a wild card (and all like cards are wild) in every player's hand. (Spit Card)

Window – The card exposed or flashed at the end of a player's closed hand.

Window Dressing – A card purposely flashed in one's closed hand.

Winging – Having a winning streak.

Wired – A pair, trips or four of a kind dealt consecutively to a hand . . . usually a stud hand starting with the first card.

Woolworth – When all 5's and 10's are wild.

You Roll Two – See New Guinea Stud.

X Marks the Spot – See Criss-Cross.

Z-Game – The lowest stake game in the house.

The above glossary lists 854 separate terms.

APPENDIX D

ODDS

This Appendix compiles the following *card* odds:

1. Rank of Hands
2. Pat Hand Odds
3. Draw Odds
4. Stud Odds
5. Lowball Odds
6. Wild Card Odds

Card odds can be expressed in several ways as shown in the following example:

EXAMPLE

Card Odds for Three of a Kind

Odds For (Frequency)	*Deals per Pat Hand*	**Before Draw**	*Lower Value Hands per Pat Hand*	*Odds Against*
1 in 47	47	(on 5 cards)	46	46 to 1

To convert: Subtract (-1) →

← Add (+1)

Odds For (Frequency)	*Draw per Catch*	**After Draw**	*Misses per Catch*	*Odds Against*
1 in 8.7	8.7	(3 cards to a pair)	7.7	7.7 to 1

To estimate the number of hands possible, divide the deals per pat hand into the total number of hands possible:

$$47 \overline{)\,2{,}598{,}960} \approx 55{,}000 \text{ hands}$$

1. Rank of Hands
(highest to lowest)

Rank	*Hand*	*Example*	*Hands Possible*
*	Five Aces (with Bug)	AAAAB	1
*	Five of a Kind (with Wild Card)	8888W	13 (Joker Wild) 672 (Deuces Wild)
*	Skeet Flush	2S 4S 5S 8S 9S	24
1	Royal Straight Flush	10H JH QH KH AH	4
1	Straight Flush	4C 5C 6C 7C 8C	40
2	Four Aces	XAAAA	48
2	Four of a Kind	X7777	624
*	Big Bobtail	X 8D 9D JD QD	144
*	Blaze Full	QQKKK	144
3	Full House	66JJJ	3,744

** = Not a normal hand (Freak Hand)*

1. Rank of Hands (cont.)
(highest to lowest)

Rank	*Hand*	*Example*	*Hands Possible*
4	Flush	DDDDD	5,108 (n.s.)
*	Big Tiger (Big Cat)	8- - -K	4,096 (i.f.)
*	Little Tiger (Little Cat)	3- - -8	4,096 (i.f.)
*	Big Dog	9- - -A	4,096 (i.f.)
*	Little Dog	2- - -7	4,096 (i.f.)
5	Straight	78910J	10,200 (n.f.)
*	Round the Corner Straight	32AKQ	3,060 (n.f.)
*	Skip Straight (Dutch Straight)	579JK	6,120 (n.f.)
*	Kilter	A- - -9	35,840 (i.f.)
*	Five and Dime	5 - - -10	4,096
*	Skeet (Pelter)	2-5-9	6,144 (i.f.)

*** = Not a normal hand (Freak Hand)***

1. Rank of Hands (cont.)
(highest to lowest)

Rank	*Hand*	*Example*	*Hands Possible*
6	Three of a Kind	XX10 10 10	54,912
*	Little Bobtail	XX6C 7C 8C	3,120
*	Flash	HDSCB	685,464
*	Blaze	PPPPP	792
7	Two Pairs	X3399	123,552
*	Four Flush with a Pair	DDD5D5	34,320
*	Four Flush	XHHHH	111,540
8	Pair	XXX88	1,098,240
9	No Pair (+)	XXXXX	1,302,540
9	Ace High (+)	- - - -A	502,860
9	King High (+)	- - - -K	335,580

*** = Not a normal hand (Freak Hand)***

1. Rank of Hands (cont.)
(highest to lowest)

Rank	*Hand*	*Example*	*Hands Possible*
9	Queen High (+)	----Q	213,180
9	Jack High (+)	----J	127,500
9	Ten High (+)	----10	70,360
10	Nine Low (++)	----9	71,860
10	Eight Low (++)	----8	35,840
10	Seven Low (++)	----7	15,360
10	Six Low (++)	----6	5,120
10	Five Low (++)	A2345	1,024
	Total Hands Possible with a 52 Card Deck		2,598,960
	Total Hands Possible with a 53 Card Deck (with a Joker)		2,869,685

Code:
* = Not a normal hand (Freak Hand)
B = Bug card (Joker)
W = Wild Card
P = Any picture card
H = Heart; D=Diamond; S=Spade; C=Club
A = Ace; K=King; Q=Queen; J=Jack
X = Any non-paired side card
- = A specific non-paired side card
(+) = No straights or flushes, Ace is high
(++) = Including straights and flushes, Ace is low
i.f. = Including flushes, n.f. = no flushes; n.s. = no straights

2A. Pat Hand Odds

(VARIOUS HANDS)

Hand	Hands Possible	Pat Hands per 100,000 Deals	Deals per Pat Hand	Deals per Pat Hand or Better
Royal straight flush	4	.15	649,740	649,740
Straight flush	36	1.4	72,193	64,974
Four of a kind	624	22	4,165	3,914
Full house	3,744	144	694	590
Flush	5,108	196	509	273
Straight	10,200	392	255	132
Three of a kind	54,912	2,113	47	35
Two pairs	123,552	4,754	21	13
One pair	1,098,240	42,257	2.4	2
No pair	1,302,540	50,118	2	1
Total	2,598,960	100,000		

(HIGH PAIRS)

Hand	Hands Possible	Pat Hands per 100,000 Deals	Deals per Pat Hand	Deals per Pat Hand or Better
Aces	84,480	3,250	31	9
Kings	84,480	3,250	31	7
Queens	84,480	3,250	31	6
Jacks	84,480	3,250	31	5

2A. Pat Hand Odds (cont.)

(DRAW HANDS)

Hand	*Hands Possible*	*Pat Hands per 100,000 Deals*	*Deals per Pat Hand*	*Deals per Pat Hand or Better*
Four straight* (any)	408,576	15,625	6.4	-
Four straight* (inside)	332,800	12,821	7.8	-
Four straight* (outside)	92,160	3,571	28	-
Four straight* (inside-outside**)	16,384	767	159	-
Four flush*	111,540	4,347	23	-
Four straight flush	144	5.5	18,048	-
Three straight flush	3,120	120	833	-
Pair with an Ace	253,440	10,000	10	-

**Including four card straight flushes.*

***Inside-outside draw hand is when the draw can be made to either an inside or an outside straight (i.e. 2,3,4,5,7).*

2B. Pat Hand Odds

(TWO PAIRS)

Hand	*Hands Possible*	*Hands Higher*	*Hands Lower*
Aces up	19,008	0	104,544
Kings up	17,424	19,008	87,120
Queens up	15,840	36,432	71,280
Jacks up	14,256	52,272	57,024
- - - - - - - - - - - - - 50%			
Tens up	12,672	66,528	44,352
Nines up	11,088	79,200	33,264
Eights up	9,504	90,288	23,760
Sevens up	7,920	99,792	15,840
Sixes up	6,336	107,712	9,504
Fives up	4,752	114,048	4,752
Fours up	3,168	118,800	1,582
Threes up	1,584	121,968	0
Total	123,552		

3. Draw Odds

(ODDS ON DRAWING)

Original Hand	*Cards Drawn*	*Final Hand*	*Approximate* Draws per Catch*
Ace	4	Two pair or better	14
Ace-King (same suit)	3	Two pair or better	14
Pair	3	Any improvement	4
	3	Two pairs	6
	3	Trips	9
	3	Full	100
	3	Four	380
Two flush	3	Flush	100
Pair + kicker	2	Any improvement	4
	2	Two pairs	6
	2	Trips	13
	2	Full	125
	2	Four	1100
Pair + Ace	2	Aces-up	9
	2	Two pairs (lower)	18

3. Draw Odds (cont.)

(ODDS ON DRAWING)

Original Hand	*Cards Drawn*	*Final Hand*	*Approximate* Draws per Catch*
Trips	2	Any improvement	10
	2	Full	16
	2	Four	24
Three straight flush, double open	2	Straight or better	12
	2	Straight flush	1100
Three straight flush, KQJ or 432	2	Straight or better	14
Three straight flush, AKQ or 32A	2	Straight or better	21
Three straight, double open	2	Straight	24
Three flush	2	Flush	25
Two pairs	1	Full	12
Trips + kicker	1	Any improvement	12
	1	Full	16
	1	Four	48

3. Draw Odds (cont.)

(ODDS ON DRAWING)

Original Hand	*Cards Drawn*	*Final Hand*	*Approximate* Draws per Catch*
Four straight, open both ends	1	Straight	6
Four straight, inside or one end	1	Straight	12
Four flush	1	Flush	5
Four straight flush, open both ends	1	Straight or better	3
	1	Straight flush	24
Four straight flush, inside or one end	1	Straight or better	4
	1	Straight flush	48

**Approximate values rather than precise values are reported for the following reason: Consider, for example, the odds on a four-card draw to an Ace. ...Do you assume a blind draw into a 47 card deck that would give a precise value of 12.8 draws per catch of two pair or better? Or do you assume a draw into a 51 card deck (a deck with one Ace missing) that would give a precise value of 15.6 draws per catch of two pair or better? Now there is a twenty percent difference between these two precise values, and no basis for selecting one assumption over the other (47 card deck versus 51 card deck). Furthermore, neither assumption represents the actual situation. . . the draw is not blind from a 47 card deck; and the draw is not from a 51 card deck. An accurate and precise value is obtained only by defining each of the four discarded cards then drawing from a 47 card deck. This would not be practical because a complete table of draw odds to the Ace alone would consist of hundreds of thousands of values. All these values do, however, lie somewhere between the values for the blind draw into the 47 card deck and the draw into the 51 card deck. The above values are, therefore, taken intermediate to the two extreme precise values and then rounded off. This is the only practical way to report these data in an accurately defined manner.*

4A. Stud Odds
(SEVEN CARD STUD)

Hand	*Hands Possible*	*Approximate Hands per 100,000 Deals*
Straight flush	37,444	28
Four of a kind	224,848	168
Full house	3,437,184	2,590
Flush	4,051,784	3,030
Straight	8,466,876	6,330
Three of a kind	6,374,520	4,760
Two pairs	30,834,000	23,050
One pair	56,851,296	42,500
No pair	23,470,608	17,500
Total Hands	133,748,560	

4B. Stud Odds
(IMPROVING IN SEVEN STUD)

	Misses per Catch of a		
Start With	*Straight (outside)*	*Flush*	*Full House or Fours*
FFX	66	31	13
FFXX	106	275	19
FFXXX	-	-	38
FFGG	53	137	4
FFGGX	-	-	7
FFGGXX	-	-	11
FFF	4	4.5	1.5 (11 for fours)
FFFX	8	9	1.7
FFFXX	22	23	2
FFFXXX	-	-	4
FFFF	1.5	1	-
FFFFX	2	2	-
FFFFXX	5	4	-

F or G = a flush, straight (outside) or a paired card
X = a non-helping card

5. *Lowball Odds*

(CARD ODDS)

Highest Card in five cards	*Pairless Hands Possible*		
	Including Straights and Flushes, Ace is Low	*No Straights and Flushes, Ace is Low*	*No Straights and Flushes, Ace is High*
Ace	-	-	502,860
King	506,880	502,860	335,580
Queen	337,920	335,580	213,180
Jack	215,040	213,180	127,500
Ten	129,024	127,500	70,360
Nine	71,680	70,360	34,680
Eight	35,840	34,680	14,280
Seven	15,360	14,280	4,080
Six	5,120	4,080	-
Five	1,024	-	-

(DRAW ODDS)

four cards →	*five cards*	*One Card Draws per Catch*		
Ten	Ten	2	2.03	2.45
Nine	Nine	2.4	2.45	3.10
Eight	Eight	3	3.10	4.30
Seven	Seven	4	4.30	7.53
Six	Six	6	7.53	-
Five	Five	12	-	-

5: Lowball Odds (cont.)

(DRAW ODDS)

Highest Card in five cards		*Including Straights and Flushes, Ace is Low*	*No Straights and Flushes, Ace is Low*	*No Straights and Flushes, Ace is High*
		Two Card Draws per Catch		
three cards →	*five cards*			
Eight	Eight	7.35	7.59	13.44
Seven	Seven	12.50	13.44	30.75
Six	Six	24.50	30.75	-
Five	Five	73.50	-	-
		Three Card Draws per Catch		
two cards →	*five cards*			
Seven	Seven	30.63	31.91	95.15
Six	Six	76.56	95.15	-
Five	Five	306.25	-	-
		Four Card Draws per Catch		
one card →	*five cards*			
Seven	Seven	65.08	70.02	244.96
Six	Six	195.24	244.96	-
Five	Five	976.17	-	-

6. *Wild Card Odds*

(VARIOUS HANDS)

Hand	*Deals to Get on First Five Cards*			
	No Wild Cards	*Joker Wild*	*Deuces Wild*	*Deuces Wild, Hands Possible*
Five of a kind	-	220,745	3,868*	672
Royal straight flush	649,740	119,570	5,370	484
Straight flush	72,193	14,666	575	4,072
Four of a kind	4,165	920	81*	30,816
Full house	694	438	205	12,672
Flush	509	362	159	13,204
Straight	255	221	38	66,236
Trips	47	21*	8*	355,056
Two pairs	21	23	27	95,040
Pair	2.4	2.4	2.4	1,222,048
No pair	2	2.2	3.4	798,660
Total				2,598,960

**With deuces wild, five of a kind is easier to get than a straight flush, four of a kind is much easier to get than a flush or a full house, and three of a kind is easier to get than two pairs.*

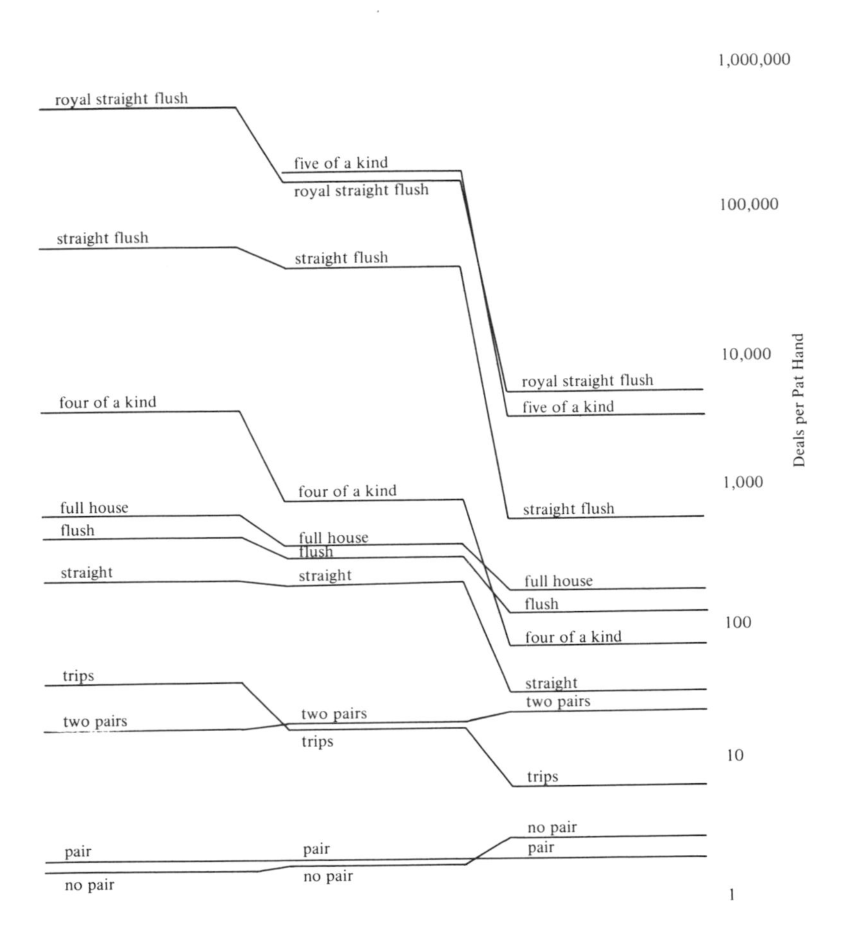

Various Hands

APPENDIX E

REVIEW

Before each poker game, read this review . . . it will be worth your time in dollars.

	Page
– Anyone can get rich by playing poker.	III
– The opportunities are great, and the income is unlimited.	V
– First understand the definitions.	1
– Remember, poker is not a card game . . . it is a game of money management over which luck has no influence.	1
– Differentiate between *card* odds and *investment* odds.	3
– Use the *edge* odds to evaluate performance.	8
– Differentiate between betting *stakes* and betting *pace.*	10
– The good player is rare; he is different from all other players. . . .In method of thought, the good player is right and the poor player is wrong.	13
– Emotions control most poker players, but never the good player.	18
– The common concepts of poker can be costly; the advanced concepts can be worth a fortune.	21
– The technique of good poker is *discipline, thought* and *control* - The DTC technique.	31
– How valuable is discipline? Did you ever eat a $750 sandwich?	40

Page

- Thought is the labor of good poker. What is the labor worth? 41
- Control is the result of good poker. The good player seizes control of the game and then wins all the money. 44
- Use strategy to win maximum money. The key is deception. 49
- Three ingredients of strategy are: understand the game, know your opponents, be aware of the situation. 49
- Tailor-make the game to yield maximum advantage; make the game expensive and wild. 56
- Adjust behavior for maximum profit. Be unfriendly or congenial, practice deceit and lie, create a reckless atmosphere, read opponents and peekers; spot cards reflected in eyeballs, look for flashed cards and ghost hands; be a fake, do anything to gain an advantage . . . except cheat. 67
- Proper policies result in fewer mistakes and better decisions. Get more money in the game, make credit easy, collect bad debts, keep rules sloppy, avoid arguments. 90
- Welcome cheaters; they are worth money and easy to spot. 103
- Remember all honest cards are marked. 104
- What about taxes and laws? 111
- Your opponents are your assets. Treat them with respect and extract maximum money from them. 124
- Get opponents emotionally and financially involved. Keep them from quitting. 124

	Page
– Exploit opponents through their weaknesses.	128
– Bribe with favors.	132
– Make weird bets.	133
– Use hypnosis.	134
– Create distractions.	135
– Win slower to win more.	139
– Bigger and more games mean greater profit.	145
– Find new games, then raise the stakes.	145
– Organize the game; make it exciting and play all night.	149
– Watch out for an armed robbery.	157
– Expand the game by finding new players; then keep the losers and reject the winners.	159
– Remember that more players quit because of injured pride than because of hurt finances.	160
– Beware of women players.	165
– Keep the game healthy by making it attractive and by boosting the morale of losers.	168
– For unlimited income, run major and minor league poker games with a farm system.	174
– Win a million dollars at poker.	177
– Is poker moral?	178
– Know the history of poker.	179
– Refer to the poker literature.	183
– Be familiar with poker terms.	203
– Check over the card odds.	248
– Review the Advanced Concepts of Poker.	264
– Read MAN'S CHOICE.	276

This book is epitomized by the following triangle:

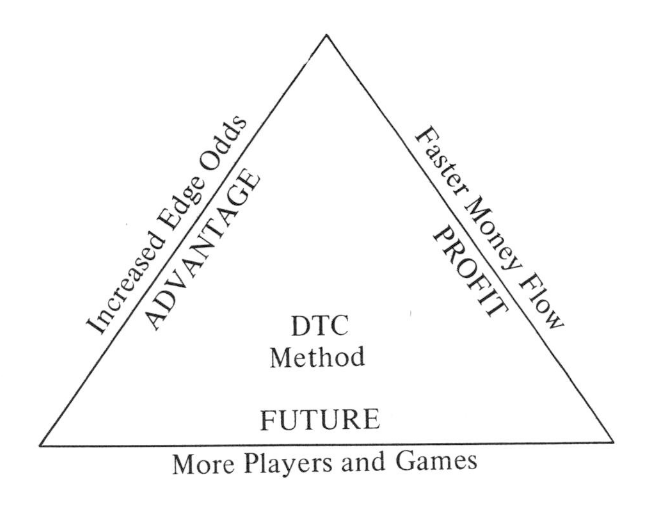

* * *

The publisher and author assume no responsibility for the use of any information in this book.

* * *

MAN'S CHOICE

(see page 276)

Unearned guilt
Cruel hoax of two thousand years.
Abandon it and live for your own happiness.

René Po

INDEX

Acting 68-69
Action 168
Additional cards 60
Advanced concepts V, 29-30
Aggressiveness 10
Agreements 138
Alcohol 31, 127, 136
Analytical thinking – See Thought
Ante 16, 24, 65, 169
Appraising 49-54
  example of 50
  game 50, 53
  hand 53
  opponents 49-50, 51, 52, 53
    changes 52
    classification 51
    mixture 51-52
  position 53
Arguments - See Emotions
Armed robbery 157-158
Assets 124, 165
Atmosphere 75-77, 80, 168
  carefree 75-76
  pleasant 76
  relaxed 76
  unpleasant 69-71, 95
Attitude 73, 75, 171
  poor 90-91
  proper 90

Bad debts - See Credit
Bankrupt player 93
Banks 125
Bath 40
Behavior 67-90
  friendly 71
  in game 67-88
  non game 88-90
  tough, unfriendly 69-71, 95
Bet or get 60
Betting 10-13, 23, 45, 48, 79, 91, 132
  defensive 133
  feeler bet 85
  indirect 133
  manipulations 45
  offensive 133
  pot limit 61
  side bets 138
  table stakes 16, 61
  weird bets 45
Betting pace 10, 11-13, 56, 72, 75, 91, 129, 169
  examples of 12, 13
  game pace 11
  hand pace 11
  optimum pace 12
  ratios 12
Betting stakes 10, 11, 56, 62-65, 73, 129
  increases 62-63
    example of 63
  raising 152
  temporary increases 62
Bibliography 183-202
Black book 9, 50, 79, 98, 129
Blandness 68-69
Bluffing 22, 24, 28, 43, 45, 46, 69, 84, 109, 130, 166
Bonds 125
Books - See Poker Books
Bragging 28, 127
Bribes 132
Bug card - See Joker
Burning bridges 102
Business 1, 125
Business contacts 160

Card odds - See Odds
Cards 168
Card sequence 17
Cash 91
Cash position 97
Character 178
Character catalyst 178
Cheaters and Cheating 17, 30, 82, 102, 103-110
  accepting cheaters 105
  cost of 105-106
  detection 109-110
  eliminating cheating 106
  exposing cheaters 107
  rejecting cheaters 106-108
  Robin Hood 108-109
  stealing money 103, 107
    example of 107
  techniques 103, 105
    betting agreements 104

card switching 103
collective 107
deck stacking 103
marked cards 104
mechanical devices 104
money stealing 103
partnerships 108
Check raising 59
Checks (bank) 95
bounced checks 95
cashing checks 95
check winnings 98
Chips - See Poker Chips
Cleaning woman 157
Companionship 127
Complaints 168
Concealing - See Deception
Concentration 31, 86
Concepts - See Poker Concepts
Conclusion 178
Confidence 19
Conflicts 176
Contacts 148
Control 44-48, 94, 126, 145, 154, 176
Craps 126
Credit 22, 27, 91, 92-95, 132, 169
bad debts 93, 95-98
absorbed 96
legal recourse 96
maximum 96
buying loans 97
credit rating 98
extending credit 94
reciprocating loan 93
refusing credit 94
risks 95
Credit rule 92-93
exception 93, 96
Cutting pot 126, 157

Dealer advantage 27, 55
Dealer or dealing 79, 83
house dealer 126
Debts - See Credit
Deception and deceit 1, 30, 49, 72-75
concealing desires 72-73
concealing facts 73-74
lying 74-75, 87
Decisions 6
Definitions 1-30
betting 10-13
emotions 18-20
odds 3-10
poker 1-3
poker concepts 21-30
poker players 13-18
Derivation of poker 181
Deterioration 32
Diamond 65-67
Discipline 31-41
Discouragement 176
Disputed plays - See Rules
Distractions 135-138
examples of 137
Drawing 80, 83
odds for 256-258
Draw poker 56, 81
Drinking - See Alcohol
Drop - See Fold
DTC method 31-48
control 44-48
discipline 31-41
thought 41-44

Early bet 59
Edge odds - See Odds
Edge percentage - See Odds: Edge Odds
Effort 41-42
Emotions 18-20, 86, 103, 105, 109, 110, 124, 172
arguments 102-103, 168, 169
disputes 102
emotional characteristics 20
emotional involvement 124, 127, 128
fear 19, 60
hurt feelings 160, 176
influence 19
personal problems 102, 169
reactions 19
resentment 173
scaring 160
stresses 20
Encouragement 160
Erroneous ideas 90-91
Errors 17, 33, 109, 132
Ethics 70, 83

Evaluations 34-39
outlines 34-39
semi-annual game notes 36-37
semi-annual player profiles 38-39
weekly game notes 34-35
Evasions 178
Evolution of poker 180
Expansion 159-167
Exploitation 128-138
Eye movements 78, 86
Eyeshades 168

Farm system 174, 176-177
Favors 132
Fear - See Emotions
Finances 176
Fines 151
Flashed cards 82-85, 86
also see Intentional Flashing
statistics 83
Flattery 89, 160
Fold 83, 88, 132
Food 40, 46, 76, 131, 135, 168
Formulae 6, 8, 12
understanding 6*n*, 12*n*
Freak hands 60, 249-252
Future earnings 48

Gamblers and gambling 13, 32, 95, 124-126
books on 197
craps 126
definition of 124
gambling intensity 126
gambling situations 126
horses 126
house dealer 126
lottery 126
numbers 126
poker in casinos 126
roulette 126
slot machines 126
Game - See Poker Game
Game modifications 56-62
Game notes - See Evaluations
Game rules - See Rules
Ghost hands 81-82
Gifts 168
Glossary 203-247

Goal III
Good players - See Poker Players: Good Players

Health 153, 176
High-low poker 23, 58-59
qualifiers 59
History 179-182
Holding cards 87
Hold Me 60
Honest marked cards 104
Honest poker 104
Horses 91-92, 126, 135
House dealer 126
House rules - See Rules
Hoyles 183
Hypnosis 134-135

Illness 172-173
Immoral concepts VI
Impulses 14
Individualism 178
Influence - See Control
Insurance 144
Intentional flashing 85
Investment odds - See Odds
Investment situations 125
banks 125
bonds 125
business 125
intensity 125
situation 125
stocks 125
winner 125
Invitations to games 147, 165
Involvement 124-128, 150
emotional 124, 127, 128
financial 127-128

Job 153
Joker 61, 131
Justice 178

Kibitzers - See Peekers

Late hours 32, 152-153
Laws - See Taxes and Laws
Laziness 18, 19, 132
Liabilities 146, 161
Library of Congress 187-197

Loans - See Credit
Location 76
Losing streak 19, 32
Losers 94, 126, 127, 159, 178
  helping 169-170
Losses 176
  on purpose losses 144
Lottery 126
Lowball draw 60
  odds for 260-261
Luck 1, 16, 18, 22, 24, 26, 89, 91, 128
Lying - See Deception
Maintenance 168-173
Major league game 174-177
Manipulations 45-46
  betting 45
  defensive 45-46
  offensive 45
Man's Choice 276
Marker (buck) 55
Maximum value hand 60
Maximum win approach III, 21
Mechanics of poker 49
Memorizing 31, 81-82
  discards 81
  in draw 81
  in stud 81
Minor league game 174-177
Money III, 21, 90, 91, 178
  money management 1
  unattached money 30
Money extraction 139-144, 148
Money flow or money patterns 45, 48, 56, 139-144
  controlled 142-144
  ideal 140
  uncontrolled (normal) 139-143
Morale 144, 149, 170-172
Motives 128
Mystical attitude 18

Nap 40
Negative activity 178
Negative qualities 178
Nervousness 41, 76, 77
Newspaper 136
Non-game behavior 88-90
Non-game contacts 88-90
Notes - See Evaluations
Novel games 60
Numbers 126

Observation 77-88
Objective attitude 18, 178
Objective thinking - See Thought
Odds 3-10, 248-263
  accurately defined 258
  calculations of 248
  card odds 3-6
    examples of 4
    low hands 4
    statistics 5-6
  draw odds 256-258
  edge odds 8-10, 44, 48, 63, 64, 65, 67, 101, 105, 124, 142, 147, 152
    formula 8
    statistics 9, 10
  graph of 263
  investment odds 6-8, 44, 133
    examples of 7, 15
    formula 6
  lowball odds 260-261
  pat hands 253-255
    draw hands 254
    high pairs 253
    two pairs 255
    various hands 253
  rank of hands 249-252
  stud odds 259
  tables of 248-263
  wild card odds 262-263
Off days 172-173
One million dollars 177
On purpose losses 144
Opponents 49-50, 51, 52, 73, 124-144
  changes in 52
  classification of 51
  disintegration of 52
  family of 89
  stimulating poor attitudes in 90-91
  wife of 89-90
Optimum pace 12
Other games 73
Organization 149-158

Peekers 83, 85-88, 157
Penalties 23, 151, 178
Personality 69-72
friendly 71
friendly traditions 71
split 71, 89
unfriendly, tough 69-71, 95, 148
Physical movements 68
Pick up checks 59
Place-and-show-tickets-split-pot-with-twist-your-neighbor 60
Player notes - See Evaluations
Players - See Poker Players
Poker III, V, 1-3, 25, 178
derivation of 181
evolution of 180
good poker 14, 49
history 179-182
Poker books V, 21-29, 185-202
gambling books 197
in Library of Congress 187-197
Poker chips 75, 91, 136
Poker concepts 21-30
advanced 29-30
common 21-29
new 175
Poker income 127
Poker in gambling casinos 126
Poker game 145-177
attendance 167
breaking up 149
collapsing 150, 154
expanding 159-167
farm system 174, 176-177
fast game 135
filled game 167
financial potential 149
high stake 175
irregular games 150
leaving early 173-174
location 157-158
different 157
permanent 157
major league 174-177
making attractive 168-169
maintenance 168-173
minor league 174-177
new games 145-146
one shot games 148
organizing 149-158
other games 145-148
quitting 148
small stake 175
Poker players 13-18
bankrupt 93
breaking in 175
contacting 153-156
desirable 94, 146
financial limits 149
good players 13-15, 48, 71, 125, 146, 178
playing against 14
two in a game 14
helping 160
irregular players 167
keeping 160-161
losing tolerances 150
new players 159-160
permanent players 145, 147-148
poor players and other players 15-18, 25, 26, 72, 146
potential 89, 159, 175
recruiting 145, 149
rejecting 161-165
selecting 175
women players 165-167
Poker rules - See Rules
Police 158
Policies 90-103
Pornographic literature 135
Position 53-55
fundamental 47, 53
seat 54-55
technical 54
Positive qualities 178
Posture 31
Pot limit - See Betting
Pride 94
Probabilities - See Odds : Card Odds
Profit 63, 64
poker income 127
profit motive 14, 16, 67
Psychology 20, 21, 46, 88

Qualifiers 59
Questions and responses 78, 80
Quitting a game 148
Quitting time 28, 151-153

Radio 135
Raising 23, 45, 79
Rank of hands 249-252

Rationality 178
Rationalization 18
Readable patterns 68, 79-81, 85, 86
Reading opponents 77-81
Recruiting players 145
Reflected cards 84
Relative performance - See Odds: Edge Odds
Remembering - See Memorizing
Responsibility 266
Resting place 175
Review 264-266
Rewards 178
Right to bet 59
Robbery 157-158
Roulette 126
Rudeness 161
Rules 1, 17, 98-103, 169, 183
  disputed plays 99-100
    exposed card 99
    misdeal 99
    out of turn 100
  game rules 98, 100, 101
    equitable interpretations 98
    problems 98
  house rules 98, 100-101
  Hoyles 183
  inequitable rules 100
  modified rules 99
  ruleless situations 99
  standard rules 99

Seat position 54-55
  arrangement 55
  swapping 55
Self-control - See Discipline
Self esteem VI
Shave 40
Shuffling 82
Side bets 138
Slot machines 126
Social contacts 160
Spectacular plays 46
Spectators 157
Split pot - See High-Low Poker
Squeezing cards 41
Starting time 150-151
  indefinite 150
  firm 150
Statistical value 53
Stocks 125
Strategy 49-123, 73, 86
  ingrediants of 49
    immediate or action 49, 53
    long range 49
    short range 49
Strength, estimated 53
Stud poker 56, 80, 81
  five card 61
  odds for 259
Superstitions 130
Systemization 68-69

Table stakes - See Betting
Tailor-made games 56-67
Tattletale 96
Taxes and laws 111-123
  federal excise tax 111
  federal income tax 111
    tax form 123
  state laws and taxes 111-122
Technique 31-48
  control 44-48
  discipline 31-41
  DTC method 31-48
  thought 41-44
Telephone calls 153-156
  telephone outlines 155, 156
Television 135
The Diamond 65-67
Thought 41-44, 129, 178
  analytical thinking 41
  objective thinking 41
Tight playing 26, 73
Time 178
Time limit 17
Tough behavior - See Personality: Unfriendly
Triangle 266
Twist 57-58
  double twist 58
  giant twist 58
  unlimited twist 58

Understanding poker 49
Unexposed cards 82-85
Unfriendly game 41

Verbal expressions 68
Vocal tones 68, 78

Weaknesses 128-132

Welching 27, 96
Whims 178
Wild cards 60
  odds for 262-263
Wild games 16
Winners 125, 127, 178
  also see Poker Players: Good Players
Winning 139
  rate 139
  too fast 139
Winnings 73
Win one million dollars 177
Win streak 19, 32, 128, 176

Yearly income 42

A SPECIAL OFFER TO OWNERS OF DR. WALLACE'S POKER MANUAL

- A Valuable Supplement -

I & O Publishing Company has the exclusive rights to Dr. Wallace's new novel, MAN'S CHOICE. This novel is important to all owners of the Poker Manual who wish to expand their knowledge of human behavior in order to outperform their competition in poker and business. In an exciting, quick-moving plot, a colorful spectrum of poker players springs to life. Owners of the Poker Manual will recognize the principal characters as those who acted out the various examples in the Manual. In fact, here is the key:

Poker Manual		*MAN'S CHOICE*
John Finn	=	John Flagg
Sid Bennett	=	Sid Glickman
Ted Fehr	=	Ted O'Breen
Quintin Merck	=	Quintin Marini
Scotty Nichols	=	Scotty Drummond
Aaron Smith	=	Aaron Silver
Mike Bell	=	Mike Morgan
Charlie Holland	=	Max Pursyman
Boris Klien	=	Boris Krupp

With vivid psychological exposés of these characters, the novel delivers a crystal-clear understanding of each type of human mind from the confident, consistent winner to the unhappy, self-defeating loser. This book demonstrates that the choice to be a winner or a loser is always open to every man. MAN'S CHOICE is an invaluable aid to analyze yourself and others. This $6.95 hardbound novel is available to owners of the Poker Manual at a special price of $5.95 (postpaid) from the I & O Publishing Company.

I & O Publishing Company, Box 644, Wilmington, Delaware 19899

ADDENDUM NOTES

1. What Happens When All the Players Own the Poker Manual?

As sales of the Poker Manual expand, more and more players are asking, "What will happen when all the players own the Poker Manual?" Will the advantage gap between the good and poor players narrow? Will the earning potential for the player applying the Advanced Concepts of Poker diminish?

The answers to the last two questions are no. The profit opportunities for most good players should increase as the circulation of the Poker Manual grows. This phenomenon can be explained by examining the nature of the game, the good player, and the poor player:

Tens of thousands of these Manuals are already in the hands of poker players. The Manual is gradually and permanently changing the game of poker. For the first time, the true nature of poker has been delineated. The identifications made in the Manual are quietly dispelling the errors, misconceptions and myths that have beclouded the game since its inception. As the cloud lifts, so lifts the mystical concepts (both overt and subliminal) that impede the good player's efforts to create faster pace, higher profit games. The fundamental resistance against fast-pace games involving split pots, twists, qualifiers, etc., is being cut at the roots (e.g., by dispelling the false notion that pace-increasing variations change poker from a game of skill to a game of luck). As the distribution of the Poker Manual continues, the more lucrative, fast-paced games will become more acceptable and easier to create. This will allow the good player to increase his profits more rapidly.

But will the identifications about poker also dispel the misconceptions and myths that poor players themselves hold, thereby improving their performance and decreasing the edge odds for the good player? On the whole, the answer would be no. Only a few poor players will benefit to any significant degree from the Advanced Concepts of Poker. While these concepts will serve to dissipate the misconceptions about the game in general (e.g., dispel the myth that good players never indulge in high-low games or use the twist), only a small percentage of poor players will ever directly apply these concepts to themselves. Why? Consider the nature of the poor player. Most have developed deeply entrenched habits that militate against the ingredients of good play—*discipline, thought* and then *control*. To suddenly apply the Advanced Concepts (that by nature demand intensive concentration and thought) would require a continuous, excruciating effort from the poor player. This would be highly unlikely since most poor players have through years of default built an elaborate rationalization mechanism to avoid this very type of effort. They seek to "relax" their minds in poker. To apply the Advanced Concepts would be a complete contradiction to the poor player's nature. The effect of exposing most poor players[1] to the Advanced Concepts of Poker would be similar to exposing alcoholics to the logical advantages of being sober or to demonstrate the unbeatable horse race or casino odds to inveterate gamblers. Very few losers will change their self-destructive habits when confronted with their errors. Those who have read MAN'S CHOICE can

[1] *On exposure to the Advanced Concepts of Poker, the loser may temporarily become more wary of the good player and alert to some of his techniques. In most cases, however, this cautiousness and alertness quickly fade and the loser sinks into an even lower state of awareness because of his "confidence" that he now knows the good player's techniques and is savvy to the tricks of the game. He lets himself forget that these "tricks" continue to be used with the sole purpose of extracting maximum money from him and the other losers.*

grasp this unwillingness of losers to change by visualizing the effect of exposing poor players such as Ted Fehr and Rocco Torri to the Advanced Concepts of Poker. The beneficial effect on them would be nil.

The transformation of Scotty Nichols, on the other hand, demonstrates that any loser *can* choose at any time to use his mind and alter his habits to make himself a winner. Winners make themselves winners. And losers make themselves losers by defaulting in the proper use of their minds.[2] The mind is the instrument required to utilize the Advanced Concepts of Poker.

The advantage of the good player would decrease, of course, if he encountered other players who had read the Poker Manual and were properly applying its concepts. Even with complete distribution of the Manual, however, the probability of two or more good players in a game would remain low. Even with this possibility increasing with the growing circulation of the Poker Manual, the advantages of dispelling the myths about poker should outweigh the potential decrease in edge odds caused by encountering opponents applying the Advanced Concepts.

2. Who is Buying the Poker Manual?

Analysis of sales data indicates that more winners than losers are buying the Manual. By far, the highest percentage of sales develop from ads placed in sophisticated, business-oriented publications (e.g., FORBES, FORTUNE, WALL STREET JOURNAL, etc.). A scanning of the letterheads suggests that successful, well-to-do individuals (generally men who have chosen to use their minds effectively) are the primary buyers of the Poker Manual. In other words, winners are more interested in improving their performance than are losers. This is logical.

For many losers, the Manual represents a threat by exposing their well-ensconced mechanisms of self-deception. Thus lies the nature of the controversy behind the book. I & O Publishing Company receives about 1% negative feedback on this Manual. Many of the negative reactions reveal deep-seated fear and anger. A few reactions involve vitriolic letters accompanied by threats of violence. For the most part, these are the losers who are trying to strike back at what the Manual has exposed. Their facade of self-deception has been stripped away for all to see. Basically, their reaction is fear followed by a deep repression of the crucial identifications made in the Manual. As long as they repress these identifications, they will remain losers.

While it is obvious that poker losers are self-made fools[3] for not using their minds, perhaps the biggest fool is the good player. With his efficacious mind and willingness to exert effort, he is profligating his most precious possession . . . his time . . . time needed to pursue expanded, long-range goals that he is capable of achieving. So perhaps the biggest loser at the poker table is the good player.

3. If the Author Could Gain a Considerable Income by Applying His Advanced Concepts of Poker, Why Does He Reveal this Information in a Book?

In addition to the answer provided above (that unlimited exposure of the Advanced Concepts should not diminish the profit potential for the good player

[2] *This does not mean* intelligence . . . *it means the* use *of the mind. A genius can (and often does) default on the use of his mind and make himself a loser. On the other hand, any man with mediocre intelligence can elect to honestly and efficiently use his mind to make himself a winner against competition of superior intelligence.*

[3] *This does not include men who have lost or failed through honest errors in non-poker pursuits.*